Rebel by vocation

Manchester University Press

Rebel by vocation

Seán O'Faoláin and the generation of *The Bell*

NIALL CARSON

Manchester University Press

The right of Niall Carson to be identified as the author of this work has been asserted by him in accordance with the Copyright, Designs and Patents Act 1988.

Published by Manchester University Press
Altrincham Street, Manchester M1 7JA

www.manchesteruniversitypress.co.uk

British Library Cataloguing-in-Publication Data
A catalogue record for this book is available from the British Library

ISBN   978 0 7190 9937 3 hardback
ISBN   978 1 5261 3375 5 paperback

First published in hardback by Manchester University Press 2016
This edition first published 2018

The publisher has no responsibility for the persistence or accuracy of URLs for any external or third-party internet websites referred to in this book, and does not guarantee that any content on such websites is, or will remain, accurate or appropriate.

Typeset by
Servis Filmsetting Ltd, Stockport, Cheshire
Printed in Great Britain by
CPI Group (UK) Ltd, Croydon, CR0 4YY

Contents

Acknowledgements   *page* vi

1 Introduction: Rebel by vocation   1
2 Beginnings and blind alleys: O'Faoláin and his circle   11
3 A broken world: Church and state in *The Bell*   50
4 The mart of ideas: O'Faoláin and literature   96
5 The thin society: O'Faoláin and the descent of *The Bell*   129
6 Conclusion: Signing off   156

Works cited   162
Index   174

Acknowledgements

This monograph is the result of several years study and work at the Institute of Irish Studies at the University of Liverpool; it is a fantastic institution, in a fantastic city. During my research I have had several small but welcome grants from the Institute of Irish Studies and the School of Histories, Languages and Cultures at the University of Liverpool and from the British Association of Irish Studies and I wish to acknowledge this debt here. I would like to thank the Sydney Jones Library, Liverpool; the National Library of Ireland, Dublin; the Boole Library at University College Cork; the Howard Gotlieb Archival Research Center at Boston University; the John J. Burns Library at Boston College; the Harry Ransom Center at the University of Texas at Austin; the University of Reading Library, Reading; the British Broadcasting Corporation written word archive, Reading; and the Dublin Writers Museum, Dublin for access to their collections. I wish to express my gratitude to my colleagues and students at the Institute of Irish Studies for making it such an intellectually vibrant place to work. At Liverpool, I have had the privilege of making some lasting friendships and I would like to thank Maurice McColgan, Jimmy Fennessy, John O'Shea, Roland Enmarch, Paddy Hoey, Alex Pelavan, Anna Pilz, Jane Davison, Chris Kedge, Tony Halpin, Laura Green, Kati Nurmi, Maija Salokangas, Bryce Evans, Sonja Tiernan, Stephen Kelly, Brian Hanley, Andrew Tierney and Tom Waldron amongst others who have greatly enriched my experience here. I am indebted to Julia O'Faoláin for her support of the project at an early stage by providing access to restricted materials. I have been very lucky in having the benefit of talented proofreaders who have given their time to read over badly written drafts, and I would like to thank Sr Deanna Bartolomei OSF, Ciaran O'Neill, Whitney Standlee and Robert O'Brien for all their hard work. Matthew Staunton kindly provided me with a striking cover image. Manchester University Press has been a pleasure to work with and I thank their readers for their insightful comments and support. Special mention must also go to Frank Shovlin for his support and friendship over many years; this work would not have been possible without his contribution. However, the greatest debt for this project lies with my family and their collective support; in particular, I would like to thank my parents Hugh and Mary Carson for their love and encouragement throughout. Finally, this book is dedicated to the irrepressible Anne-Claire Leydier.

Every effort has been made to obtain permission to reproduce copyright material, and the publisher will be pleased to be informed of any errors and omissions for correction in future editions.

1

Introduction:
Rebel by vocation

A whole generation since 1922 has gone rotten like fruit badly kept or evaporated like your da's whiskey. (Seán O'Faoláin)[1]

In the summer of 1947 the writer Frank O'Connor returned home to Ireland to find a country still locked in an atmosphere of post-war stagnation; for him, it was one that was in direct opposition to the dynamism and progression of Clement Attlee's Britain, which had undertaken a programme of nationalisation that would culminate in the formation of the National Health Service in 1948. As an artist O'Connor felt that this national quiescence was reflected in Irish literature, and a whole generation of artists had failed to deliver on the promise of the cultural revival to develop a great national art:

> I'm only back from England and in a state of complete disillusionment with this country. The first thing I did was re-order my books so that the complete Irish section now forms portion of a larger English unit. What's the point of pretending that Sean [O'Faoláin] or Peadar [O'Donnell] or any of the lads after Yeats is anything except a damp squib? 'Irish Literature' is simply a dope we give ourselves to reassure ourselves of the continuity; … none of us will get anywhere until we say 'I'm a writer in my own right, and I hate every son of a bitch in this country, and be jasus I'll kick it into culture before I die.' I haven't yet reached that point; only the disillusionment and the loathing of the smugness on part of the boys.[2]

O'Connor's dismissive assessment of the condition of Irish letters is telling, in that it points to a sense of failure and hopelessness on behalf of the generation of Irish writers who had worked in the shadow of W.B. Yeats and James Joyce, and had struggled to survive in an indifferent Irish market under a frustrating state censorship. It also points to something of O'Connor's own volatile character and oscillating moods. By 1947 he had finished his association with Ireland's premier literary magazine *The Bell* (1940–54) and was still frustrated by what had been, on his part, an acrimonious split. O'Connor, along with Seán O'Faoláin and Peader O'Donnell, was part of the original editorial board of *The*

Bell, a magazine that had been formed with the express intention of kicking Ireland into culture.

This book contextualises the magazine within the Irish society of its day, and looks at the coterie of writers that gathered around *The Bell* under its first editor and most important figure, Seán O'Faoláin. Why these writers felt compelled to launch a magazine is the subject of some debate, and their place in the Irish literary canon is also much misunderstood. Critically, authors such as O'Faoláin, O'Connor and Liam O'Flaherty have been sandwiched between the colossal figures linked with modernism in Yeats, Joyce and Samuel Beckett, and for some time remembered as the reactionary writers of twee short stories about 'wee Anne going to her first confession, stuff about country funerals, old men in chimney nooks after 50 years in America, will-making, match-making', and yet this is not the complete story.[3] Beckett too was dismissive of O'Faoláin and the other writers within his circle; writing to his friend Thomas McGreevy he complained: 'In the train from Bray, vainly unrecognized, the pestiferous Michael Farrell fresh from Kilmacanogue & next doordom to All Forlorn [Seán O'Faoláin] (whose elucubration on Coriolanus at the Abbey I trust you read at the Chelsea Library). He is finishing a work, really very beautiful, & admired by All Forlorn, himself naively 5 minutes later extolled by Farrell as a critic!'[4]

Despite this hostility, O'Faoláin and the generation of writers that assembled around him in *The Bell* were among Ireland's most internationally celebrated authors within their own time and formed a recognised role within its cultural elite. Their work is much less popular today, partly because of the hostility with which it was viewed by a contemporaneous generation of writers (like Flann O'Brien and Samuel Beckett) who were reacting against their prominence, and partly because of a critical misreading within the academy of their work that neglects them by interpreting the history and, by extension, the culture of post-independence Ireland as stifled, muted and isolated. It is this misreading that this book attempts to rectify. For some, the 'introspective literary scene of the Free State was understandably largely absorbed in adjusting to the often disheartening realities of independence, as shown in the commitment of many to what were essentially mimetic modes of writing – the short stories of Seán O'Faoláin and Frank O'Connor.'[5] For mimetic here read imitative, restricted and, ultimately, inferior; a generation of diverse and complicated writers are contrasted with an expansive, experimental and progressive modernism embodied, in Ireland's case, in Yeats and Joyce. However, this is to do a disservice to O'Faoláin and his contemporaries who wrote from a range of perspectives and for a variety of reasons, as *The Bell* itself demonstrates. That their first love was the Russian realists was a matter of choice; O'Faoláin's most prized books were the fifteen-volume collected *Novels of Turgenev* published between 1894 and 1899 and translated by Constance Garnett. It was not through ignorance of the challenges of modernist experimental writing that this choice was made. At least that is how they viewed themselves, and there were few as immersed in the traditions of international literature as O'Faoláin, and indeed his close childhood friend, O'Connor.

O'Connor was a committed supporter of Yeats, and although he was later in life dismissive of Joyce, he did take the opportunity to seek out the great writer in Paris as a young man.[6] O'Faoláin, for his part, was unashamedly supportive of both writers, beginning a PhD on Yeats and writing frequently of his admiration for Joyce, although like many other readers he baulked at the complexity of *Finnegans Wake*.[7] It is the writers of *The Bell*, with O'Faoláin to the fore, that are examined here, especially in light of their own conception of themselves as a generation and the concomitant pressures and reactions that this entailed. In one of his less disconsolate moods, O'Connor was able to conceive of the burden that he seemingly shared with O'Faoláin to produce something of a national literature, but at an international standard. He felt the baton had been passed from Yeats to the younger writers, and it was their responsibility to hand it on to a younger generation. It was this desire which was made manifest in *The Bell*:

> Anglo-Irish is a different subject, and it's no use pretending I can teach it, though I do my best. The trouble is John, it's all Yeats, whatever you say; Joyce only slinks in as a negation of Yeats – Yeats as he might have been if he'd only had talent and no brains, no character and no decency. I am beginning to feel a respect for Sean and myself. At least we are not a mere negation of Yeats; we are like Paul and the apostles, poor devils who do the best we can to make intelligible the preposterous ideas of that Sligo Christ [Yeats], adopting them to history and to Cork.[8]

O'Connor's naming of Cork is significant here, criticism of O'Faoláin and O'Connor was tied to their presence in Dublin as interlopers from Éire's second city. Their own sense of friendship and loyalty had been honed under the tutelage of Daniel Corkery (a man whom they would later bitterly resent and attack) as two young students who were aspiring artists in post-Civil War Cork. This tension between the local and the universal, so admirably articulated by Patrick Kavanagh in 'Parochialism and Provincialism',[9] plagued the post-independence generation of writers as the nation struggled to express its own identity on an international stage.[10] The fear of accusations of provincialism worried Cork men going to Dublin and Dublin men going to London, and this was especially acute with the added stresses of the Second World War in a globalised world that was rapidly tearing itself apart.

That Cyril Connolly equally worried in London about the isolation that war imposed on the metropolitan artist was of little consolation in Ireland; yet with the benefit of hindsight we can see that this isolation was not as complete as it appeared to those who experienced it at the time. Connolly, O'Faoláin, and a whole host of other international literary editors and artists, such as

R.P. Blackmur, formed part of a network or exchange that was remarkable for
its productivity, despite their claims about isolation and other 'enemies of promise'.[11] They were, in effect, part of an Atlantic world of letters that struggled
to make sense of their time, and to promote the production of art under trying
circumstances. Even W.H. Auden felt the pressure that war exerted on artists
and felt sure that no great novel would be produced for its duration, claiming:

> Times of crisis, like our own, are unfavourable to the art of the novelist. The
> realistic novelist, trying to write about Europe to-day, is like a portrait-painter
> whose model refuses to sit still. He may hope to catch certain impressions, jot
> down a few suggestive notes – but the big, maturely considered masterpiece must
> wait for better times. Most of what passes for fiction is, of necessity, only a kind
> of high-grade news-reporting. The writer is far too close to his violently moving,
> dangerous subject.[12]

Auden's nod to news-reporting here is noteworthy, as journalism was the mode
of choice for many writers during the war, including O'Faoláin.

That O'Faoláin and those around him appealed so vocally and consistently
in their journalism against the perceived indifference and philistinism of Irish
society has led to their artistic output being considered as an extension of their
political writings. They are now seen as naturalists in the same mode as Émile
Zola and their work concerned with exposing the hypocrisy and bad faith of
Irish society; as one critic has argued:

> No one can doubt that the social and sexual problems depicted in naturalism were
> actual and pressing. The issue is not that naturalism invented or even exaggerated
> the social grimness that would become the trademark topic. But what can be
> questioned is the inference that the communities thus depicted were so helplessly
> paralysed, so bereft of internal dissident forces and resources, as naturalism would
> typically suggest ... It was as if the colourless monotony of the society – as the
> naturalists conceived of it at least – could only be conveyed in a drab, colourless,
> monotonous aesthetic. When compared to the altogether more outward-looking
> and experimental modernists, the naturalists seem to replicate the very conditions
> of backwardness or inward-looking provincialism their own works protest.[13]

There are several points worth considering here in this criticism of the Irish
naturalists (O'Faoláin, O'Connor and others of *The Bell* generation). First, the
critic is right to point out the points of resistance to social inertia in Irish society. There was a vibrant popular culture at work in post-independence Ireland,
as is evidenced by the sheer numbers of dance halls, cinemas and sporting
arenas that sprang up across the country at that time. Second, there is nothing
in naturalism as a form that inherently ties a monotonous society to a 'monotonous aesthetic'; after all, Zola's own gritty realism was produced at the height
of *belle époque* France.

Irish artists may have felt obliged to develop a readership for their work, and may have suffered under censorship, but the real issue was indifference from the public to what was perceived as elitist artistic production in the main, something that has been present throughout modern western history, and not just in Ireland. That said, this criticism of writers such as O'Faoláin is wrong to depict a coherent or developed school of naturalistic writing against an experimental, progressive modernism, even in aesthetic terms. Much of O'Faoláin's writing is not naturalistic nor is it even overtly political. It is concerned with aesthetics, mystery, romance and Catholicism as well as politics, and would not fit easily within a naturalistic definition. O'Faoláin himself regularly identified a romantic streak to his writing that was more in line with writers of the Revival and his youth than with any naturalistic school:

> The romantic [O'Faoláin] doesn't give a damn if nobody is looking at him. He's looking at himself. He's seeing God looking at him – the Gods, and the Glory, and if he were all alone on a desert island he'd dress up in regimentals and wave a soword [*sic*] and shout, 'To glory. Follow my white plume' – and start fighting the waves. If he were an Irishman he'd then sit down and laugh himself sick at himself.[14]

Seen in this light then, O'Faoláin and the writers he gathered round him lived in a complex relationship to those of the previous generation, and in a complex relationship to modernism as a movement so defined by us today. Modernism and its connections with O'Faoláin and *The Bell* are problematised by this study; the traditional opposition between an outward-looking modernism and an inward-looking naturalism are challenged here. Mark Quigley has defined O'Faoláin's work as inhabiting a place on a late modernist spectrum, one that deploys 'postcolonial realism' that 'constitutes at once a critique of mainline modernism and an alternative late-modernist practice'.[15] However, this study sees debates around modernism as placing O'Faoláin and his generation at a critical disadvantage, caught between the vice of James Joyce and Samuel Beckett abroad and domineered by W.B. Yeats at home. The writers of *The Bell* had their faults, but they also had a difficult literary landscape to navigate in post-independence Ireland.

Internationalist or European has long been a synonym for modernist within literary criticism, especially when comparing Irish writing to some of the giants of high modernism, such as T.S. Eliot, Virginia Woolf, Joyce or Ezra Pound. But in doing so the force of critical interpretation places O'Faoláin and the generation of *The Bell* at a loss. They came to maturity at a time when Yeats and Joyce were at the height of their powers and struggled to define themselves in an Irish world of letters being canonised around these two figures. However, this is not to say that their own work was reactionary or that they rejected the challenges set by a modernist aesthetic. Rather, no one argues persuasively why they should have accepted that challenge in the first place; they wrote of what they knew, in a mode that they had mastered. Both writers were well aware of their reputation as being excessively in thrall to the Russian realists. As O'Connor wryly remarked to their joint friend, the Harvard Professor John V. Kelleher, 'the atmosphere of Dublin was lovely, relaxed and not too hostile, the only discord being an article in the I.T. [*Irish Times*] which suggested that Irish literature had been put astray when Sean and I got Turgenev out of the Cork public library and referring younger writers back to the real Irish source – Samuel Lover!'[16]

Their writing came from a Russian base, through a French model, and in an Irish context; it is hard to see a more European or internationalist set of influences on Irish writing. Their critical exclusion from wider movements in global literature is unusual, especially as some of their contemporaries, such as Elizabeth Bowen, are now considered at the forefront of Irish modernism.[17] Not that O'Faoláin's work should be considered modernist in itself, it is not, but just that, outside of Yeats and Joyce, he was arguably the most recognised figure in post-independence Irish letters at an international level for several decades. The term 'internationalist' is used in this book to mean that the writers of *The Bell* generation had lived abroad, were alive to the artists and literary traditions of other countries, and were in connection and exchange with their international peers. It also aims to show that if modernism in an Irish context is wide enough to include the paintings of Basil Rakoczi or the architecture of Barry Byrne then *The Bell* also included writers within that mode, or who were knowingly operating within that tradition, with Nick Nicholls and Freda Laughton perhaps being the most prominent examples. Their presence, along with other experimental writers, undermines the claim that 'while avant-garde experimentalism thrived in continental Europe … it is difficult it trace any such tendency in Ireland'.[18] If modernism had seen its apotheosis in 1922 then its impact was well understood by the time O'Faoláin and his contemporaries were in the ascendant in the 1930s; to put his writing in context, his second novel *Bird Alone* was first published in 1936, two years later than Henry Miller's *Tropic of Cancer* in 1934. If anything, the debate around the usefulness of modernism as a helpful critical term in understanding Irish writing and writers in the twentieth century is drawn into focus when discussing a little magazine that ran for fourteen years across so many authors and fields.[19] For example, *The Bell* contained some important works of the distinctly modern but also distinctly unmodernist Patrick Kavanagh.

Kavanagh, perhaps more than any other Irish author responding to Joyce and Yeats, showed the way to escape from their shadow. The distinctive lyrical force of his work puts him outside the formal experiments of high-modernist poets such as T.S. Eliot, yet his poetry is among the most distinctly modern writing in *The Bell*. His calm confidence in writing of the 'ordinary plenty' of Irish life gave a younger generation of writers, such as Seamus Heaney, the 'permission to dwell without cultural anxiety among the usual landmarks of your life', and avoid the epic mytho-poetic dominance of Yeats.[20] So *The Bell* and its writers exist in a position of resisting easy categorisation, inhabiting a space that is critically difficult to define and draws into question the suitability of modern critical models to delineate such an elusive subject as that little magazine. As Edna Longley has shown for Yeats, but in an argument that could equally be applied to *The Bell*:

> Some critics distance what they call 'modernism' from Ireland. Others collapse it into Ireland. If Yeats's poetry slips through the cracks, the remedy may not be to talk of 'modernisms' or 'poetries' but rather to revisit the inter-national dynamics that created modern poetry in English.[21]

Similarly, this book looks to the international dynamics that created the modern literary magazine that informed the composition of *The Bell* and the writers who made up its editors and contributors, including those who chose to engage with the style that we now identify as modernist, but just as importantly, those that did not. As the literary public house replaced the literary at-homes as the main source for social interaction between artists, *The Bell* stands as the printed testimony to this transition from writers who had cut their teeth under the gaze of Yeats and AE (George Russell), to a new type of artist with a more public and less elitist reputation as best embodied by Brendan Behan or Patrick Kavanagh.

For O'Faoláin *The Bell* was about producing a sustained, low-key criticism of life and art in Éire. He wanted to slowly build up standards in line with other international magazines by publishing the best of Irish talent alongside the best of international talent. As he reminded O'Connor, *The Bell* was not a blast of explosive experimentalism, but the slow boil of creative criticism:

> We do not keep a dog that barks. You will recollect that we set out to be a natural sort of sane, and quiet, and constructive paper such as any normal country should produce – to use one of your own phrases when 'breathing naturally'. I do not know that we are thereby 'getting anywhere'. It is just a corner of sanity and intelligence and decency. A tiny piece of construction. Barking is not our line. It was not the AE line in the Statesman. I do not notice that it is the line in any periodical I know – Yale Review, Virginia Quarterly, Horizon, Life and Letters, London Mercury. Are all these 'dead ends'? You see – you want controversy, dramatics, fight, explosions.[22]

This book focuses on these writers, led by O'Faoláin and O'Donnell in their capacity as editors, who contributed to *The Bell* and formed part of the cultural vanguard of Irish writing, that sought to develop Irish standards, both aesthetic and critical, to match their ambitions. This project was, from the outset, self-consciously about the formation of a group capable of leading Ireland in its cultural rejuvenation:

The breech is made … If I can get the *Bell* to take in every sort of person from
Kerry to Donegal, and bind them about you and me and Peadar [O'Donnell] and
Roisin [Walsh] do you not see that we are forming a nucleus? Take the long view
– bit by bit we are accepted as the nucleus. Bit by bit we can spread ideas, create
REAL standards, ones naturally growing out of Life and not out of literature
and Yeats and all that. It is going to take years and years. Explosions and rages
get nowhere. You sit down there on your backside and do the highfalutin' artist,
while up here, painstakingly, I am doing a spot of real construction.[23]

The construction of a new Irish identity is what O'Faoláin felt *The Bell* would
contribute to the world of letters, but also to Irish society in general. The magazine was much more than an outlet for writers in Ireland, it was also engaged
politically, which explains its tendency towards Mass Observation inspired
articles and direct criticism, albeit limited by what wartime censorship would
allow. No attempt has been made to address *The Bell*'s theoretical underpinnings in the world of sociology, nor to evaluate the contribution of Mass
Observation to its composition, and this is a gap that is addressed here.

O'Faoláin, *The Bell* and Irish literary periodicals have seen some renewed
interest from the academy since the publication of Frank Shovlin's seminal
The Irish Literary Periodical 1923–1958 (2003) and an upswing in awareness
on O'Faoláin around the centenary of his birth in 2000.[24] The publication of
new studies into magazine culture and journalism in Ireland has also brought
some much needed perspective to the field and widened our understanding of
the period.[25] This work has been supplemented by the publication of letters
from O'Faoláin that add to the earlier foundations set by Maurice Harmon
in O'Faoláin criticism.[26] Most recently, we have seen the publication of two
considerable contributions to our knowledge on *The Bell* and O'Faoláin in
Kelly Matthews's *The Bell Magazine and the Representation of Irish Identity*
(2012) and Paul Delaney's *Seán O'Faoláin: Literature, Inheritance and the 1930s*
(2014).[27] This book seeks to add to the work already done here and contribute
to our understanding of O'Faoláin as a writer and *The Bell* as a magazine.
This is done through a biography of the magazine itself, with its first editor
O'Faoláin to the fore, also analysing those who wrote for it. It throws some
light on the Ireland of the period and complicates the picture of an inward-
looking, isolationist island bereft of humour. By putting O'Faoláin, O'Donnell,
and those who gathered around them in *The Bell* into focus, those writers are
placed not only in their international framework, but also into the local, in the
petty and provincial backbiting that characterised much of their interactions.
It follows the work already set down for writers such as W.H. Auden or Cyril
Connolly in a British setting, but widens the scope to include Ireland, putting
O'Faoláin in the proper context of his international peers.[28] If R.F. Foster
has recently shown that those who took up arms in 1916 were a diverse and
complex group, then this study shows that the generation that followed them

were equally divergent and complicated in their motives and ambitions. Theirs was a new Ireland to make, and O'Faoláin and *The Bell* generation were at the forefront of the cultural elite that sought to establish itself in the decades after the revolution and civil war.[29]

Notes

1 Seán O'Faoláin to John V. Kelleher (22 August 1948), John V. Kelleher Correspondence, Boole Library, University College Cork, BL/L/JVK/25. Hereafter referred to as UCC.

2 Frank O'Connor to John V. Kelleher (June 1947), UCC, BL/L/JVK/152.

3 Myles Na Gopaleen, 'Cruiskeen Lawn', *Irish Times* (4 October 1954), p. 4. Myles Na Gopaleen is one of several pen names for Brian O'Nolan. Where possible the given spelling is maintained.

4 Samuel Beckett to Thomas McGreevy (16 January 1936) in Martha Dow Fehsenfeld and Lois More Overbeck (eds), *The Letters of Samuel Beckett: Volume 1: 1929–1940* (Cambridge: Cambridge University Press, 2009), p. 299.

5 Alex Davis, 'The Irish Modernists', in Matthew Campbell (ed.), *The Cambridge Companion to Contemporary Irish Poetry* (Cambridge: Cambridge University Press, 2003), p. 78.

6 Richard Ellmann, *James Joyce* (London: Oxford University Press, 1961), p. 563.

7 See Seán O'Faoláin, '50 Years After Bloomsday', *New York Times* (13 June 1954), pp. 5, 24.

8 Frank O'Connor to John V. Kelleher (26 February 1952), UCC, Bl/JVK/179.

9 Patrick Kavanagh, *Kavanagh's Weekly: A Journal of Literature and Politics* 1:7 (24 May 1952), p. 2.

10 Antoinette Quinn (ed.), *A Poet's Country: Selected Prose* (Dublin: Lilliput Press, 2003), p. 237.

11 Cyril Connolly, *Enemies of Promise* (London: Routledge & Kegan Paul, 1938). Connolly's work is preoccupied with the social conditions that prevent the production of great art, a topic O'Faoláin would return to again and again in his editorial work in *The Bell*.

12 W.H. Auden and Christopher Isherwood, 'Young British Writers – On the Way Up', in Edward Mendelson (ed.), *The Complete Works of W.H. Auden Prose: Volume II 1939–1948* (Princeton: Princeton University Press, 2002), p. 21.

13 Joe Cleary, *Outrageous Fortune: Capital and Culture in Modern Ireland* (Dublin: Field Day Publications, 2007), p. 98.

14 Seán O'Faoláin to John V. Kelleher (September [1948]?), UCC, BL/L/JVK/26.

15 Mark Quigley, *Empire's Wake: Postcolonial Irish Writing and the Politics of Modern Literary Form* (New York: Fordham University Press, 2013), p. 68.

16 Frank O'Connor to John V. Kelleher (n.d.), UCC, BL/L/JVK/172.

17 The *Cambridge Companion to Irish Modernism* does not mention Seán O'Faoláin, or *The Bell* in any detail despite discussing the White Stag Group, and the importance of editors, magazines and collectors to Irish modernism. See Joe Cleary (ed.), *The*

Cambridge Companion to Irish Modernism (Cambridge: Cambridge University Press, 2014).

18 Frank Shovlin, 'From Revolution to Republic: Magazines, Modernism, and Modernity in Ireland', in Peter Brooker and Andrew Thacker (eds), *The Oxford Critical and Cultural History of Modernist Magazines Volume 1, Britain and Ireland 1880–1955* (Oxford: Oxford University Press, 2009), p. 735.

19 Fionna Barber sees *The Bell* as important in supporting modernist painting in Ireland, especially the White Stag Group during the war. See Fionna Barber, *Art in Ireland since 1910* (London: Reaktion, 2013), pp. 95–106.

20 Patrick Kavanagh, 'Advent', in *Patrick Kavanagh: Collected Poems*, ed. Antoinette Quinn (London: Penguin Books, 2005), p. 110; Seamus Heaney, *Finders Keepers: Selected Prose 1971–2001* (London: Faber & Faber, 2002), p. 140.

21 Edna Longley, *Yeats and Modern Poetry* (Cambridge: Cambridge University Press, 2013), p. 44.

22 Seán O'Faoláin to Frank O'Connor (n.d.), Frank O'Connor Collection, Gotlieb Archival Research Centre, Boston University (Box 3, Folder 6). Hereafter referred to as Gotlieb.

23 Seán O'Faoláin to Frank O'Connor (n.d.), Gotlieb (Box 3, Folder 6).

24 See Frank Shovlin, *The Irish Literary Periodical 1923–1958* (Oxford: Clarendon Press, 2003); Donatella Abbate Baden (ed.), *Seán O'Faoláin: A Centenary Celebration: Proceedings of the Turin Conference, Università di Torino, 7–9 aprile 2000* (Torino: Centro studi celtici, Dipartamento di scienze del linguaggio, 2001).

25 See Brian Fanning, *The Quest for Modern Ireland: The Battle for Ideas, 1912–1986* (Dublin: Irish Academic Press, 2008); Malcolm Ballin, *Irish Periodical Culture 1937–1972: Genre in Ireland, Wales, and Scotland* (New York: Palgrave MacMillan, 2008); Mark O'Brien and Felix M. Larkin (eds), *Periodicals and Journalism in Twentieth-Century Ireland: Writing Against the Grain* (Dublin: Four Courts Press, 2014).

26 See Munira H. Mutran (ed.), *Sean O'Faoláin's Letters to Brazil* (São Paulo: Associacão Editorial, 2005); Maurice Harmon, *Sean O'Faoláin: A Life* (London: Constable, 1994); Maurice Harmon, *Sean O'Faoláin: A Critical Introduction* (Dublin: Wolfhound Press, 1984).

27 Kelly Matthews, *The Bell Magazine and the Representation of Irish Identity* (Dublin: Four Courts Press, 2012); Paul Delaney, *Seán O'Faoláin: Literature, Inheritance and the 1930s* (Dublin: Irish Academic Press, 2014).

28 See Michael Shelden, *Friends of Promise: Cyril Connolly and the World of Horizon* (London: Hamish Hamilton, 1989); Samuel Hynes, *The Auden Generation: Literature and Politics in England in the 1930s* (London: Viking Press, 1977).

29 R.F. Foster, *Vivid Faces: The Revolutionary Generation in Ireland 1890–1923* (London: Allen Lane, 2014).

2

Beginnings and blind alleys:
O'Faoláin and his circle

I soon found out that what they really needed was not instruction in the art of writing but in the art of living. (Seán O'Faoláin)[1]

I am really without a standard of measurement in myself as to what constitutes a good book. (Peadar O'Donnell)[2]

The above epigraphs from *The Bell*'s two editors, Seán O'Faoláin and Peadar O'Donnell, reflect their differing attitudes to writing and point to the differences of character that combined so fruitfully in the production of this literary journal. O'Faoláin's mind was that of teacher and educator. It was expansive in its outlook, consistently seeking to elaborate and complicate his instruction from a position of distant authority. O'Donnell, on the other hand, disavowed specialist knowledge, preferring the mantle of man of action to man of letters. His writing was less that of the great artificer and more that of a force of nature. Between them, they would work to help establish *The Bell* as one of Ireland's most important periodicals and to establish the careers of a new generation of Irish writers, publishing them alongside some of the most important literary figures of their day. Although O'Donnell remained editor for longer than O'Faoláin, the style of the magazine and its publication culture had already been established, and O'Donnell's tenure is marked by a decline in the consistency of publication quality. While not taking away any of the credit from O'Donnell, who was the only permanent presence with the magazine throughout its life, Seán O'Faoláin was the magazine's guiding light, as Vivian Mercier argued in an early analysis of its achievements: 'Seán O'Faoláin *is The Bell*. He is not just a figurehead – he is the magazine.'[3]

The initial connection between these two men lay with Edward Garnett, who had been introduced to O'Donnell through Liam O'Flaherty, and had subsequently introduced O'Donnell to O'Faoláin. Their shared experience of writing under a reader and editor as gifted as Garnett would give them the confidence and insight to put themselves forward as senior figures in the Irish literary landscape after the passing of W.B. Yeats in 1939 and James Joyce in 1941. Their attitude in *The Bell* was always one of support for writers embarking on the first steps of a literary career. However, they were at pains to distinguish themselves from this next generation of aspiring artists in Ireland, seeing their role in *The Bell* as that of paternalistic overseers rather than active participants. Both authors had already set out their hopes for the future of Irish writing, as seen in their publications in journals such as *The Commonweal* and *Ireland To-Day*, and in doing so bemoaned the lack of an advanced critical apparatus within Ireland to interpret modern writers and disseminate their ideas to a wider audience.[4] The effect of this distinction between more established writers and their younger counterparts was the creation of a false temporal binary, which elided the true nature of literary production, in that it failed to acknowledge that different artists produce work at different ages and of differing quality. The veracity of this distinction was demonstrated by O'Faoláin's own literary career and his attempts to downplay his achievements in *The Bell* in favour of his later literary work and O'Donnell's own fruitful output after his association with the magazine had ended. Ironically, it is this false distinction that gave O'Faoláin and O'Donnell the confidence to see themselves as the voice of the literary establishment in Ireland, and in doing so they fulfilled their own prophesy in becoming that establishment. In this way, the success of *The Bell* endowed it with a formidable reputation and established it as the most obvious route to literary recognition in Ireland during the years of its operation 1940–54. Such was its reputation that the story of *The Bell* is the story of Irish literature from the beginning of the Second World War to the 1960s. That is to say that all Irish writers of that generation, be they regular contributors or entirely absent, were in some way involved with the coterie who wrote for *The Bell*.

In order to understand how O'Faoláin could come to see himself as ideally suited to lead a new generation of Irish writing from the self-proclaimed wilderness to literary salvation, one must first look at his own early professional formation. O'Faoláin's first substantial published work was the collection *Midsummer Night Madness and Other Stories* (1932). It was published by Jonathan Cape, a firm established in 1922 by the eponymous book salesman and his Cambridge-educated friend George Wren Howard. The success of this firm was defined by its production of high quality books, and was greatly assisted by the astute eye of Edward Garnett in his role as its chief reader. O'Faoláin was suggested as an author to George Howard by Garnett, and an offer to publish *Midsummer Night Madness and Other Stories* with an accompanying two further books was made on the 10 August 1931: 'I may say with what personal interest and pleasure', wrote Howard, 'I have read some of the stories in *Midsummer Night Madness*.'[5] Such a substantial offer for three books from a publisher of Jonathan Cape's standing made a deep impression on O'Faoláin who replied in humbled terms of gratitude. In a letter to Howard, most likely written in October 1931, O'Faoláin gave some insight into his mindset at that time:

I await the proofs of the new story, 'The Patriot'. Has Mr. Garnett handed it to you? He approves of it. He has mentioned my correcting his preface ... Most of my corrections have been due to your alterations in my method of indicating *oratio recta*, i.e. a hyphen followed by a capital, e.g. – Yes, he said. Instead of 'Yes', he said. ... You will observe that I have humbly accepted your alterations but I hope that you will allow me to use my preferred method in my novel. It is, I believe, regularly used by Joyce. By the way, can you manage to get two accents into my name: see title page, i.e. for Seán O'Faoláin. These accents indicate length of vowel in Gaelic. My name is pronounced therefore as Shawn O'Faolawn. Without the accents it would be Shann O'Faolann. I don't much care how people pronounce it but I do care how it is spelled.[6]

This letter is instructive as it points to some significant facts about O'Faoláin and his writing. First, it resolves the debate about the correct spelling and use of O'Faoláin's name, which has changed through the different printings of his works.[7] Second, it shows O'Faoláin had prior knowledge of Garnett's preface wherein he attacked Irish literary censorship, another indication that he was deliberately being provocative with this collection. Finally, it points to a close study of James Joyce and his writing by O'Faoláin as early as 1931, and an attempt to emulate his work at least stylistically. This is important because Joyce is conspicuous by his absence from *The Bell*. For example, *The Bell* contained no obituary for Joyce when he died on 13 January 1941, despite his international fame, and yet O'Faoláin could show the good grace to include an obituary of F.R. Higgins and publicise his memorial fund.[8]

Although Elizabeth Bowen did publish a biographical sketch of Joyce two months after his death, Joyce remained a figure whom O'Faoláin had difficulty reconciling with his theories of Irish society and literature.[9] The Joycean method of using a hyphen to indicate direct speech is present throughout *A Portrait of the Artist as a Young Man* (1916) and *Ulysses* (1922), although not in *Dubliners* (1914). O'Faoláin was hopeful that he could follow Joyce in using this method for his proposed novel, but Howard was reluctant to change the publisher's preferred style: 'personally I find your method which as you say is used by James Joyce more difficult to read'.[10] It seems that Howard was insistent on this, as when O'Faoláin's next submission to Jonathan Cape, his novel *A Nest of Simple Folk* (1933), was published, it retained the more common method of inverted commas for direct quotations. This letter also shows that O'Faoláin's short story 'The Patriot', set in the seaside town of Youghal where O'Faoláin holidayed as a child, was added later to the collection and not present in the original manuscript. As a matter of literary interest, O'Faoláin also based the character Edward Bradley on Daniel Corkery, while the protagonist, Bernard, has autobiographical echoes. He wrote: 'I put it, quite explicitly, into the story in M.N.M. called "The Patriot", in which I, as the hayro, go to bed with a girl while Corkery, as the old patriotic sentimentalist, goes off speechifying.'[11]

If O'Faoláin was young and eager to please Jonathan Cape, his experiences in dealing with the Irish book market as a travelling salesman had left him clear-eyed as to the vagaries of Irish reading culture. Between the truce in 1921 and the outbreak of civil war in 1922, O'Faoláin had worked as a travelling salesman for a 'publisher that specialised in school texts: the Educational Company of Ireland' and this experience gave him a unique understanding of the Irish publishing industry.[12] Consequently, when he was accepted for publication, he felt qualified to instruct Jonathan Cape as to the pitfalls of the Irish market and as this letter shows, was beginning to see Ireland in the manner later expressed in *The Bell*:

> I was for a year a traveller in Ireland for the Talbot Press so I know a little about things here. I am eager to get my books into the out of the way places ... We are beginning to think that more Irish literature is being read than formerly and want to develop the people's habits of reading – above all reading us ... The new Civil Service and the "bourgeois" civilisation of post-revolutionary years has money to buy books <u>if encouraged</u>. Advertising is no good here – at present anyway. It's the trade that sells books, reviews, and talk.[13]

The Educational Company of Ireland was an imprint of the Talbot Press, producing books for schoolchildren. A newly emergent Irish bourgeoisie was clearly the target market on which O'Faoláin based *The Bell*'s readership, especially if one considers its didactic tone and attempts to educate its subscribers to higher standards and tastes. This middle-class culture was later to return to frustrate O'Faoláin by its inward looking myopia and cultural philistinism. It was this hypocritically pious society that later accepted the banning of several authors, including O'Faoláin himself, under state censorship. However, it also illuminates some of the hard-nosed cynicism with which O'Faoláin drove *The Bell*, in that he had already identified its market as set among those whom the magazine would spend most of its time attacking. These early formative experiences are key to understanding the legacy of *The Bell*. O'Faoláin's grassroots understanding of the Irish publications market afforded him an insight into what would and would not work in an Irish context, and goes some way to explain the success of the magazine, especially when coupled with Peadar O'Donnell's capacity to source timely cash injections for the venture.

If O'Faoláin was disappointed and downbeat by the subsequent banning of *Midsummer Night Madness* he certainly showed no evidence of this in his correspondence with Cape. On the contrary, his letters betray a new-found confidence, an enthusiasm he developed that would give him an air of authority when editing *The Bell*. After its banning, O'Faoláin submitted *A Nest of Simple Folk* to Jonathan Cape for publication. This novel was epic in its scope and was O'Faoláin's attempt to emulate his role model, Ivan Turgenev, in his intragenerational novel *Fathers and Sons* (1862). The title is also a nod to Constance Garnett's translation of Turgenev's novel *A House of Gentle Folk* (1894). *A Nest of Simple Folk* runs to 413 pages, and the sustained effort O'Faoláin must have endured to finish it within a year of the publication of his first collection left him with a sense of achievement which removed his critical distance from the work. Writing to Cape, he showed his pride in its completion: 'As I read over I fear I was over-optimistic about expecting a wide reception. It's far too good. Much better, I think, than E.G. [Edward Garnett] realises. I am very pleased with it.'[14] Or again, when he was asking for its circulation among other authors: 'I wonder could you help me out by sending an advance copy to [B.W.] Huebusch of the corrected version of my great novel?'[15] Such was O'Faoláin's belief in the novel that he even wrote to Cape suggesting that they hold back the publication of another Irish author for fear it would influence his own sales: 'Kate O'Brien has finished a sequel to *Without My Cloak* and lest it clash with my book – for both that and this cover the same country and her novel, also was a chronicle of generations, I thought you might like to forestall her book.'[16]

O'Faoláin's obsession with detail and capacity for self-promotion was clearly at work at this early stage, traits that would prove invaluable in establishing and maintaining *The Bell*. He wrote to the production manager, demanding that free copies be sent to W.B. Yeats and angrily criticising her decision to pass the design for the book: 'The design has no merits whatever. It is neither original nor even as unoriginal pleasing in itself. It is devoid of imagination, absolutely … An arrangement of lines existing in the vacuum of a brain that has no associations of any kind the design is even then tawdry. A scroll across a harp! Some idle blocks of green!'[17]

Although O'Faoláin was clearly disappointed with the presentation of the book, it seems it was printed in accordance with the publisher's wishes anyway, as the harp remained embossed on the cover of the first edition. Despite O'Faoláin's prickly correspondence with Jonathan Cape, he was still considered a worthwhile author to have in their stable, even if his pleas for more money were draining: 'O'F is a very good bet and I should not at all mind helping him further … But he must not think that books go on selling at the same pace for ever and he must be alive to the dangers (for him more than for us) of mortgaging his future too heavily.'[18] What is striking about O'Faoláin's relationship with Jonathan Cape is his ability to hold out for better terms and his commercial insight. This allowed him to maintain a working relationship with the publisher until 1974, when the final profit and loss account on his collection *The Talking Trees and Other Stories* (1971) was tallied. O'Faoláin's hard-nosed pragmatism was what sustained *The Bell* and made it such a success under his stewardship, even if this sometimes rubbed publishers up the wrong way. In a confidential letter written in 1938, G. Wren Howard warned Harold

Raymond of Chatto & Windus of O'Faoláin's arrival in London to circulate his manuscripts for better terms:

> I suspect that the future work of a certain author, Sean O'Faolain, for whom we have hitherto published, may be offered to you shortly. I ought perhaps to remind you in the first place that he is an Irishman, and to tell you, in the second place, that he has just placed his work in the hands of A.D. Peters. The situation is, unhappily, not an uncommon one. We have for many years provided O'Faolain with a regular income, but the royalties earned by the sale of his books have never yet covered the total advance payments we have made.[19]

Despite the somewhat sinister aspect of Howard warning Raymond that O'Faoláin was Irish, which reveals a degree of prejudice within the English publishing world, this letter also shows O'Faoláin at his resilient best. Augustus Dudley Peters was a famous literary agent who proved to be the scourge of publishing houses throughout Great Britain for his ability to get better terms for his authors.[20] O'Faoláin's tenacity of spirit and aggressive self-promotion allowed him to sustain a lifestyle in Ireland that was beyond the reach of many of his contemporaries. It served him well when he turned his eye to Irish society and examined it for what it was, and what he felt it should be. *The Bell* is a testament to his unremitting examination of Irish life, where he attempted a truthful account of what he saw as an inert culture in its infancy, and requiring development and instruction from its artistic leaders. The legacy of the magazine to budding Irish artists was one of high editorial standards and demanding expectations for their work. However, it also left an imprint on Irish culture through the type of article that this ostensibly literary magazine would publish. The first hints of the artistic network that would eventually drive *The Bell* towards success came more than five years before its foundation.

At the beginning of March 1935, Frank O'Connor delivered an open lecture to the Irish Academy of Letters on 'Irish Democracy and the Gaelic Tradition' at the Abbey Theatre.[21] Present at the lecture was a large crowd, including members of the general public, members of the Academy and other writers, including Brinsley MacNamara (Chairman), Peadar O'Donnell, F.R. Higgins, Michael Farrell and Seán O'Faoláin. In his lecture O'Connor argued that his contemporaries in the Irish revival bardic school of poetry were part of a long tradition that praised both 'race and place'. However, O'Connor suggested, this tradition became calcified by the arrival of Christianity, which divorced the traditional Irish bardic classes from any sense of change in their environment and insulated them from this change by a flight towards sponsorship from the Irish aristocracy. The result of this stagnation was a separation from the life blood of poetry in the voice of the ordinary people. The voice of Irish democracy, O'Connor argued, did not surface again until the Wexford songs of 1798, songs from English-speaking towns. O'Connor saw this force of traditionalism as being on the rise in Ireland again, prising art away from its roots within the people and isolating it as a form of grand delusion.

After the lecture, Peadar O'Donnell moved to have the speaker thanked for his contribution but added the caveat that the Irish ruling elite were as deficient as the colonial rulers they had superseded. He went on to suggest that, while they could certainly be seen as forthright in their support for the Church and law and order, there remained a profound ignorance within their ranks that relied on the combined forces of Church and nationalism to protect their own interests, before finally adding: 'If a person to-day wants to attack anything, he must wrap the green flag round him and have holy water shaken over him.' This claim, following on from O'Connor's pointed lecture was too much to bear for some members of the crowd, and there were shouts and interruptions from the floor. One elderly gentleman who was wearing a Fáinne shouted: 'A little holy water sprinkled over you would do you a lot of good.' These interruptions were sufficient for the chairman of the debate, Brinsley MacNamara, to appeal to O'Donnell and to ask him to keep his remarks relevant to the subject of the lecture. However, further lively scenes ensued when O'Faoláin stood up to second O'Donnell's proposal and said: 'There was not in Ireland a capacity for being objective with regard to our own conditions, and the result was that we were unwilling to submit our traditions to any kind of criticism whatsoever.' O'Faoláin continued to argue that the 'modern Gael dressed in clothes of the usual sort, with the Fainne in the lapel of their coat, and wearing spats ... had to realise that his traditions cannot continue in a world like the present'.[22] For O'Faoláin and this developing group of writers, Ireland was failing its youth in refusing to acknowledge the realities of the modern world.

O'Faoláin's claims echoed Flann O'Brien's famous quip about 'the Gaelic morons here with their bicycle clips and their handball medals' and it was received as a direct attack on Irish nationalism by some sections of the crowd.[23] His speech was punctuated with shouts of, 'you are wrong', 'you are very insulting', and one among the crowd who claimed that 'he had come there to receive an education, but was now disgusted by what he had heard from the *Intelligentsia*.' O'Connor, in his typically combative style, seemed to enjoy the commotion he had caused and finished by thanking all members for the debate, stating that. 'We have had a brave night, a bonny night, and a rushin' night.'[24] Unfortunately for O'Faoláin, this would not be the last time he would be asked to defend himself or others from a hostile crowd at the Abbey. During the staging of his play *She Had to Do Something: A Comedy in Three Acts* (1938) he had to take to the stage to admonish sections of the crowd who were booing. The play depicts a Frenchwoman who tries to bring a Russian ballet into an Irish country town. Horrified by the appearance of such a strange and immoral new art form the local priest drives the company away. O'Faoláin was indignant that his own work would receive similar treatment to his literary creation and took to the stage arguing that:

> Fifteen years ago, George Russell the poet said, "As soon as the Abbey theatre ceases producing plays that provoke a portion of the audience, it might as well go into literary Limbo." I am glad to re-baptise this little pagan so that it should not continue to exist solely on the applause of the foolish.[25]

The attack only reinforced O'Faoláin's sense of frustration and indignation with the Ireland which he saw developing around him and added fuel to his desire to effect a change. O'Connor's lecture is indicative of the way in which many Irish writers were beginning to see their society. Such nights shone a light on the emergence of a difficult and petty bourgeois class in Irish culture that could only see their identity in terms of a long history of struggle against English repression, the class of people whom W.B. Yeats had earlier identified as constituting the main body of support for Griffithite nationalism.[26] Conversely, such an occasion would also have helped to form a bond among the emerging writers who began to see themselves as an island of progressive thinking, isolated from the flow of ignorance and conservatism in Irish society. This reactive culture among O'Connor, O'Faoláin and O'Donnell was the inspiration for their attempts to effect a change in Irish identity through the formation of a magazine of intellectual honesty and ameliorative social practice. This desire would later be made manifest in *The Bell*.

This meeting and the heated debates it sparked continued when the triumvirate of O'Faoláin, O'Connor and O'Donnell first wrote together in the periodical *Ireland To-Day*. Thereby, they effectively entered into a proving ground for their future literary efforts while simultaneously creating a blueprint for *The Bell*. This periodical was first released in June 1936 under the editorial guidance of James 'Jim' L. O'Donovan, a former Irish Republican Army volunteer. Although *Ireland To-Day* would have a relatively short life, producing only twenty issues before closing in 1938, it would have a profound influence on the formation and format of *The Bell*. *Ireland To-Day*, like *The Bell*, was an open journal that sought to include a variety of different voices, covering a large range of subjects. It was more politically committed than *The Bell* would be, and it had a more identifiable leftist agenda. O'Donovan employed O'Faoláin as its books editor, and from the start of his first submission the themes that were to dominate his later editorials in *The Bell* were present. His first two-page review of Lord Dunsany's *Up in the Hills* (1935) identified the difficulties that might arise from a light-hearted treatment of the Civil War, and complained of an Irish inability to address such historical issues in an objective manner, with nationalism clouding Ireland's capacity to joke at itself:

> Our trouble is that it deals with our Troubles and it hits a dark spot in us that is a very tender spot, yet. It is typical of the equivocal condition of modern Irish

intellectual life that I cannot for the life of me say whether or not it is in bad taste
to play the Rakes of Mallow on our grave-stones … The implication is obvious,
namely, that literature needs a very free atmosphere to move in; wherefore, let
us enjoy Dunsany's pleasantries lest we find our Nationalism turning our hearts
sour.[27]

O'Faoláin, in the same review, follows this attack on nationalism with an attack
on censorship, criticism of Professor Daniel Corkery's theories of Irish literature, and a commitment to 'Anglo-Irish' writing. Professor Corkery had an
interesting relationship with O'Faoláin, being first his literary mentor and then
his great nemesis; he beat the young O'Faoláin to the Chair in English Language
and Literature at University College Cork. He also introduced him to Frank
O'Connor.[28] O'Faoláin's anger towards Corkery did not diminish with age; he
wrote to John V. Kelleher saying: 'perhaps it is that the very name of Corkery
makes me squirm. I can't remember what I ever felt about him beyond intense
admiration and gratitude at being permitted to consort as an equal with a great
man, followed swiftly by the awful realisation that he was a frustrated bloody
romantic who couldn't write for toffee.'[29] O'Faoláin's difficulty with Corkery
and his sense that Irish nationalism oppressed the development of a native
critical faculty were themes that he would return to throughout his writing life.

O'Faoláin's mission statement in *The Bell* was to capture what was essential
to Irish life and, in particular, to its identity. As he saw it 'our only job was to
encourage Life to speak. When she speaks, then *The Bell* will itself become a
symbol, and its "policy" will become self-evident.'[30] This desire to capture an
honest account of Irish life is foreshadowed in his mission statement for the
book section of *Ireland To-Day* and accounts for the type of submission that
O'Faoláin was hoping to attract for both publications:

> In this section of *Ireland To-Day* we hope to disclose the existence of a flexible,
> informed, individual, and unprejudiced criticism. We shall search for the type
> of critic who does not think that his own pleasure or displeasure at the opinions
> or approach of a writer is sufficient for approval or disapproval, and we may,
> thereby, in time, succeed in articulating reasonably the basis of our own peculiar
> instinct of life.[31]

A similar appeal in *The Bell*'s manifesto shows the extent to which O'Faoláin
had formulated his ideas on the role of the literary journal in Irish society
during his time with *Ireland To-Day*. As early as March 1936 O'Faolain had
already developed an understanding of the aesthetic objectives of a literary
magazine and saw fit to lecture his editor on its role: '[t]hey must be made [to]
realise that we are the high-water mark of the new Ireland, and we must, in
brief, cut out all competitors at their own game … Your job, partly, is that of
finding the future intelligentsia of the new Ireland.'[32] This clear-sighted and
business-like attitude to writing typifies O'Faoláin and his work. His pragmatic

and industrious disposition helped him to generate a comfortable income for his family when most writers in Ireland were struggling or maintained another profession. Such was his professionalism that many writers had little difficulty in working for him when he made the transition from *Ireland To-Day* and started *The Bell* two years later.

It was this personal gravitas and the maintenance of thematic concerns that would see other writers follow both O'Faoláin and O'Donnell to *The Bell*. The Dublin University lecturer Owen Sheehy Skeffington submitted a regular piece to *Ireland To-Day* on 'Foreign Commentary' and he was later asked to do the same for *The Bell*. Such an easy transference of writers among journals is partly accounted for by the lack of quality outlets for their publications, but it is also testament to the circle of associates that O'Faoláin and O'Donnell were developing, from which they could draw sophisticated submissions. The editors' connections to wider international literary circles was a source of material, and by the time of its final issue *The Bell* had attracted writers of international repute, such as George Bernard Shaw, William Saroyan, Louis Aragon, Jean-Paul Sartre, Ernst Wiechert, Ernst Schroedinger, Osbert Sitwell and Yeh Sheng-Tao, as well as more local figures, such as Owen Sheehy Skeffington. O'Faoláin's friendship with Skeffington was to last until he died, and O'Faoláin even delivered his graveside oration, seeing Skeffington's most enduring characteristics as those which he had identified as a journalist: '[l]et us salute then a man who, in a country and a time not rich in moral courage, was a giant of honesty who never swerved or changed and who kept his youthful spirit to the very end.'[33] Throughout *The Bell*'s run O'Faoláin sought to make room for writers who he felt challenged hegemonic political or social discourses, especially where they demonstrated a forthright bravery in their opinions. Owen Sheehy Skeffington fell into such a category, and O'Faoláin was moved to support him both as a friend and publicly through his editorials in *The Bell* when he later became embroiled in controversy.

Peadar O'Donnell also contributed to the early editions of *Ireland To-Day*, writing a symposium on the Spanish Civil War. O'Donnell's submission had the typically straightforward title of 'What I saw in Spain' and would later form part of the book on his experiences in Spain during July 1936, *Salud! An Irishman in Spain* (1937). This book differed from work being produced on Spain in that period by lacking any of the angst associated with young British writers and their issues of commitment, O'Donnell having seen enough of war to be purged of that particular emotion.[34] If O'Donnell's response to the tragedy unfolding in Spain was a fact-finding mission and unwavering support for the government then O'Faoláin's response was typically more controversial; he responded to *Left Review*'s survey on the Civil War, *Authors Take Sides on the Spanish War* as one of the few authors, along with T.S. Eliot and Ezra Pound, to declare themselves neutral. He superciliously declared:

DON'T BE A LOT OF SAPS. If X and Y want to cut one another's throats over Z why on earth must people who do not believe in the ideas propounded be either X, Y, or Z have "to choose between them"? If you want to know, I do think Fascism is lousy. So is your Communism, only more so. But there are other ideas in the world besides either of them – thank God (whom neither of you believe in). For the love of Mike cut loose from this fixation that the artist no longer can have the guts to be what every artist worth his salt has always been – *an individualist.* … (May I say how much I like your postal address?) Yours contemptuously.[35]

It is interesting that O'Faoláin's experience of the Irish Civil War had left him more cynical of all wars than the older O'Donnell, something that would become apparent in their editorial styles in *The Bell*. It is also worthwhile to note that O'Faoláin mentions God at a time when he had just published his distinctively Catholic novel *Bird Alone* (1936). But for O'Donnell, his article on the Spanish Civil War tried to discredit some of the extreme propaganda that had been circulating in the Irish media with an anti-communist bias. O'Donnell was himself a known communist, so such a position was not unusual. However, he was at pains to defend the democratically elected coalition of the left in the Spanish Civil War against charges of anti-Catholic atrocities in the Irish papers. Although he was willing to admit that there had been some attacks on priests and church property, these were isolated incidents rather than the norm, and emphasised that the true attack on western values came from the fascist foreign legion and their Moorish allies: 'It is important that we all remember that the people of Spain rid themselves of the monarchy in a perfectly constitutional way in 1931 … And that it is against this democratic government that the foreign legion and the Moors are waging their war for "Christian Ideals".'[36]

Such direct commentary had added to O'Donnell's infamy in Irish society as a communist, and although he was never banned by the censorship board, there was a de facto restriction on his works owing to their tainted reputation. O'Donnell was known to the authorities for his subversive opinions and this carried a certain notoriety. Once while driving through Dublin he was stopped by a member of the Garda: 'You may be a fuckin' Red', lectured the Garda, 'but you can't drive through a red light.'[37] It would seem that such infamy was not always a positive experience in O'Donnell's life as he would continue his open disputes with the political establishment in *The Bell*. O'Donnell had his own reasons for engaging with a literary journal and he remained convinced that *The Bell* could act as a guide to the Irish in expression of their natural genius. His faith in the youth of Ireland to rise up and implement a new Irish literature in English was expressed in an unusual source early in his career when he published an article called 'Young Irish Writers' in the Catholic journal of the liberal arts, *The Commonweal*.

Although O'Donnell is characteristically remembered as a man of action, and an effective counterpoint to O'Faoláin's more effusive and lofty personality, his interest in creating a magazine was also theoretically informed. By 1933 O'Donnell had identified a sea change in Irish literature, one that saw the passing of an old guard and its superseding by a growing force in Irish culture: 'The ANGLO-IRISH school of writers is passing. We are just on the edge of a period when Irish life will find its way into literature, written in English, but of Ireland and by Irish writers.' Even though O'Donnell believed that there was a great deal of genius in the Anglo-Irish school of literature, such writing could not truly capture the experiences of the great bulk of people in modern Ireland. Their champions would appear from under the yoke of British colonial rule and express the universal truth of Irish experience for its people: 'They will be much more easily accepted by their countrymen than the Anglo-Irish school that preceded them. Some resistance to interpretation is inevitable in a small country fighting its way out of slavery.' However, it would also seem that O'Donnell had in mind a very particular form of Irishness that would be expressed by these new writers. Although they were Gaelic, and presumably Catholic, and reflected the attitudes of the people, O'Donnell conceived of these writers coming from a working-class social background, and expressing new visions of Irish life. He was deliberately fighting against the newly formed petty bourgeois Irish:

> I think that the sharp ear of the great mass of plain people out of whom the
> new literature is arising are quickly catching the Gaelic note our schoneenized
> middle-class are unable to understand, and that they will sponsor our new writ-
> ers. For the new literature will shock many, just because it is informed with
> Gaelic values of life. The aftermath of English puritanism lives on in Ireland as
> an invasion of rugged language with a sickly varnish.

O'Donnell's communist and nationalist credentials are exposed here, seeing the main resistance to this new literature as coming from a conservative middle class who embodied the remnants of British colonial rule through their sham squire pretensions and faux sophisticated mannerisms. However, it is also evident that he held a true belief in the strength of young Irish writers coming to the fore in post-independence Ireland.

O'Donnell was also well aware that if this movement were to thrive it would need the support of all the critical organs open to its distribution. Thus, there should be an emphasis on maintaining strong links to publications that would promote these writers and provide them with the opportunity to express themselves fully:

> We are on the edge of a great literary achievement in Ireland, and it is the duty
> of those journals that have not shut themselves out from the fermentation out of
> which these voices come to give space to the message, even when the message
> itself is a bit bewildering. Ireland is all right, and the youth of Ireland is a great
> youth.[38]

Having identified this great need to promote younger writers, *The Bell* can be seen as an attempt by O'Donnell to ameliorate the plight of this new talent. This article in *The Commonweal* is neglected in O'Donnell scholarship, but it is of prime importance in situating O'Donnell's work as a writer who saw writing as another means of dismantling British imperialist influence in an Irish context. O'Donnell's dynamism found the perfect foil in O'Faoláin, and together they would make *The Bell*, in spite of its difficulties, a success story. O'Donnell's role in *The Bell* is often considered secondary to that of O'Faoláin, and in many ways it was. However, he was also the senior artist of the two, and had been someone O'Faoláin looked up to in the world of letters.

While living in London in June 1933, where he had been working as a lecturer at St Mary's College, Richmond, O'Faoláin wrote to Edward Garnett, asking for an introduction to O'Donnell, his fellow republican writer. At St Mary's, O'Faoláin was understandably at pains to hide his republican past and went under his original name of John Whelan; when writing to Lincoln Kirstein of the *Hound & Horn* he warned her to, 'keep it *Whelan* – I keep my more unconventional side to myself *there* [St. Mary's College]'.[39] He used his publisher's connections to meet the authors whom he highly admired: 'I received the note of introduction to Miss Somerville and to Peter O'Donnell, and I met O'Donnell twice in Dublin.'[40] O'Faoláin deeply admired O'Donnell and sympathised with his work, especially his account of his IRA activities as depicted in *The Gates Flew Open* (1932). He could identify the raw power of O'Donnell's writing at its finest: 'Thanks many times for The Gates Flew Open. It is the most virile bit of writing I have read in many a long day. As always this fellow makes me feel effeminate and "aesthetic". I toil and toil and scratch and scratch and he by sheer force of personality just gets over on foul [?] style & everything theoretically wrong. He's an amazing personality, and a damn fine writer. I've written to tell him so.'[41] This appreciation for O'Donnell was the foundation on which would blossom an excellent working relationship within *The Bell*. At this stage, O'Faoláin respected O'Donnell as an artist, and for his accomplishments as a writer. However, O'Donnell mainly identified himself as a political activist and thus was happy to have O'Faoláin as the man to lead the magazine and give it the artistic prestige which would be vital to its success.

When later reflecting on his life, Seán O'Faoláin saw as his primary achievement for 1940 the publication of his novel *Come Back to Erin*. This novel was pivotal in his development as an artist in that it reflected his decision to return to Ireland to work and, he argued, it 'revealed a turning point in my life'. However, 1940 was also the year in which O'Faoláin began his journey into what he dismissively called the production of '61 portentous manifestos written between October 1940 and April 1946 as editor of the monthly magazine *The Bell*.[42] This odd attitude towards his own achievement in *The Bell* is typical of O'Faoláin's autobiography and is, on the whole, at odds with the impressive success of such a quality literary magazine during the difficult wartime period in Ireland. These '61 portentous manifestos' formed the backbone of a magazine that was, under O'Faoláin, Ireland's most consistently politically engaged literary journal in the middle decades of the twentieth century. *The Bell* was an outstanding achievement in terms of the quality of submissions it produced and the talent it was able to draw from, forming a core around which the intellectuals and artists of Irish society could express their opinions and publish their work, placing them side by side with more established writers of international repute. The first edition alone was one of considerable strength, containing submissions from enduring artists, including Frank O'Connor, Flann O'Brien, Lennox Robinson, Patrick Kavanagh, Jack B. Yeats, Peadar O'Donnell, Elizabeth Bowen and Ernie O'Malley. It also contained the now renowned editorial 'This is Your Magazine' and the short story 'Janus' from O'Faoláin himself. For a magazine of such talents, and with its comparatively successful print run, the exact origins of *The Bell* remain difficult to place. However, what is certain is that *The Bell* began its life on October 1940, with a business address at 43 Parkgate Street, just off Wolfe Tone Avenue near Dublin's north quays; it was priced at the reasonable amount of one shilling.

Its price must be considered in the context of the time and of equivalent publications. Cyril Connolly's *Horizon* was also launched in England during 1940 and was priced at two shillings and sixpence, while *Ireland To-Day*, first published in June 1936 was priced at a shilling.[43] As a counter to its low cost *The Bell*'s production values were never of a high quality and it was caught in the double bind of restricted paper imports and inflationary wartime prices.[44] Also at 43 Parkgate Street were the offices of Cahills, Dublin's only large-scale letterpress. Cahills was owned by J.J. O'Leary, a successful Wexford businessman who had moved to Dublin and employed O'Faoláin as editor-in-chief for all of his publications, something O'Faoláin's developed sense of aesthetic snobbery found distasteful. Having accepted O'Leary's offer of a IR£1,000 a year, O'Faoláin's initial reservations concerning his new employer developed into a grudging respect:

> I was told that he had achieved a monopoly of the market for Bibles in every African language – to the printing of bus timetables, the breakneck late-night printing of each day's Dail debates for early morning distribution, the printing of confidential end-of-term scholastic examination papers, of each month's the *English Digest*, which he imitated with his own the *Irish Digest*, the ruthless abridgement of famous novels in paperback, ranging from *Robinson Crusoe* to *The Last of the Mohicans* to cheer up Britishers starved of fiction during the war. And so on. If this random list of a few of J.J.'s activities suggests a versatile character (I do not say versatile mind) it points also to both his flair for spotting the urgency of a public need and his salesman's skill in simultaneously promoting himself as the best man to fulfil it.[45]

O'Faoláin's role within O'Leary's publishing business also afforded him the opportunity to utilise the office space at Cahills, something which would have been a boon to any fledgling magazine.

Although the magazine was published by Cahills, and O'Faoláin was working for O'Leary editing his publications, including his *Irish Digest*, the vital financial support for *The Bell* came from Joe McGrath. McGrath was, like O'Faoláin, O'Donnell and O'Connor, a former IRA volunteer, and he had made his money through the Irish Hospitals' Sweepstakes, where he was company director of the Hospitals' Trust. McGrath had a colourful and politically influential past. Having served in the 1916 Rising, he formed part of the delegation that travelled with Michael Collins to debate the treaty. McGrath had also served four terms as a Teachta Dála (TD), three times with Sinn Féin, before finally returning for Cumann na nGaedhael between 1923 and 1927. During his time as a TD, McGrath had served one term as Minister for Labour and two terms as Minister for Trade and Commerce. As such, his influence was felt across several spheres of Irish public life. During the Civil War he stood on the pro-treaty side before being elected to the fourth Dáil with Cumann na nGaedhael under William T. Cosgrave. Some of McGrath's fellow party members included figures such as Professor Eoin MacNeill, Professor Michael Tierney, Kevin O'Higgins, Alfred O'Rahilly, Richard Francis Hayes (later Film Censor) and Ernest Blythe (Minister for Finance and, later, director of the Abbey Theatre).[46]

McGrath was highly unusual in Irish politics as he was able to maintain his associations with both his pro-treaty political allies and his former colleagues in the IRA. He could therefore use his considerable wealth to maximise his political influence and yet employ many of his former republican associates in his Hospitals' Trust. The Hospitals' Trust was directly under McGrath's control in his capacity as managing director. McGrath operated under a policy of employing close friends from his days as an Irish revolutionary: Charles Dalton was circulating manager, and had been prominent in the Dublin Brigade during the War of Independence. P.J. Fleming was manager of the Foreign Department, and he had played an active role for the IRA in Laois and Kilkenny. His director of publicity was Jack O'Sheehan who had been an active Sinn Féin organiser. Finally, Eamon Martin was controller of sales, and he had been a 1916 veteran and close associate of Peadar O'Donnell. Most unusually, many of McGrath's senior associates in the sweepstake had taken the republican side in the Civil War, and would have fought against the government in which McGrath had played such a prominent role.[47] Such an impressive achievement demonstrates the personal charisma that McGrath must have had, and it also says something of his nature that he would be approachable for a financial contribution from his potential political opponents. McGrath's success as a businessman and his interest in the arts were what led him to generously support *The Bell*, offering

O'Donnell IR£1,000 towards its production costs. This was not an insignifi-
cant amount considering that O'Faoláin was earning the same for his work with
O'Leary on an annual basis. O'Donnell organised the approach through Eamon
Martin, with whom he had been interned as a prisoner of war in Mountjoy
during 1922, and together they made the suggestion to McGrath.[48] As with all
serious businessmen McGrath's support came at a cost and by 1942 *The Bell*'s
editorial board had to sign over its remaining shares to his deputy Martin for
IR£360 in order to ensure paper supplies. As was usual in the dynamic of their
relationship, O'Donnell struck the deal, while O'Faoláin was left to apply his
more subtle skills in persuading the rest of the original editorial board:

> We are running into lots of shallows and sheals [shoals?] in this magazine. The
> essential one at the moment is that we can only get continuing supplies of paper
> if we pay for it in advance. We need approximately £360, cash down, at once. In
> addition to that we need more funds. That walking cornucopia Peadar believes
> he can get it. And if he cannot we cannot go on. His business friends, in the way
> apparently of business men, want some quid pro quids, even if it is only nominal,
> and the essential thing is that even if they put up £360 plus more funds they
> want a business man's control. They guarantee that there will be no interference
> with the Editorial side. What this boils down to is that we must all make over our
> shares to one of their number. I suppose you have no objection? I am collecting
> the other signatures to this transfer which is urgent, i.e. Roisin's, Peadar's, Mossy
> Walsh's, and my own. I will be at Don Jupiter on Monday night and bring this
> document for signature.[49]

O'Donnell's eye for a business opportunity was vital and he provided the
initial impetus to get a magazine off the ground. In this O'Donnell showed
his accomplished organisational skills by securing the talent of 'Ireland's pre-
eminent "man of letters", Seán O'Faoláin, as editor, a crucial factor in giving
the new venture the "stature" that O'Donnell wanted for it',[50] This account
would certainly tally with that of the authors themselves, or at least it would
after the passage of some years. In a letter to the editor of the *Irish Times* in 1970
O'Faoláin placed the plaudits for the creation of *The Bell* firmly at O'Donnell's
feet:

> Sir – I am touched and flattered by Monk Gibbon's amiable poem wishing me
> a happy seventieth birthday (February 21st). The note appended to it, however,
> embarrassed me a little in saying that I founded the *Bell*. This magazine was,
> from start to finish Peadar O'Donnell's creation, and as it was his inspiration,
> neither could it have gone on appearing without his tireless guidance and most
> inventive support. Long after I ceased to edit it, he kept it going, for fourteen
> years in all, from 1940 to 1954, a remarkable feat for what may fairly be called, in
> his name, a one-man Little Magazine.[51]

O'Faoláin's praise is indeed flattering, and he was at pains to stress that
O'Donnell was the source and driving force behind *The Bell*. However, his

own contribution is not to be underestimated; whatever the material challenges faced by O'Donnell in founding and running a successful literary magazine, *The Bell* took its artistic guidance and moral authority from O'Faoláin in his role as editor. If we also consider O'Faoláin's own dismissal of *The Bell* years in his autobiography we can begin to see how he attempted to downplay its significance.

Yet the publication of a newspaper article sixteen years after *The Bell* ceased production crediting O'Donnell with the honours entirely could also be read as an example of good grace between two old friends. O'Donnell, to his credit, was willing to acknowledge as much. He also identified O'Faoláin's contribution to be one of central importance, and he saw *The Bell* as shaped in O'Faoláin's own image, directed by the force of his personality. Moved by O'Faoláin's attempt to deny his role in *The Bell*, and by his self-deprecation, O'Donnell decided to reply in kind. Writing also to the *Irish Times*, but in his more direct style, O'Donnell described the formation of *The Bell* as he recalled it:

> Sir – The *Bell*, as the public knew it, was Sean O'Faolain's creation. He gave it 'its recognisable gait of going'. The idea of a magazine was mine. With Eamon Martin's help I brought it to Joe McGrath. Without his help it would have remained an idea. I think – I even thought at the time – that the *Bell* should have ceased publication when O'Faolain decided to end his editorship of it. The decision to wind up the *Bell* in 1954 was mine. I only hope Sean O'Faolain found it as easy to work with me as I found it rewarding to work with him.[52]

Whatever the origins of *The Bell*, what is clear is that here were two men writing some sixteen years after it ceased publication who were still proud of their involvement with their 'little magazine'. Despite, perhaps, an element of false modesty on behalf of both O'Faoláin and O'Donnell, what is important is the synergies that these writers were able to bring to *The Bell*. Certainly, by 1939 O'Faoláin was already sounding out potential contributors for a magazine that would look to the United Kingdom and *The New Statesman* as a model. While journeying through Ireland for his travel book *An Irish Journey* (1940) O'Faoláin revealed his intentions to Ernie O'Malley:

> Last night Sean O'Faolain and Dr Collins called here. Sean is writing a guide book to Ireland. His stay in Connaught was two days: however, he knows the craft well enough to be able to write about anything. They talked about a paper to carry on the work of 'The New Statesman'. I did not ask what was the idea behind it but F. Packingham (spelt wrongly, I fear) is behind it and ready to put up some money. I'm sure you could do weekly art critiques. I'll suggest your name as soon as I hear from O'Faolain. Evidently the people concerned are going about the venture in a rather thorough way, slowly covering the ground. We need a paper badly here but I do not know the real reason behind it, the motive or its direction: a purely literary paper does not interest me now.[53]

What is most important is that in both their roles as founders and subsequently as its editors, the combination of personality and opinion that O'Donnell and O'Faoláin shared ensured a vitality and enthusiasm to which their reading public could respond. Their achievement in the formation of a new literary magazine is a testimony to their determination to promote the best of Irish culture regardless of political allegiance, as O'Faoláin would later state: 'Whoever you are, then, O reader, Gentile or Jew, Protestant or Catholic, priest or layman, Big house or Small House – *The Bell* is yours.'[54]

With O'Faoláin at the helm, the project of collecting material for a magazine was made less difficult. Already by the age of 40 he had assumed an air of cosmopolitanism and success that few, if any, other Irish writers were able to achieve. In addition, he was well connected both in Irish and international literary circles. O'Faoláin's reputation as a writer of talent exceeded any of his Irish peers during this time. At a very young age he had met and befriended some of the most powerful players on the literary scene in the English-speaking world, and counted, among others, Edward Garnett (who had died in 1937), as a close friend. From his time studying at Harvard he also was on close personal terms with R.P. (Richard Palmer) Blackmur (editor of the *Hound & Horn*) and one of America's most prominent literary critics. These connections were in addition to his association with more established Irish artists in W.B. Yeats and George Russell (AE). By 1940 O'Faoláin had submissions accepted internationally for prestigious publications such as *The Criterion, The London Mercury, The Virginia Quarterly Review* and the *Yale Review*. He had published in the Irish journals *Folklore, Ireland To-Day, The Dublin Magazine* and the *Irish Statesman*.

O'Faoláin's standing at the forefront of a new wave of Irish literary talent was cemented when he joined the group of illustrious names who had succeeded in making the list of authors whose work had been banned by the Irish state. Under the Censorship of Publications Act (1929) his collection of short stories *Midsummer Night Madness* (1932) and novel *Bird Alone* (1936) were banned and this would kick-start his campaign against literary censorship. O'Faoláin needed writers of quality for the first edition of *The Bell*, and with this in mind he asked his old friend Frank O'Connor to contribute. The need for a vehicle to express their criticisms of Irish society must have appealed to both men. O'Faoláin and O'Connor identified a stifling atmosphere in Irish society, and a sense of hostility towards their own work that would drive them both to fight back. But O'Faoláin's and O'Connor's presence in the magazine together strengthened their position as at the forefront of Irish cultural identity, and nowhere is this more evident than in their relationship with the English poet, John Betjeman.

Betjeman had been posted to Éire during the Second World War as a press attaché, although his real work was writing reports for the British Ministry of

Information and supporting efforts to spread British propaganda throughout Ireland. In effect, this turned out to be a much gentler form of propagandising than might be imagined. It seems that Betjeman was particularly effective in promoting British goodwill and gathered around him a large number of personal friends among Éire's political and intellectual elite. He nurtured friendships with many writers from *The Bell* set, including O'Faoláin, O'Connor, Patrick Kavanagh and formed a deep and lasting friendship with Geoffrey Taylor. As was the case with Elizabeth Bowen, Betjeman's presence in Ireland was deemed suspect, and speculation was rife that he was a spy. He even managed to avoid being shot by an IRA assassin, who decided not to kill him after reading some of his poetry and concluded that no spy could write so well.[55] Betjeman's role crossed both countries as he also had some success in preventing journalistic attacks on Irish neutrality within the British press, seeing how counterproductive such articles were. As part of his cultural mission Betjeman also promoted Irish writers within England, and was directly responsible for pushing the Irish edition of Cyril Connolly's *Horizon*, which contained Frank O'Connor's embittered attack on the future of Irish writing and the first draft of Kavanagh's epic poem 'The Great Hunger'.[56] Connolly had spent the summer of 1941 in Ireland as a guest of Betjeman, and circulated with O'Faoláin and others as part of his literary tour of Dublin's important writers and sites, including the Palace Bar. Connolly forms part of a British journalistic tradition that saw the neutral Éire as a plentiful utopia, isolated from the war, entirely unaffected by its violence, and it brought to mind the uneasy topic of commitment which had dogged his generation in the previous decade:

> Returning to England, in fact, from the lovely island of 1938, with its lights and its crowds, its huge trees and cloudscapes, its shops full of food, and newspapers full of nothing, and its wise ruler struggling with the insoluble problem of the future of small nations, is not unlike going back from Southern France to the Spanish War. The examination in the shed, the soldier with a revolver who goes through one's letters ... carries one back to reality, to the five-year sentence in gregarious confinement which we are all serving. I thought of my friends in Dublin, their kindness and intelligence, their attitude of mingled curiosity and pity, together with a kind of uneasiness about their neutrality.[57]

Connolly's *Horizon* is filled with concerns about the limiting effects that confinement has on the artist during the war, and this is a topic that O'Faoláin would return to in *The Bell* with his own editorials. Betjeman, on the other hand, had a much more unromanticised view of the Irish and their habits. Echoing G.B. Shaw's inversion of supposed English and Irish characteristics, Betjeman, at least to other Englishmen, tried to stress the pragmatism of the Irish, and in particular their position on neutrality: 'The English are the poets, the Irish are the non-dreamers.'[58] This personable approach and sympathetic goodwill towards Ireland made Betjeman many friends among writers during his time there.[59] If Betjeman had been successful in getting exposure for Irish writers in England, they were perfectly capable of getting it themselves in Ireland. However, this was not always for the right reasons, as the example of Frank O'Connor aptly demonstrates.

On Monday 10 March 1941, the Abbey Theatre opened with Louis Lynch D'Alton's new play *The Money Doesn't Matter* (1939). D'Alton had been a playwright and director at the Abbey and had already written and produced four other plays before *The Money Doesn't Matter*. The play was a commercial success, running for forty-nine performances over a period of eight weeks.[60] D'Alton's play was a comedy and was well received critically for its portrayal of modern Irish life and the difficulties facing the expanding Catholic middle classes. The play's plot was based around the character Tom Mannion who had worked hard to amass a fortune and was struggling to secure his legacy through his family. The dramatic tension comes from the failure of Tom's family to live up to his expectations for them, and in particular on his daughter, who rejects his attempts to find her a suitable suitor and decides to lead a life of religious contemplation as a nun. The play was reviewed in the *Irish Times* the following day and its reviewer saw an underlying theme of human tragedy in its protagonist's plight: 'It has a serious subject, a theme of importance, and the dramatist does not too soon begin to see its rich comic side. The story of Tom Mannion, who, becomes the big man of Annakill, has an immediate suggestion of tragedy.' The star of the show, however, was Tom's son Philip who 'loves music and the bottle in unequal proportions' and for his portrayal of this character the 'highest acting honours of the evening fell, no doubt, to Denis O'Dea for his most diverting performance'.[61] The play was also reviewed by *The Bell*'s first theatre critic Denis Johnston, who briefly mentioned it in his column 'Plays of the Quarter'. Johnston, who was familiar with O'Faoláin from his time working at the British Broadcasting Corporation (BBC), was theatre critic for *The Bell* before leaving in February 1942 for a role with the BBC as a war correspondent.

Johnston's contributions ran alongside Michael Farrell's who wrote 'The Country Theatre' column, while Johnston stuck to the plays performed in the big theatres of Dublin. For Johnston, D'Alton's play was an amusing side piece that gave the company the opportunity to fully express their comedic potential. Johnston noted how the play worked on a humorous level, without detecting any of the tragic undertones of the *Irish Times* reviewer:

> They were at their best [the Abbey team] again in Louis D'Alton's new play [the] *Money Doesn't Matter* – an amusing piece of foolery which, without professing great profundity, proved an excellent vehicle for the Company and gave an opportunity for one or two rather scandalous but very funny characters.[62]

Another of *The Bell*'s contributors also took notice, and in particular, Denis O'Dea's performance as Philip Mannion caught the eye of Frank O'Connor.

These 'scandalous but very funny characters' provoked O'Connor sufficiently to write an article for *The Bell* which would lead him to protest against the play and its critical reception. O'Connor had tendered his resignation to the board of the Abbey in 1939, which was duly accepted, and he carried a personal grievance against them which he often chose to air in public.[63] The cause of the resignation was political machinations on the part of the board of directors. O'Connor had been editing a special edition of *The Arrow*, the Abbey journal of which he had been appointed editor by W.B. Yeats. However, in Yeats's absence the board voted to have O'Connor's work submitted to them for review before publication. This act effectively removed the last influence O'Connor had on the board, and his pique was such that he offered his resignation, which, to his surprise, was accepted.[64] The June edition of *The Bell* 1941 carried an article in the 'Public Opinion' section titled 'The Stone Dolls'. This article was written by O'Connor and coupled with a further submission called 'The Abbey Theatre' by Denis Ireland. Both were highly critical of the Abbey's board of directors and, in particular, of Louis Lynch D'Alton's *The Money Doesn't Matter*.

O'Connor began his letter by stating that Louis D'Alton was 'a writer I admired' and a dramatist who 'knows how to choose a dramatic theme and has the technical skill to handle it'. He then proceeded to analyse the play and, after offering a plot synopsis, suggested that it lacked sufficient depth of characterisation to work. He felt that the internal conflicts and dilemmas of all human interaction were not present and this robbed it of its tragic potential. As such, the play externalised these dramatic moments and (echoing his mentor Yeats's line 'out of the quarrel with ourselves we make poetry') the tension was reduced to the level of simplistic human interaction: 'It is from the conflict within ourselves that all great tragedy springs – Hamlet, the dreamer who would be a man of action and avenge his father's murder – but in this play of Mr. D'Alton's the conflict is completely externalised.'

However, O'Connor's real focus of attack came with the portrayal of Denis O'Dea's character Philip Mannion. Philip was an alcoholic, and O'Connor objected to the treatment of alcoholism in such an unreflective and cheap manner; having grown up with an alcoholic father himself, O'Connor was acutely aware of the impact alcohol could have on family life. Mannion's character and O'Dea's depiction of it removed any element of humanity from the role and stole the dignity of anyone who struggled to deal with its consequences: 'worse than that was the coarseness and facetiousness with which the dipsomaniac was treated … here there was no pity, no horror, no sense of right or wrong. It was treated as a very good joke and so the audience accepted it.'[65] O'Connor was spurred to write against this play by the memory of Yeats's bravery in objecting to the revival of George Shiels's play at the Abbey, *Cartney and Kevney* (1930). Although Shiels's plays were popular, Yeats objected on

aesthetic grounds because he found his 'plays [were] without plots'.[66] O'Connor
was consciously emulating Yeats's 'noble indignation' at the horror of artistic
representation lacking in an informed morality; he disapproved of any art that
'displayed a series of base actions without anything to show that its author
disapproved or expected us to do so'. This crass and tasteless production was
exacerbated by O'Dea's performance as the hapless drunk, affecting the habits
and mannerisms of a famous Dublin character: 'the actor who played the part
of the dipsomaniac and thief was caricaturing a well-known figure'. The figure
ridiculed in this performance was none other than Lennox Robinson, playwright, regular contributor to *The Bell*, and fellow Cork man. To make matters
worse, Robinson was a former director and manager of the Abbey and was on
its board of directors, and had given O'Connor his first job with the Carnegie
Library Trust. This grievance was too much for O'Connor to bear and he took
it on himself to argue on behalf of Robinson whose dignified silence was admirable. However, this did not absolve the culpability of the Abbey board with
whom he served: 'yet they allow the stage of the national theatre to be used to
portray a public figure as a thief and a dipsomaniac! The victim has chosen to
ignore it, as he was fully entitled to do, but no amount of magnanimity on his
part can acquit the members of the board of an unusual degree of thoughtless-
ness.'[67] O'Connor's own confrontational character was evident here and his
outrage soon boiled over from an attack on the play to an attack on his own
colleagues within *The Bell*.

O'Connor was disgusted that Denis Johnston in his review saw this play as
affording the opportunity for some funny caricatures, and he drew a comparison with O'Faoláin's editorial in the same edition which discussed censorship
and found it to be 'natural' and 'easy to forgive'.[68] In both of these sentiments
O'Connor detected an urbane sophistication that belied a moral cowardice and
elided 'a common absence of any desirable vision of life'. Returning from a
recent trip around Ireland where he had studied the ruins of ancient Norman
and Irish monasteries, O'Connor was horrified by the petty and mean nature of
Irish art, as embodied by a sculpture of the Twelve Apostles from the fifteenth
century. This he contrasted with the Norman sculpture from two centuries
earlier which was, to him, much more sophisticated and aesthetically pleasing.
These Twelve Apostles were the twelve stone dolls that gave their name to his
essay, and when he reflected on the nature of art in fifteenth-century Ireland,
controlled by the Irish themselves, he found uncomfortable comparisons with
today: 'Yet when I began to think what it was [in] the Censorships which
Mr. O'Faoláin finds so "natural" and the scandalous caricatures which Mr.
Johnston finds so "funny" had in common, it was these horrible dolls who
floated before my mind's eye by way of answer.'[69] O'Connor's attack was a
reaction to the idealisation of Irish peasant life, and against the concept of Irish
culture as a *sui generis* society, isolated and apart from other world cultures. As

with his earlier article in *Ireland To-Day*, O'Connor's historical analysis had a specific message for his contemporary audience.

This must also be seen as part of O'Connor's own contrary and irritable character, seeing nothing wrong with attacking his own editor and colleagues within *The Bell*. However, in this particular case, O'Connor's attack was direct and personal, singling out individually D'Alton, Denis O'Dea and O'Faoláin as complicit in the fall in Irish cultural standards. His criticisms of O'Faoláin for condoning censorship are particularly harsh and unusual, especially considering that *The Bell* was set up specifically with the project of rejuvenating Irish cultural life. It is a credit to O'Faoláin that he published the article as it stood, when he was one of its principal targets. O'Faoláin had the article reviewed by a solicitor in order to 'protect the magazine from libel'. O'Connor had first offered the article to R.M. Smyllie, the flamboyant editor of the *Irish Times* and subject of one of *The Bell*'s interviews by 'The Bellman', H.L. Morrow.[70] However, it was *The Bell* that published the article and carried the responsibility for the criticisms of one of its founding members.

Published alongside this article under 'Public Opinion' was an open letter from Denis Ireland also criticising Louis Lynch D'Alton's *The Money Doesn't Matter*. Ireland was critical of the play because of its low artistic merit, and found it unworthy of production at the Abbey. He enjoyed the play as a comedy and had to 'admit that I got several good laughs in the course of the evening', but did not think this suitable for the Abbey to produce, seeing it more in the vaudeville tradition than as a play of true artistic merit. On leaving the play, Ireland, like O'Connor before him, was forced to question the value of Irish cultural production as a whole, when the hallowed shrine of the Abbey was reduced to producing crowd pleasers of dubious artistic merit:

> What we asked ourselves was this: Has the State-supported Irish National Theatre become simply a kind of laboratory where experts in Mass-Observation can test their theories about the vacuity of the twentieth-century Irish mind, counting every manufactured laugh as a hit? If it has, then does this not amount to a complete reversal of Yeats's original policy, which was to go on giving us the best until we began to like it?[71]

These two articles published together were a substantial criticism of the Abbey and its board of directors. They also are indicative of a kind of misreading of Yeats's legacy only two years after his death, one in which this new generation of Irish artists strove to distinguish themselves from the past, and yet, paradoxically, position themselves as the natural inheritors of a cultural continuation. Yeats was, after all, perfectly willing to compromise his artistic standards when faced with tough decisions at the Abbey.[72] O'Faoláin was aware of the reactionary potential of such publications and, by way of engaging the victims of the attack in an open debate, invited both Louis Lynch D'Alton and Denis

Johnston to reply in the next issue. He also signalled his intent to publish an in-depth interview with Ernest Blythe who was at that time the manager of the Abbey. However, such ameliorative gestures were insufficient to prevent the controversy which ensued.

The July edition contained the replies of both Louis Lynch D'Alton and Denis Johnston. D'Alton was indignant at O'Connor's criticisms of him. For him, O'Connor's letter marked a new low point in criticism, just as O'Connor felt D'Alton's play was a new low point in Irish culture: 'this is the very nadir of critical inanity'. D'Alton felt that O'Connor was completely unfair in his criticism and was misreading the play in suggesting that it lacked an interior quality that would allow it to transcend its limitations. For D'Alton, O'Connor's comparison with *Hamlet* was a telling one, because it demonstrated his misapprehension of the play's central motivation, namely comedy: 'five pages of splendid fol-de-rol to prove that the comic method employed in *The Money Doesn't Matter* does not conform to the tragic method of *Hamlet*! And I am to suppose that this needs answering! Mr. O'Connor doesn't need answering, what he needs is instruction.' D'Alton followed this observation with a direct attack on *The Bell* itself, questioning the right of a new magazine to sit in judgement on others. D'Alton implied that the prominence of a few critics in *The Bell* was a measure of its dependence on a small literary clique and indicated its literary provincialism, exactly the charge that O'Faoláin wished to deny: 'So What? So *The Bell* which is to be the New Arbiter of Taste is to become a species of kindergarten in which the criticised are required to instruct critics like Mr. O'Connor on the rudiments of their job!' D'Alton next accused O'Connor of sycophantic name dropping in that he used Yeats to bolster his own argument. According to D'Alton, this ruse had so often been used in debates surrounding the Abbey that it had become something of a cliché:

> And throughout this piece of critical sleight of hand we have Mr. Connor's exploitation of what I will now define as the Yeats Racket, subtitle Great Minds Think Alike. Every ambitious literary man who now wants to bolster up a bad case invokes the shade of the great man, on the supposition that we shall all become goggle-eyed with admiration and mentally paralysed. That we shall all worship the other side idolatry, and falling flat on the ground be incapable of seeing anything but only of hearing the august voice speaking in a reincarnated Cork accent.[73]

D'Alton rejected O'Connor's claim that the Abbey had become commercial and faded, and was particularly insightful in pinpointing O'Connor's penchant for evoking Yeats and the sense of moral responsibility which he felt towards him. The letter also demonstrated the resentment generated by the two Cork friends in O'Connor and O'Faoláin, who had pushed themselves to the forefront of the artistic avant-garde and then dominated one of the few gateways to critical exposure by their positions within *The Bell*. O'Connor's justification for his continued antagonism towards the Abbey came from his belief that Yeats had entrusted its artistic guidance to O'Connor himself and he was thus obliged to ensure that its standards were in keeping with Yeats's expectations. D'Alton mocked O'Connor for his continued claims of an insight into Yeats's artistic vision, but it was something which O'Connor himself took very seriously. Writing six years later after another public spat with the Abbey board of directors in which O'Connor had embroiled himself, he was to declare that:

> I've been ill and even and idle these months past. As you've probably read, Val Iremonger and Roger MacHugh [*sic*] made a public protest in the Abbey and I got involved on their side – naturally enough, as I was the only person who knew enough of the interior to defend them from the attention of people like P.S. O'Hegarty and Farren. Also I have a guilty feeling about the theatre, seeing that on his death-bed Yeats relied on me to save it.[74]

The incident referred to was an open complaint made by Dr Roger McHugh of University College Dublin and the poet and diplomat Valentin Iremonger on the night of 9 November 1947.[75] The protest was against the drop in the artistic standards of the Abbey under the leadership of Ernest Blythe and Roibeard O'Farachain (Robert Farren). Iremonger protested that 'when the poet Yeats died, he left behind him to the Irish nation as a legacy his beloved Abbey Theatre, then the first theatre in the world in acting, in production and in poetic impulse of its tradition. To-day, eight years after, under the utter incompetence of the present directorate's artistic policy, there is nothing left of that fine glory.'[76] For O'Connor, these public spats with the board were all the more vicious because of his proximity to those involved, and although he felt distant from the Abbey board by this stage he still took some pleasure in seeing it criticised, 'it's encouraging to see the young fellows kicking against that pestilential bastard [Ernest Blythe] and his stooges'.[77]

During the term of O'Connor's involvement with *The Bell*, Louis D'Alton, Denis Johnston, Lennox Robinson, Valentin Iremonger, Roger McHugh and Robert Farren were all contributors. D'Alton's reply is insightful because it points to a truth both about O'Connor in his relationship to Yeats and about *The Bell* itself. That is to say that *The Bell* was dependent on a small number of writers for its regular contributions and that these personalities were involved in a large number of other institutions, such as the Abbey, or the Irish Academy of Letters. However, where D'Alton's criticism sees this as a weakness, O'Faoláin believed that it was its strength, and saw close-knit peer interaction as a force for good.[78] D'Alton continued to criticise O'Connor and *The Bell* itself by claiming that they had set themselves up as the arbiters of good taste, and as head of a pseudo-intellectual group that was less than generous in its assessment of its peers: 'Mr. O'Connor seems to be a notable exponent of that highbrow school of lack-of-thought which supposes comedy

to be an inferior art, and people that enjoy comedy an inferior people.' D'Alton
went on to dismiss out of hand Denis Ireland's criticism as following O'Connor
in supposing comedy to be unsophisticated and degenerate, and mocked *The
Bell* for its pretensions towards the development of new standards in Irish
culture, while simultaneously publishing criticism as inane as O'Connor's and
Ireland's: 'Well, Mr. Editor what is it to be – a bull, howler – or perish the
thought – an inane idiocy! Remember that it is of importance to the cultivation
of the new standards and taste that we should be guided to a true appreciation
of such exquisite niceties!'[79]

The very fact that O'Faoláin would publish such negative press is a testament to *The Bell*'s openness and breadth of vision. However, D'Alton did
tap into a resentment surrounding O'Connor's and O'Faoláin's literary pretensions by other Dublin writers. They were two Cork friends who seemed
to be suggesting to Dublin writers that their work was not up to standards.
It must have been difficult to take for D'Alton who was prolific in his output
and had enjoyed relative success with his Abbey productions. Writing to Sean
O'Casey three months after his reply in *The Bell*, D'Alton identified the aloof
and condescending air with which the Dublin literary set perceived O'Faoláin
and O'Connor. Although the letter is long, it is worth reproducing for a picture
of how some regarded the two writers and their literary ambition in *The Bell*:

> O'Connor and O'Faoláin are a sort of literary Marx Brothers, high class patter
> artists and cross talk comedians. Their efforts to constitute themselves the new
> AE and W.B. Yeats is a source of sardonic amusement to the queer fellas, and of
> course Dublin in its dear old way isn't letting them get away with anything like
> that, and for once it's right. But they are a most industrious pair of log rollers, and
> supreme exponents of high-falutin'. O'Connor has since the death of Higgins,
> who gave a colourable imitation of the external Yeats, adopted all the great man's
> mannerisms. All they need is the recognition that Dublin and other cities gave
> Yeats to be well away – but they are not getting it! They are quite obviously clever
> sort of chaps, with the push of the very devil – They want to be claimed as men of
> supreme genius, but the world at large is not to be codded. The pretentiousness
> of the beggars on the strength of a few short stories and one or two middling kind
> of novels is woeful. They'll never be able to get over the idea of the fascination of
> being able to put words on paper. They never give themselves a rest from being
> literary men, and they hate like mischief to have anyone else attract attention for
> awhile. In fact Dublin is at the present time infested with the most mediocre pack
> of pretenders and second rate minds. We were never worse off in our lives from
> that aspect than we are, and what we never were in our history – we're compla-
> cent as hell.[80]

Although D'Alton is highly critical of both O'Connor and O'Faoláin he does
seem to suggest that there was a need for what they were trying to rectify in
The Bell, that is the identification, encouragement and support of new writ-

ers of individual genius within Ireland. Even though D'Alton was infuriated by O'Connor's criticisms, enough to deride him to O'Casey, his backbiting should not detract from his achievements. D'Alton was not the only target of O'Connor's ire, and he also attacked fellow writer in *The Bell*, Denis Johnston. This whole saga indicates the extent to which literary Dublin was caught up in minor cliques and alliances. It is also testament to the productivity of such a hotbed of critical rivals within a small proximity.[81] A side effect of little magazine publication is that these spats are captured under the guise of objective criticism, the petty side of which is supported by their personal correspondence. To O'Faoláin's credit, he also gave a right of reply to Denis Johnston, whose review had been targeted by O'Connor for its superficiality.

Johnston's retort was, on the whole, much less emotive than D'Alton's, as was befitting a man who had undergone a legal education at Cambridge University and whose mind was trained for argument. Johnston simply pointed out that O'Connor's own play *The Invincibles* (1937) was itself in bad taste, taking the Phoenix Park murders as its subject. As such, O'Connor was hypocritical in denouncing D'Alton's work, when he repeated the same mistakes in his own: 'according to his view it is degrading to invite an audience to laugh at drunkenness and larceny, but it is quite proper to encourage them in the belief that perhaps murder isn't so bad after all – provided, of course, it is political murder, and not a matter of sordid personal gain'. He was also quick to point out that O'Connor's plea on behalf of protecting Lennox Robinson's dignity was having the opposite effect, instead drawing attention to his alcoholism and publicly humiliating him. Johnston was keen not to further contribute to this debate and saw O'Connor's actions as 'grimly determined to commit an unsolicited rescue, even if first of all he has to shove some-body down the nearest drain in order to have the pleasure of pulling him out ... I shall not be a party to any further ventilation of such an unnecessary and ill-mannered argument.'[82] Johnston's reply was calm and direct, and he seemed not to have taken the assault personally, qualifying his dismantling of O'Connor's argument to soften the blow. However, one person who did take the criticism personally was the Abbey actor Denis O'Dea, whose depiction of Philip Mannion had been found so disagreeable by O'Connor.

O'Dea took the article to Denis Johnston and asked him for his legal opinion and to review 'The Stone Dolls' to see if it was libellous.[83] Whatever Johnston thought of the article, O'Dea certainly felt that it was, and subsequently took O'Connor, O'Faoláin and J.J. O'Leary, in his capacity as printer, to court for libel. O'Dea's case was successful and he received a small amount of compensation along with a full apology printed in *The Bell*:

> The attention of the Editor of the above magazine, has been drawn by the Solicitors of Mr. Denis O'Dea, Actor, to certain passages in a recent Article

in *The Bell* which have caused pain and inconvenience to Mr. O'Dea, in so
much as they suggested that Mr. O'Dea deliberately caricatured a well-known
public figure, while acting in Louis D'Alton's play 'The Money Doesn't Matter.'
We have been satisfied that no such caricature was intended and we, therefore,
express our sincere regret that Mr. O'Dea should have suffered pain and annoy-
ance by reason of this article.[84]

O'Faoláin must have felt troubled that the magazine would find itself in the
dock so early after its inception. The printing of such a grovelling apology
would have been difficult for any editor interested in maintaining the dignity of
his publication, and O'Faoláin was exasperated by O'Connor and his belligerent
attitude: 'to me you are a magnificent anarchist. You drop out of the Academy,
you want to drop out of *The Bell*. You will probably drop out of Cuala. A grand
time for a bit of excitement and let somebody else do the patient work.'[85] This
incident was the final straw for O'Connor as he finished in his capacity as poetry
editor from this edition onwards, and was replaced by his friend and manager at
Wicklow County Library, Geoffrey Taylor.

O'Connor was also becoming tired of what he perceived to be O'Faoláin
playing a grandiose role in his capacity as editor. Formal correspondence from
an old friend was too much to bear for a man as sensitive to criticism as
O'Connor: 'I gave up writing for *The Bell* when O'F started sending me letters,
written by the office boy, beginning Dear Michael and ending per and pro
S. O'Faoláin. Among the forms of hallucinations of grandeur I never heard
of a man that thought himself a limited company.'[86] However, O'Faoláin was
obviously intent on keeping O'Connor involved with *The Bell* in some capacity
as he appeared on the editorial board proper soon after.[87] Privately, however,
O'Faoláin was disgusted with O'Connor's resignation and wrote to him to
complain about his inability to work with others in any constructive capacity:

> See you at Cuala. You make me yawn. I never have yet seen you *DO* anything.
> Academy, Abbey, Bell, Drama League, and I am sure in time Cuala – you will
> enjoy yourself blowholing at them all, and then chuck them. I suppose you think
> you are the Strong Man? To me you are, in these matters of practical work, just
> one gigantic bubble of fart. That is your role – to stand up on the ditch and roar,
> and be the bullfrog blowing himself out, and saying all the time, 'I am the Big
> Noise. All these other chaps are mean little whinging whining vacillating con-
> spiring do nothings'. You co-operate with nobody, work with nobody, resign in
> a huff when you get tired, and go off feeling pure and noble. You are, I am tired
> of saying it, a genius: though if you let your work get infected by your character
> you will indubitably kill your genius: but as for working with other human beings
> – and God in heaven knows I am no great shakes at it – you are a complete wash-
> out. Your letter is going in (is gone in) as I said it would, and my leader with it.
> What the frigging hell more do you want? I told you, frankly, as friend to friend,
> what happened at a conference, I told you objectively and reportorially what hap-

pened, truthfully and exactly. I told you that Johnston will choose his own time to expose the Abbey. And I trust Lord God that Your Highness has no objection to doing whatever he thinks best? I told you that the attack will develop. Do you think the *Bell* is a sort of rubber balloon which you can blow up and up and up all in one second? Jesus Christ but you make me tired. As for you and the Abbey have you not got enough native wit to see that the people to whom you want to appeal inevitably *must* say that you have a sore toe about it? You are a silly ass. Go away and write masterpieces. And grow up.[88]

Interestingly, O'Faoláin also suggests that Denis Johnston was unhappy with the Abbey board but was biding his time before attacking it, which shows that at least some of O'Connor's public convictions were shared by others, albeit in a more private and less controversial manner. Both O'Faoláin and O'Connor were frustrated by Irish society and its institutions, yet O'Faoláin had a wider vision and was dispositionally less inclined to perceive such frustration as a form of personal persecution. O'Connor's anger would eventually lead him to try and escape to America through teaching contracts organised by John Kelleher at Harvard. The visiting American Catholic writer J.F. Powers, who became a regular guest at the O'Faoláin household, captured the distinction between their two personalities well:

I had dinner at the Bailey – a restaurant in Dublin – with Sean O'Faolain and Frank O'Connor the other night. Liked them both. O'C. is going to the U.S., hopes to settle there, can't live or write here, he says, because of 'personal troubles,' meaning his marital troubles, I guess. He now has an English wife, an Irish one here, numerous children etc. O'F. is riding it – being happily married, it appears – riding it out on purer lines, the problem with being a writer in Ireland I mean. O'C. said it would be impossible for him or O'F. to live anywhere but in Dublin, in Ireland; O'F. seemed to agree they'd be in physical danger in Cork, where they both come from … O'F. is very calm, cool, and, I suspect, long-suffering … O'C. great admirer of A.E. Coppard and Saroyan. O'F. might have been a Dublin businessman, from his dress, dark suit, white shirt; O'C. raffish, orange wool shirt, wool tie, blue tam. O'F. in good health. O'C. has trouble with his liver, his wife tells him what he can eat, drinks light wines and lime juice. He paid the bill.[89]

This sense of personal persecution demonstrates why O'Connor found it difficult to work with others and why O'Faoláin was better suited to the methodical work of editing *The Bell*.

At this early stage of production, and despite the controversies, *The Bell* must be considered a runaway success, its circulation figures reputedly reaching 5,000 copies, so it would seem that O'Connor's departure as poetry editor cannot be attributed to the stresses and infighting that come when a magazine is faced with declining numbers.[90] By comparison, and to put these numbers in context, Cyril Connolly's *Horizon*, also launched in 1940, had sold 5,000 copies

despite a potentially much larger audience and easier access to paper under
wartime rationing.[91] One critic puts *The Bell's* circulation figures as high as
30,000 by its fifth year, although this figure would have afforded the editors an
unlikely annual income of IR£15,750 at a price of one shilling and sixpence.[92]
The circulation figure of 5,000 copies is now critically accepted, and it is also
commonplace to acknowledge that the magazine probably had a circulation
beyond its sales figures.[93] However, there are good reasons to doubt the validity
of such numbers, as it was obviously in the interest of any magazine to boast to
its advertisers that its circulation numbers were high, and privately its board
members were less assertive; O'Connor claimed that O'Faoláin admitted to
him that 'they <u>never</u> sold it out!!'[94] Whatever its actual circulation numbers
it is obvious that *The Bell* was prominent in the minds of literary Dublin, as
evidenced by the quality of its board of directors and the standard of writers
willing to publish in it.

   O'Connor was not the only author with a growing reputation who featured
heavily in the early issues of *The Bell*. Elizabeth Bowen – by 1940 a writer of
international fame, closely associated with the Bloomsbury group and with
influential contacts throughout the publishing world in Great Britain – was
also present from the first edition. Bowen was friends with Cyril Connolly,
and another source of contact between Connolly and O'Faoláin, which would
result in *The Bell* and *Horizon*'s closeness as publications, often carrying advertisements for each other and sharing many contributors. *The Bell* even tried
to publish an English writers' edition in response to Connolly's Irish edition
of *Horizon*, but was unable to source the contributors due to the constraints
of the war. As a result, O'Faoláin decided instead to run an international
number, with contributors coming from France, Russia, Germany, England,
Italy, America, Ireland, Spain and Norway. Why contributors from these countries should be easier to source during the war remains unclear.[95] O'Faoláin's
admiration of Bowen as a writer would lead to their meeting and eventually
becoming lovers. In his autobiography, O'Faoláin recalled travelling to Euston
Station, London in 1937 from his home in Killough House in Co. Wicklow,
where he was mulling over the impossibility of producing the great Irish novel.
He had searched for a model on which to base his own works, but was unable
to find such a framework in Irish writing. In his boredom he chanced on a book
that offered to him an insight into the possibilities for Irish art, similar to the
one which Turgenev had offered to Russia.

   Enthralled, he read straight through the night and arrived at his destination
exhausted, but alive to the new vista which had opened up before him: 'I found
myself reading a novel that seemed to me to solve all of my problems by demonstrating that one could actually be Turgenev when writing in holy, simple pie-
tistic, peasant, bogtrotting, jansenistic, lower lower middle-class agricultural
Ireland.' The author of the work in question was a woman and he immediately

recognised it as a 'beautifully written work of romantic genius composed realistically.' The novel to which he was referring was Bowen's *The Last September* (1929), and he saw in it a counterpoint to his own collection *Midsummer Night Madness and Other Stories* (1932), which had also dealt with the conflicts and pressures of the Irish War of Independence, although treated from the perspective of the Big House inhabitants. By the time O'Faoláin had arrived at Euston station he was 'bleary-eyed from reading, but I was excitedly wide awake to the realisation that I had fallen utterly in love with this author'.[96]

O'Faoláin shared his new-found enthusiasm for Bowen's writing with his friend Derek Verschoyle, publisher and literary editor of *The Spectator* between 1932 and 1939. Verschoyle was at this time married to the beautiful and pioneering Fleet Street journalist, Anne Scott James, and it was through a meeting at the Savage Club, where they were members, that O'Faoláin was first introduced to Bowen.[97] Although O'Faoláin was impressed by Scott James's good looks, he was disappointed to find that she 'proved to be more outstanding for her beauty than her brains', and resented her description of Bowen as 'horsey'. O'Faoláin was impressed by Bowen at this meeting where she cut a figure of 'worldly self-possession' and remained enamoured of her until the onset of war forced a sustained separation.[98] Even though O'Faoláin's account of his 'discovery' of Bowen on a sleepless train journey to London has a romantic allure, it is most certainly a construct or mistakenly remembered on his behalf.

The truth was that by 1937 O'Faoláin had already been in contact with Bowen and she by that time had been impressed enough with *Midsummer Night Madness* to include it in a collection of modern short stories that she was editing for Faber & Faber. Writing to her friend William Plomer she claimed of O'Faoláin's collection: 'I do think [*Midsummer Night Madness*] grand' and asked 'have you met him? Is he nice? He might possibly be quite dim.'[99] O'Faoláin's correspondence with Bowen had begun as early as spring of 1937 and he had already read *The Last September* before embarking to meet her. In a letter to Bowen on 22 April 1937 from his home in Killough house, O'Faoláin claimed, 'I finished LAST SEPTEMBER this morning ... I envy you your control, and your sense of drama in small things. I feel so vulgar and "screamy" before your books ... I could smell the hay, the wet, the mountain-line. It's entirely Irish – if that matters a damn. (We're so sick of hearing our Nazionalists [*sic*] ask for Irish literature – so thirsty for just literature.)'[100] O'Faoláin's relationship with Bowen seems to have accelerated quite rapidly, so much so that he went with her to the Salzburg festival in the summer of that year, along with Isaiah Berlin, Stuart Hampshire, Sally Graves and Cyril Connolly.[101] The sense of loss for these transnational literary excursions often surfaces in the work of O'Faoláin and Connolly during their writings of the war, and are particularly acute with O'Faoláin who had a strong sense of the cultural isolationism that he felt neutrality imposed on the Irish artist. O'Faoláin identified in this letter to Bowen the more romantic tendencies in his own work, and especially in *Midsummer Night Madness*, where he touches on some of the frustrations that he was feeling at home. He also shed some light on the inspiration behind the formation of *The Bell*, in that he claimed to resent the increasing xenophobia of nationalism in Ireland.

The letter also deals with a recurring theme in Bowen's own writing, that of the isolation of the Big House from the rest of the country. O'Faoláin was concerned about the tension that existed after the Anglo-Irish had become newly disenfranchised as a political power. As such, he appealed to Bowen to write a novel which would represent the Anglo-Irish, without the convenient pressure valve of emigration eastward towards the British empire that was their traditional outlet. He wondered what could be produced if they were to channel their political energies into reform back in Ireland: 'I venture to suggest that an Irish novel (Damn this word Irish – how it slips out of me!) – that a novel about Ireland would get down to the reality of things-happening better if it chose a Big House that had no, or few, escapes; escapes to London, for example ... You will say, these people are a mess, and I cannot be bothered; this is work for a social reformer not a novelist. Still, Dead Souls did, for Gogol, link up divided worlds, and Tchekov has many stories (about doctors) that climb walls.'[102] This suggestion on behalf of O'Faoláin would develop into Bowen's first contribution to *The Bell*, titled 'The Big House'.

Published in the inaugural issue of the magazine, this short piece identifies the fears and hopes of the Anglo-Irish at the beginning of the war. Bowen's submission reads like a strange mix of guilt and prickly arrogance. In its form it is a historical explanation of the existence of the Anglo-Irish as a social class and enumerates some of their qualities as a group and their contribution to Irish society. It is written in the defensive style of one who feels under siege within her own home. It also captures the tension and sense of resentment that some Anglo-Irish must have suffered from the Catholic middle classes in Ireland: 'is it its height – in this country of low buildings – that got these Anglo-Irish houses their "big" name? Or have they been called "big" with a slight inflection – that of hostility, irony? One may call a man "big" with just that inflection because he seems to think the hell of himself.' Fittingly, considering O'Faoláin's plea, the piece ends with a hope for the future of the Anglo-Irish within the new Ireland. However, Bowen cannot help attaching a barb. She finishes on an accusatory note, sensing that the Catholic Irish are now rounding on their former political masters and behaving in an unsympathetic manner: 'The good in the new can add to, not destroy, the good in the old. From inside many houses (and these will be the survivors) barriers are being impatiently attacked. But it must be seen that a barrier has two sides.'[103]

Bowen's hesitancy here to fully embrace this new Ireland is typical of the ambiguity with which she looked on political developments in the Irish Free

State and Éire, and that is also present in her own work. When she again returned to Ireland, ostensibly for some rest and recuperation during the war, O'Faoláin managed to meet her only once. She also did the rounds among the usual circle of artists and writers within Dublin. O'Faoláin later recalled her reticence and unusual mood during their time together when 'he took her to Jammet's restaurant in either 1941 or 1942. It was not a happy lunch. She did not say why she was visiting our well-fed and neutral Ireland from her bombed and Spartan London.'[104] Bowen's reticence may have been due to the awkward silences between two ex-lovers, but it also reminded O'Faoláin of the sense of duty which Bowen must have felt towards belligerent London, and that was present throughout the Anglo-Irish as a class whose traditional political sympathies were aligned with Britain. What O'Faoláin did not know at the time was that Bowen was working for the British government writing espionage reports.

Her hope for goodwill between the Anglo-Irish and the Irish Catholic middle classes did not extend sufficiently to prevent her writing detailed accounts of their mood for the British Ministry of Information.[105] Although she worked diligently to produce reports that are astonishing in their insightful description of wartime Ireland, they also reflect on the duality of nature that is present in Bowen herself. The burden of guilt that neutrality placed on the Irish people was evident everywhere for Bowen. She read this as a moral failure which was written on the faces of the Irish and clung like a miasma on the streets of the capital: 'my general impression of Eire – or rather, Dublin – on this visit was that the country was morally and nervously in a state of deterioration. Intimidation was having malign effects. In general, people seemed to have lost face – with themselves, with each other.'[106] Bowen was right to identify, if not a sense of guilt, then at least some form of inner conflict on behalf of Irish writers. O'Faoláin himself produced a rather strange un-broadcast speech for the BBC in which he stressed that Éire was very much in the war, and Leslie Daiken's *They Go, The Irish* (1944) brought together a wide range of different writers to demonstrate Irish involvement.[107] In later years O'Faoláin would feel deep sympathy for Bowen and her actions, seeing them as the result of the pressure that war puts on people to behave unnaturally or contrary to their instincts:

> all of this is over forty years ago but I can still wince a little at us all – at Elizabeth, at myself, at some patriotic woman who wrote to the press about visiting spies disguised as harmless visitors, at Harold Nicolson, at the British Ministry of Information; or else I see the whole trivial incident as a tiny symbol of the sort of thing that war does to people. It puts an end to that civilised balance of values that normally encourages us to see everybody's dilemma from other angles besides our own ... The very thought of Ireland at war would have torn Elizabeth's heart apart.[108]

Bowen's conflicted attitude towards Ireland at this time is also evident in the interview that she gave to Larry Morrow, writing under the pseudonym 'The Bellman', and published in *The Bell* in September of 1942.

When pricked by Morrow that she might not be considered an Irish novelist, Bowen was at pains to emphasise her Irish credentials, even going as far as denying any English influence on her work: '"I regard myself as an Irish Novelist," she said simply. "As long as I can remember I've been extremely conscious of being Irish – even when I was writing about very un-Irish things such as suburban life in Paris or the English seaside ... As regards my work, if I've been influenced by anything it's by the French novelists and short-story writers of the past fifty years ... I've never been influenced by any English writer.' Bowen's own sense of displacement is evident here, feeling duty-bound to write reports for the British Ministry of Information, and yet also compelled to deny an English identity or influence on her own work. Bowen also made a case for Irish exceptionalism within a European artistic context and was caught in the double-bind that is present throughout *The Bell*. That is to say, she pleaded for a wider cosmopolitan outlook and yet struggled to demonstrate that Ireland was in some way different: 'This country is different from the other countries in Europe. It's so much more complex. It requires such an enormous amount of knowledge and experience before the foreigner begins to make an impression – even on the rim of things.'[109]

This also was the dilemma facing O'Faoláin in editing *The Bell*. He worried over the differences in Irish society that prevented the development of a literature of a uniquely national character, while simultaneously arguing for the non-existence of such differences. As such, he pleaded with the Irish writer to seek European models as a potential lead where their art might follow, but wanted them to create a distinctively Irish mode of these models. All in all, this crisis of identity under which Bowen was suffering was replicated in *The Bell*, which struggled to define a new vision of Irishness that was not the same as the exclusivist identity of Irish nationalism in the 1940s. In the same way that Bowen professed herself Irish, but reported on Ireland to a belligerent power, O'Faoláin's *The Bell* also cast itself as Irish, but sought international role models for its particular brand of Irish identity. In so doing, O'Faoláin ran the danger of repeating a reductive definition of Irishness, albeit with a more cosmopolitan outlook substituted for a restrictive nationalist one. For O'Faoláin, this cosmopolitan outlook was coupled with a sense of isolation which affected English writers from Cyril Connolly to W.H. Auden, but also those whose identity was less clearly delineated and for whom Irishness or Englishness was a difficult negotiation, such as C.S. Lewis, Louis MacNeice, or C. Day Lewis. Bowen herself is often unproblematically adopted within an English literary tradition, despite her own protestations of her Irishness.[110] But she was not the only person to feel the pressure exerted on identity by the shift in political reality. Irish people of all classifications were trying to adjust to public life in a world at war, and in a state determined to maintain its sovereignty at all costs.

Notes

1 Seán O'Faoláin, *The Short Story* (London: Collins, 1948), p. 15.
2 Peadar O'Donnell to Edward Garnett (7 July 1930), Garnett Family Collection, Harry Ransom Center at the University of Texas at Austin. MS 1542. Hereafter referred to as Garnett.
3 Vivian Mercier, 'The Fourth Estate: VI – Verdict on *The Bell*', *The Bell*, 10:2 (May 1945), p. 157.
4 See Seán O'Faoláin, 'Literary Provincialism', *The Commonweal* (21 December 1932), pp. 214–215. Peadar O'Donnell, 'Young Irish Writers', *The Commonweal* (26 April 1933), pp. 717–718.
5 G. Wren Howard to Seán O'Faoláin (10 August 1931), Jonathan Cape Ltd, MS 2446, the Archive of British Publishing and Printing, University of Reading. Hereafter referred to as Cape.
6 Seán O'Faoláin to G. Wren Howard (n.d. [1932]), Cape, MS 2446.
7 For more on this debate see Frank Shovlin, 'The Struggle for Form: Seán O'Faoláin's Autobiographies', *The Yearbook of English Studies*, 35 (2005), pp. 161–170.
8 Seán O'Faoláin, 'F.R. Higgins', *The Bell*, 1:5 (February 1941).
9 Elizabeth Bowen, 'James Joyce', *The Bell*, 1:6 (March 1941).
10 G. Wren Howard to Seán O'Faoláin (20 October 1931), Cape, MS 2446.
11 Seán O'Faoláin to John V. Kelleher (8 September [1948]?), UCC, BL/L/JVK/26.
12 Seán O'Faoláin, *Vive Moi! An Autobiography* (London: Sinclair-Stephenson, 1993), p. 150.
13 Seán O'Faoláin to Jonathan Cape (n.d. [1932]), Cape, MS 2446.
14 O'Faoláin to Jonathan Cape (n.d.), Cape, MS 2446.
15 O'Faoláin to Jonathan Cape (4 September 1933), Cape, MS 2446.
16 O'Faoláin to Jonathan Cape (n.d.), Cape, MS 2446.
17 Seán O'Faoláin to Ruth (n.d.), Cape, MS 2446.
18 Internal memo (n.d.), Cape, MS 2446.
19 G. Wren Howard to Harold Raymond (1 March 1938), Cape, MS 2446.
20 See the Oxford Dictionary of National Biography: www.oxforddnb.com.ezproxy.liv.ac.uk/view/article/31541?docPos=7 (accessed 3 March 2010).
21 This lecture was later published in *Ireland To-Day*. See Frank O'Connor, 'The Gaelic Tradition in Literature', *Ireland To-Day*, 1:1 (June 1936), pp. 41–48.
22 For a full account of this incident, see Anon., 'Lively Scenes at Lecture', *Irish Times* (4 March 1935), p. 7.
23 See Declan Kiberd, *The Irish Writer and the World* (Cambridge: Cambridge University Press, 2005), p. 32.
24 Anon., 'Lively Scenes at Lecture'.
25 Quoted in Sean McCann, *The Story of the Abbey Theatre* (London: Four Square Books, 1967), p. 154.

26 For more on W.B. Yeats's attempt to distance himself from more advanced nationalism, see R.F. Foster, *W.B. Yeats: A Life 1: The Apprentice Mage 1865–1914* (Oxford: Oxford University Press, 1998), p. 405.
27 Seán O'Faoláin, 'Book Reviews', *Ireland To-Day*, 1:1 (July 1936), p. 73.
28 For a full account of their relationship, see Maurice Harmon, *Sean O'Faoláin: A Life* (London: Constable, 1994), pp. 63–69.
29 Seán O'Faoláin to John V. Kelleher (8 September [1948]?), UCC, BL/L/JVK/26.
30 Seán O'Faoláin, 'This is your Magazine', *The Bell*, 1:1 (October 1940), p. 6.
31 Seán O'Faoláin, 'Book Review', *Ireland To-Day*, 1:2 (July 1936), p. 70.
32 Quoted in Frank Shovlin, *The Irish Literary Periodical 1923–1958* (Oxford: Clarendon Press, 2003), p. 77.
33 Quoted in Andrée Sheehy Skeffington, *Skeff: The Life of Owen Sheehy Skeffington 1909–1970* (Dublin, Lilliput Press, 1991), p. 240.
34 For more on the topic of English writers and commitment, see Valentine Cunningham, *British Writers of the Thirties* (Oxford: Oxford University Press, 1988); Samuel Hynes, *The Auden Generation: Literature and Politics in England in the 1930s* (New York: Viking, 1977).
35 Seán O'Faoláin, 'Neutral?', *Authors Take Sides on the Spanish War* (London: Left Review, 1936).
36 Peadar O'Donnell, 'What I saw in Spain', *Ireland To-Day*, 1:4 (September 1936), p. 20.
37 Quoted in Peter Hegarty, *Peadar O'Donnell* (Cork: Mercier Press, 1999), p. 226.
38 Peadar O'Donnell, 'Young Irish Writers', *The Commonweal* (26 April 1933), pp. 717–718.
39 See Seán O'Faoláin to Lincoln Kirstein (3 July 1930), in Mitzi Berger Hamovitch (ed.), *The Hound & Horn Letters* (Athens: University of Georgia Press, 1982), p. 120.
40 Seán O'Faoláin to Edward Garnett (14 August 1931), Boston College, Seán O'Faoláin Correspondence 1926–1969, MS 86–180 (Box 2, Folder 1). Hereafter referred to as Boston.
41 Seán O'Faoláin to Edward Garnett (30 January 1932), Boston, MS 89–14 (Box 2, Folder 7).
42 O'Faoláin, *Vive Moi!* (1993), p. 296.
43 For an excellent introduction into British and Irish periodical culture, see Peter Brooker and Andrew Thacker (eds), *The Oxford Critical and Cultural History of Modernist Magazines: Volume 1, Britain and Ireland 1880–1955* (Oxford: Oxford University Press, 2009).
44 Just as *The Bell* was launched, another Irish journal *The Dublin Magazine* (1923–58) was making an impassioned appeal for new subscriptions to ensure its survival. See *The Dublin Magazine: A Quarterly Review of Literature, Science and Art*, 15:1 (January–March 1940), ix.
45 O'Faoláin, *Vive Moi!* (1993), p. 321.
46 These were just some of the important establishment figures McGrath would have known through his role in the Oireachtas. For a full list of members of the

Oireachtas see the Irish Government website Houses of the Oireachtas, www. oireachtas.ie (accessed 4 February 2010).

47 For a fascinating insight into the life of Joe McGrath, see Marie Coleman, *The Irish Sweep: A History of the Irish Hospitals Sweepstake 1930–87* (Dublin: University College Dublin Press, 2009).

48 Donal Ó Drisceoil, *Peadar O'Donnell* (Cork: Cork University Press, 2001), p. 110.

49 Seán O'Faoláin to Frank O'Connor (19 September 1942), Gotlieb (Box 3, Folder 6).

50 Ó Drisceoil, *Peadar O'Donnell*, p. 110.

51 Seán O'Faoláin, 'The Little Magazine', *Irish Times* (25 February 1970), p. 11.

52 Peadar O'Donnell, 'The Little Magazine', *Irish Times* (4 March 1970), p. 11.

53 Ernie O'Malley to Thomas MacGreevy (2 July 1939), in Cormac H. O'Malley and Nicholas Allen (eds), *Broken Landscapes: Selected Letters of Ernie O'Malley 1924–1957* (Dublin: The Lilliput Press, 2011), p. 170.

54 O'Faoláin, 'This is Your Magazine', p. 9.

55 Candida Lycett Green (ed.), *John Betjeman, Letters: Volume One: 1926–1951* (London: Methuen, 1994), p. 269. This story seems apocryphal, considering the unlikely event of an IRA assassin writing to his supposed target about the beauty of poetry.

56 Cyril Connolly *Horizon: A Review of Literature and Art*, 5:25 (January 1942).

57 Cyril Connolly, 'Comment', *Horizon: A Review of Literature and Art*, 5:25 (January 1942), p. 11.

58 John Betjeman to William Rothenstein (United Kingdom Representative to Éire) (20 April 1943) in Lycett Green (ed.), *John Betjeman, Letters: Volume One*, p. 315.

59 For a nuanced account of the Irish experience of the war, see Bryce Evans, *Ireland During the Second World War: Farewell to Plato's Cave* (Manchester: Manchester University Press, 2014).

60 Production information taken from: www.abbeytheatre.ie/archives/production_detail/1747 (accessed 4 August 2010).

61 For a full review of the play, see Anon., 'New Play at the Abbey: "The Money Doesn't Matter"', *Irish Times* (11 March 1941), p. 6.

62 Denis Johnston, 'Plays of the Quarter', *The Bell*, 2:1 (April 1941), p. 91.

63 For an example of O'Connor's bitterness towards the board of the Abbey Theatre, see Frank O'Connor, *Leinster, Munster, and Connaught* (London: Robert Hale, 1950), pp. 35–49.

64 See James Matthews, *Voices: A Life of Frank O'Connor* (New York: Atheneum, 1983), pp. 124–148.

65 Frank O'Connor, 'The Stone Dolls', *The Bell*, 2:3 (June 1941), pp. 61–64.

66 R.F. Foster, *W.B. Yeats: A Life II. The Arch-Poet* (Oxford: Oxford University Press, 2003), p. 414.

67 O'Connor, 'The Stone Dolls', pp. 61–64.

68 The editorial O'Connor was attacking was Seán O'Faoláin, '1916–1941: Tradition and Creation', *The Bell*, 2:1 (April 1941), pp. 5–12. O'Connor's criticisms are reductive and unfair to O'Faoláin who was trying to account for both sides of the argument in his attempt to better articulate his anti-censorship stance.

69 O'Connor, 'The Stone Dolls', p. 67.
70 Matthews, *Voices*, p. 178.
71 Denis Ireland, 'The Abbey Theatre', *The Bell*, 2:3 (June 1941), pp. 67–68.
72 For more on Yeats's working relationship with the Abbey Theatre, see Lauren Arrington, *W.B. Yeats, the Abbey Theatre, Censorship, and the Irish State: Adding the Half-Pence to the Pence* (Oxford: Oxford University Press, 2010).
73 Louis Lynch D'Alton, 'Public Opinion', *The Bell*, 2:4 (July 1941), p. 72.
74 Frank O'Connor to John V. Kelleher (December 1947), UCC, BL/L/JVK/158.
75 Professor McHugh would later supervise the first PhD thesis on *The Bell*. See Richard A. Furze Jr, *A Desirable Vision of Life: A Study of The Bell, 1940–1954* (National University of Ireland, University College Dublin, 1974).
76 Quoted in McCann, *The Story of the Abbey Theatre*, p. 156.
77 Frank O'Connor to John V. Kelleher (November 1947), UCC, BL/L/JVK/157.
78 For a full account of O'Faoláin's attitude to this, see Seán O'Faoláin, 'Provincialism', *The Bell*, 2:2 (May 1941).
79 D'Alton, 'Public Opinion', pp. 75–76.
80 Louis Lynch D'Alton to Sean O'Casey (4 October 1941), The Sean O'Casey Papers 1917–1993, The National Library of Ireland, MS Collection List 75, MS 38,061. Hereafter referred to as O'Casey.
81 For more on this, see Seamus Deane, 'Boredom and the Apocalypse: A National Paradigm', *Strange Country: Modernity and Nationhood in Irish Writing since 1790* (Oxford: Clarendon Press, 1997).
82 Denis Johnston, 'The Theatre', *The Bell*, 2:4 (July 1941), pp. 79–80.
83 Matthews, *Voices*, p. 410.
84 'Legal Notice', *The Bell*, 3:6 (March 1942), p. 459.
85 Quoted in Matthews, *Voices*, p. 178.
86 Quoted in Jim McKeon, *Frank O'Connor: A Life* (Edinburgh: Mainstream Publishing, 1998), p. 138.
87 The editorial board is printed intermittently on the opening page of *The Bell* and notices for changes are printed randomly in the text or are entirely absent. For example, See *The Bell*, 2:4 (July 1941).
88 Seán O'Faoláin to Frank O'Connor [n.d. probably 1942], Gotlieb (Box 3, Folder 6).
89 J.F. Powers to Father Harvey Egan (8 March 1952), in Katherine A. Powers (ed.), *Suitable Accommodations: An Autobiographical Story of Family Life: the Letters of J.F. Powers, 1942–1963* (New York: Farrar, Straus and Giroux, 2013), p. 168.
90 A thank you to advertisers is printed in the back page of the April edition that puts its circulation numbers at 5,000. See *The Bell*, 2:1 (April 1941).
91 Michael Shelden, *Friends of Promise: Cyril Connolly and the World of Horizon* (London: Minerva 1990), p. 42.
92 This figure is unsupported by any reference. See Furze, *A Desirable Vision of Life*, p. 42.
93 For a critic who follows this line, and for an excellent account of *The Bell*'s material history, see Kelly Matthews, *The Bell Magazine and the Representation of Irish Identity* (Dublin: Four Courts Press, 2012), p. 69.

94 Frank O'Connor to John V. Kelleher (January 1947), UCC, BL/L/JVK/151.
95 See Anon., 'Announcements', *The Bell*, 5:5 (February 1943).
96 O'Faoláin, *Vive Moi!* (1993), pp. 301–302.
97 For an account of the interesting life of Anne Scott James, see Richard Boston, 'Obituary: Anne Scott James', *Guardian* (15 May 2009), p. 36.
98 O'Faoláin, *Vive Moi!* (1993), p. 303.
99 Quoted in Victoria Glendinning, *Elizabeth Bowen: Portrait of a Writer* (London: Weidenfeld & Nicolson, 1977), p. 119.
100 Seán O'Faoláin to Elizabeth Bowen (22 April 1937) in Elizabeth Bowen Collection, the Harry Ransom Centre, the University of Texas at Austin (Box 11, Folder 7). Hereafter referred to as Bowen.
101 See Jeremy Lewis, *Cyril Connolly: A Life* (London: Jonathan Cape, 1997), p. 303.
102 Seán O'Faoláin to Elizabeth Bowen (n.d.) Bowen (Box 11, Folder 7).
103 Elizabeth Bowen, 'The Big House', *The Bell*, 1:1 (October 1940), p. 71.
104 O'Faoláin, *Vive Moi!* (1993), p. 310.
105 The debate around whether Bowen's activities actually constituted spying is still unresolved. See Eunan O'Halpin, *Spying on Ireland: British Intelligence and Irish Neutrality During the Second World War* (Oxford: Oxford University Press, 2008), pp. 137–140.
106 Elizabeth Bowen to the Ministry of Information (20 February 1942), in Jack Lane and Brendan Clifford (eds), *Elizabeth Bowen: "Notes on Eire" Espionage Reports to Winston Churchill, 1940–42, with a Review of Irish Neutrality During World War 2* (Aubane: Aubane Historical Society, 2008), p. 29. Bowen was working for the British Ministry of Information compiling reports on wartime Éire and was rewarded for her service with membership of the Order of the British Empire (CBE) in 1948. See James McGuire and James Quinn (eds), *Dictionary of Irish Biography: From the Earliest Times to the Year 2002, Vol. 1 A-Burchill* (Cambridge: Royal Irish Academy, 2009), p. 694.
107 See Niall Carson, 'The Barbaric Note: Seán O'Faoláin's Early Years at the BBC', *Irish University Review*, 43:2 (autumn/winter 2013), pp. 398–413; Leslie Daiken (ed.), *They Go, The Irish: A Miscellany of War Time Writing* (London: Nicholson & Watson, 1944).
108 O'Faoláin, *Vive Moi!* (1993), p. 311.
109 The Bellman, 'Meet Elizabeth Bowen', *The Bell*, 4:6 (September 1952), pp. 426.
110 For an example of such critical appropriation, see Alexandra Harris, *Romantic Moderns: English Writers, Artists and the Imagination from Virginia Woolf to John Piper* (London: Thames & Hudson, 2010).

3

A broken world:
Church and state in *The Bell*

The man of letters who tries to avoid politics is trying to avoid life.[1] (Seán O'Faoláin)

The editorial board of *The Bell* was first published in the issue of April 1941 and consisted of Seán O'Faoláin, Maurice Walsh, Róisín Walsh, Eamon Martin, Peadar O'Donnell and Frank O'Connor as poetry editor. Of these members, all with the exception of Maurice Walsh were active in the IRA or within republican politics. Róisín Walsh was involved with republicanism and feminism throughout her life, and was key in establishing the credibility of the Irish library system in the new state through her role as Dublin city chief librarian between 1931 and her death in 1949. She was a committed political activist and moved in the same circles as Hanna Sheehy Skeffington, Mary Kettle and Maud Gonne McBride.[2] Like O'Donnell, she had travelled far and wide, even spending some time in Soviet Russia and the United States, where she undertook tours of their different circulating libraries. Her involvement with Peadar O'Donnell goes back at least as far as the formation of Saor Éire, when the IRA General Army Convention met in her kitchen in 1931 to underline their commitment to the radical new politics it embodied.[3] It is important to note that Róisín Walsh was not the wife of Maurice Walsh, they just shared the same name; indeed, it is difficult to see what this radical feminist republican would have in common with the author.[4]

Maurice Walsh was at that time one of Ireland's most successful writers and wrote the short story that would eventually be made into John Ford's film *The Quiet Man* (1952); his presence on the editorial board is the exception and was probably intended to give *The Bell* some credibility as a literary rather than political journal.[5]

The Bell carried no notice of Róisín Walsh's untimely death in June 1949 as it had suspended publication for thirty-one months between April 1948 and November 1950.[6] Her contribution to Irish society has been largely forgotten, and her role in *The Bell* almost entirely neglected. However, her presence was of vital importance and her involvement along with Lennox Robinson, Frank

O'Connor and Geoffrey Taylor helps explain the high prevalence of articles about the library system, and its dire need for increased funding.[7] Róisín Walsh was not the only member of the editorial board whose republican background has been shrouded in mystery.

There is an enticing letter from Seán O'Faoláin, marked private, written to Sean O'Casey from 17 Upper Ormond Quay in Dublin in 1917:

> Fergus O'Connor of 44 Eccles St., has sent us your song 'Grand Old Dame Britannia' in ballad form to be retailed at one penny each, but I have not put it on sale. My reason for doing so is, that I was anxious to know from you if you had consented to this, as I did not want the trick of last [August?] repeated. If you have agreed to its publication of course I don't mind in the least, but your name is not even mentioned, though Fergus knew you were the author I was not speaking to him on the matter at all. It was Mrs. W. who had the transaction with him.[8]

This letter is controversial because it places O'Faoláin in Dublin at the tender age of 17, one year after the Easter Rising of 1916, asking O'Casey for use of his anti-recruitment song 'Grand Old Dame Britannia'. What 'us' he is referring to in the opening sentence can only remain the subject of speculation, but it is tantalising to think that he had been involved with the Irish Volunteers (later to become the Irish Republican Army) as a propaganda officer much earlier than he suggested in his autobiography, where he claimed not to have been active until university.[9] At the very least, any account of why a Cork teenager would be in Dublin writing to such a subversive political activist as O'Casey is omitted from his autobiography. O'Faoláin also contradicted his autobiographical account when he wrote a letter of introduction to the BBC in 1932, claiming that:

> I have been through the Irish revolution from 1918 to 1923 when I acted as Director of Publicity for Mr De Valera's Party, then known as the I.R.A., and have since had ample opportunity of keeping in touch with all recent developments.[10]

Such deliberate attempts to obfuscate one's Irish Republican Army (IRA) connections were understandable at a time when civil war grievances were still so bitter. However, they would also come in useful at a later date when both O'Faoláin and Peadar O'Donnell would offer themselves as objective editors in publishing controversial opinions in *The Bell*. O'Faoláin was unlikely to have been director of publicity in 1918 although he was definitely active during that period. Robert Brennan, Operating Commander of the Sínn Féin press bureau between 1918 and 1922 claimed: 'In Cork there was no lack of publicity personnel, amongst my helpers being Daniel Corkery, Frank O'Connor and Sean O'Faolain.'[11] That Daniel Corkery was mentioned first here is significant, and perhaps he was more responsible for O'Faoláin's and O'Connor's military as well as intellectual radicalisation then is now recognised, especially when we

read autobiographical stories such as O'Faoláin's 'The Patriot' over which the
shadow of Corkery looms large. If Corkery was responsible for encouraging
the young Cork writers into taking up arms then this would go some way to
explaining O'Faoláin's and O'Connor's resentment of their old mentor later
in their lives. However, O'Faoláin's own republican commitment was real and
heartfelt, as is only befitting for a man who made bombs, carried a gun, and
whose wife had been shot in the neck by the Black and Tans.[12]

On release from internment in 1924, Peadar O'Donnell became a member
of the IRA army council. However, he soon found republican politics insufficiently radical to meet the needs of the prevailing political climate. Eventually,
he realised that the IRA was doomed to failure unless it promoted a socialist
solution that would politicise the working classes and guarantee their support
for the IRA as an organisation. With this in mind, O'Donnell – along with
George Gilmore, Frank Ryan and others – split from the IRA council to form
the Republican Congress, a broadly based political organisation that could be
described as a loose coalition of anti-right political activists. Its main motivation was the rejection of any physical force republicanism that was unattached
to a socialist agenda.[13] In light of O'Donnell's political sympathies it is easy to
see his commitment to broadcasting his message further afield, and *The Bell*,
in parts, was another medium through which this message could be conveyed.
Certainly, during his internment, O'Donnell was thinking of the formation of
a magazine along the lines of *The Bell* that could contain his radical political
ideals. His fellow republican prisoner and later editor of the books section in
The Bell (May 1947–October 1950), Ernie O'Malley, discussed such a magazine
with him as early as 1923:

> Did you read Peadar [O'Donnell]'s note? He was rather ill yesterday. I would
> be keen on a monthly paper I told him – to deal with articles such as [Patrick]
> Pearse might write, current European and Imperial events as seen through the
> eyes of the 'underdog', literary and art criticism, book reviews, short stories, [a]
> little history, economics, geography – a paper for the man of average intelligence,
> but which would deal primarily and perhaps unconsciously (as we take our med-
> icine best unwittingly or flavoured), with the inclusion of a spiritual doctrine. I
> feel sure that such a paper would sell well and would tend towards our general
> development.[14]

O'Donnell's training in journalistic writing intensified when he took over the
editorial duties of *An Phoblacht* between 1926 and 1929, and it was here that
he received the grounding that would later serve him so well in *The Bell*.[15] Not
that O'Donnell's opponents felt his ideas needed any further dissemination; as
he recalled himself, his reputation as a hard-line communist led to *ad hominem*
attacks whenever he expressed a political opinion, as was the case with James
Hogan.

Professor Hogan of University College Cork, who was also a member of PEN (poets, essayists, novelists) with O'Faoláin, published *Could Ireland Become Communist?* (1935) with the explicit intention of exposing O'Donnell as a subversive communist, and the threat posed by him and his close circle of friends.[16] Hogan based his book on O'Donnell's prison file and had his brother, Colonel Mick Hogan, smuggle O'Donnell's record from Mountjoy jail to provide the basis for his research.[17] Hogan's book is filled with claims that O'Donnell was pushing an anti-Catholic agenda; although he is respectful of O'Donnell as an opponent, he acknowledges his cunning in hiding his explicit communist politics: 'Not all of Mr O'Donnell's colleagues are as much at home in the Machiavellian tactics of Communism as he is.'[18] Interestingly, Hogan's pamphlet was also published by Cahill and Co. which supports O'Faoláin's claim that J.J. O'Leary was less interested in the content of what he was printing and more in the number of copies being sold. O'Donnell's reputation as a communist agitator, however, was not without merit. As Hogan's pamphlet shows, albeit in hysterical terms, O'Donnell was the most active left-wing political agitator at a grassroots level in Ireland throughout the 1930s. By the time of the formation of *The Bell* in 1940, he had become the established voice of socialist/communist politics in Irish society, and the selection of its editorial board reflects this.

For *The Bell*, the old IRA networks offered an efficient source of nourishment, be that for contributors such as Sean Murray or George Gilmore, or for vital commercial help as with Joe McGrath. This connection with the IRA, and in particular its more socialist elements, is often overlooked as a means to understanding *The Bell* as a functioning magazine. The quality of its publications, both political and literary was dependent on its editors' ability to solicit material from the leading intellectuals of Irish life. Many of those within the Irish political or intellectual spheres had been members of the IRA. The internment camps of the Irish Free State had acted as a breeding ground for radical political and artistic expression, and several of *The Bell*'s more celebrated articles, if not *The Bell* itself, had their origins within their confines. O'Donnell's left-wing reputation ensured that writers of the quality of Desmond Ryan contributed. He was editor of his own Labour journal, *The Torch*, which had closed in 1944. Although born in England, Ryan was a pupil of St Enda's School and later served under Pearse during his occupation of the General Post Office in 1916. On his capture, Ryan spent time in Stafford jail, Wormwood Scrubs and Frongoch internment camp. As such, he fits the pattern of the type of republican socialist writer that O'Donnell was supporting in *The Bell*. Their background of internment was used as a school for further improving their writing, and in particular, writing used to promote the socialist cause.

As stated, of the original editorial board all, other than Maurice Walsh, had experience within the IRA: Peadar O'Donnell had commanded an IRA unit and occupied the Four Courts during the Civil War, Seán O'Faoláin ran the IRA propaganda unit, Frank O'Connor saw active service in North Cork, Eamon Martin was a veteran of the 1916 Rising and Róisín Walsh was a committed republican activist. Among *The Bell*'s more celebrated articles lie a number that are directly attributable to its connections within this IRA framework. Brendan Behan's famous *Borstal Boy* (1958) was first published as 'I Became A Borstal Boy' in *The Bell* of June 1942. It is interesting to compare this short extract with the finished version, as some biographical details are present in *The Bell* that are absent from the finished work. For example, his prosecution at St George's Hall in Liverpool, where visitors can still retrace his steps from the cell to the dock, does not appear in the finished version.[19] Indeed, Behan's emergence as a writer was in no small part due to the support he received from O'Faoláin and O'Donnell while he was incarcerated in Mountjoy jail; O'Faoláin even encouraged Behan to seek special dispensation from the warden in order to exchange correspondence.[20]

The Bell also published an account of the death of O'Donnell's old IRA comrade in arms, Frank Ryan. This two-part submission was written by IRA activist, novelist, and husband of Iseult Gonne, Francis Stuart, and contributed greatly to the debate surrounding the IRA's role in undermining Irish neutrality during the war. This biographical reminiscence by Stuart is personal and moving. Its emphasis is on Ryan's great suffering during the last years of his life, when he was trapped in wartime Germany. However, the articles are controversial on account of Ryan's and Stuart's involvement with Hitler's Nazi government. Stuart had been working in German radio, writing propaganda speeches for broadcast, some even for Lord Haw-Haw. He initially travelled to Germany as part of a literary tour but decided to stay after the outbreak of war. Ryan, on the other hand, was a personal friend of O'Donnell's who had ended up in Germany after fighting Franco's fascists in the Spanish Civil War. He was captured by Italian fascists and imprisoned, under threat of execution, in Spain for two years. After an international campaign to secure his release, he was handed over to the German authorities who transported him to Berlin and reintroduced him to Seán Russell, who was also present in Germany on IRA business. Russell had been IRA chief of staff, and had chaired the meeting where Frank Ryan, Peadar O'Donnell and George Gilmore were court-martialled for leaving the IRA army council to form the Republican Congress in 1934.[21] Ryan and Russell were then taken by U-boat to Ireland; however, two days out Russell was taken ill and died from a ruptured ulcer, and he was buried at sea. Unusually, Ryan seems to have held no grudge against Russell, even after two years in a Spanish prison. The U-boat returned to Germany and Ryan remained there as a guest of the Nazi government until his death in 1944.[22] This article was controversial at the time of its publication as, in the post-war climate of Ireland, IRA support for Germany remained politically sensitive.

Exactly how three former republicans remained as guests of the Nazi government was also questioned. Stuart's article was an early attempt to distance Ryan from any Nazi associations. However, in doing so he also attempted to vindicate himself. The importance of Stuart's account cannot be ignored as it is a naked attempt to deny any Nazi links with an important IRA figure; it is a very moving piece of writing that focuses on Ryan's ill health and his personal bravery and kindness. For Stuart, Ryan represented nothing more than a man determined to get home. Ryan had 'a deep love of country in the old romantic sense [and] an equally deep faith in the possibility of a reign of social justice and equity'.[23] All through this discourse Stuart maintained the distance of the detached observer and was keen to stress the random hazards of war that threw them together as exiled Irishmen in Nazi Germany. Current scholarship tends to see the association of these three republicans as an act of chance, but when this article was released, only five years after the end of the war, opinions remained much more partisan and the facts were not fully established.[24] O'Donnell, who knew Ryan closely enough to give his graveside oration when he was reinterred at Glasnevin cemetery after the war, was keen to establish his socialist credentials, and his anti-fascist idealism. He wrote to the *Irish Times* fourteen years after Ryan's death to praise his lost friend:

> To understand Frank's going to Spain – he had no control over his transfer to Germany from a Spanish prison, nor over his return by submarine – it would be necessary for young people to learn of the Blue Shirt rising and the Republican resistance to it ... The picture of Ryan under interrogation on suspicion of having caused the death of Russell – the interrogator himself tells us of it – is but further light of Frank Ryan's difficult days in Germany. He was a giant of a man to have been true to himself through it all.[25]

Stuart, it would seem, was acting from a desire to humanise his position and to distract attention from his own active wartime role, if not also to eulogise his lost friend.

Michael Farrell, who wrote the long-running 'Country Theatre' series and assumed the pen name 'Gulliver' for his 'Open Window' column also had an IRA background. Although his role was minor, he still served a year in Mountjoy where he was excused from participating in a hunger strike on grounds of ill health.[26] 'The Open Window' is characterised by Farrell's flashing wit and erudite scholarship; it was a section which remained deeply popular with readers. Farrell's novel *Thy Tears Might Cease* (1963), published posthumously, draws on his experiences of growing up during the time of the troubles, and is only now beginning to receive the critical attention which it deserves.[27] *The Bell* accelerated its IRA connections under the editorship of O'Donnell; in addition to seeing the first publications of old IRA men such as Sean Murray and George Gilmore, O'Donnell also found time to promote new writers with an IRA past. Shea Murphy was a young writer, born during the 1916 Rising in Liverpool. He worked as a lorry driver before crossing to Ireland at the outset of war in 1939. He was arrested a year later for IRA activities and sentenced to seven years' penal servitude, spending time in Mountjoy, Arbour Hill, and the Curragh internment camp before his early release in 1945.[28] Murphy published five short stories under O'Donnell's editorship between March 1947 and February 1951, which deal with his experiences of prison. They also discuss his Liverpool childhood, growing up in what was a divided sectarian city at that time. His final submission to *The Bell* seems guided by O'Donnell; titled 'The Labour Exchange' it gives an account of the plight of the working man as he queues at the labour office to go to work cutting peat on a labour camp, the conditions of which were one of O'Donnell's personal bugbears.[29] Murphy's ideology is evidently that of the socialist republican with a keen eye for the suffering of humanity. His stories remain vibrant today, although he plays only a small cameo in *The Bell*.

Running side by side with his project for the promotion of young IRA writers, O'Donnell also drew on some literary heavyweights from his republican past. Liam O'Flaherty, who had himself been in the IRA and was a committed communist, was called on to produce short stories for *The Bell*. O'Flaherty had not published a substantial collection of short stories since 1937 and O'Donnell must be credited with getting him back to writing within the format. O'Donnell's no nonsense approach to organisation came to the fore here, where he ordered, good-naturedly, literary greats as he once ordered raw IRA recruits:

> Dear Sean O'Casey, Lookat. I am going to plague the life out of yourself and O'Flaherty and a few others, to pull you close in round *The Bell*. If we want to put any life into the publication, we must get into a huddle round it, all of those who have something to say and a blasphemous power of saying it. I am putting you under a geasa to let me have an occasional article every time something in the Irish scene makes you feel like boiling over.[30]

O'Flaherty submitted nine short stories in all, including 'Two Lovely Beasts', a powerful tale of class violence, set in the harsh communities along Ireland's western seaboard. O'Flaherty's contributions are all the more remarkable because his last substantial work had been *Land* (1946) and his writing in *The Bell* would eventually lead to the publication of *Two Lovely Beasts and Other Stories* in 1948. Interestingly, when O'Flaherty did return to publishing it was with Victor Gollancz, a leading left-wing publisher of the day, and not with Jonathan Cape where he had had a strong personal relationship with Edward Garnett.

O'Flaherty's stories betray the sympathies of their author and reflect O'Donnell's own political bias in that they dwell on the privations and difficulties of the Irish rural poor. In this sense they can be didactic, yet they are written beautifully and with the confidence of an artist who knows his subject intimately. O'Flaherty's absence during the O'Faoláin years is unusual in itself, especially considering O'Faoláin thought enough of him to call him his 'friend' and to write an article praising his works as early as 1937.[31] Perhaps O'Faoláin's politics as outlined in *The Bell* were insufficiently committed for a man who once occupied and flew the red flag from the Rotunda in Dublin. In any case, O'Flaherty initially found O'Faoláin to be shallow and his writing derivative, having also been introduced to his work through Edward Garnett: 'I am writing after reading your introduction to S. O'Faoláin's book. I think your fore-ward [*sic*] is great, but that O'Faoláin has little in him except a great deal of imitative cunning. Your introduction is so much stronger than he is, and your own work in *The Wind Knows the Earth*, or have I got the title wrong? Is worth ten millions of it.'[32] Although O'Flaherty revolutionary zeal had peaked by the time *The Bell* had begun, his ideological and social compatibility with O'Donnell must have left him feeling he had more in common with the rural Donegal man than with O'Faoláin, who was more effete and elitist. O'Flaherty also felt more respect for O'Donnell as an artist, telling Edward Garnett, twenty years earlier: 'I am glad you are publishing O'Donnell's book. He is the coming man in this country.'[33]

But *The Bell* was much more than a simple organ for political organisation. The breadth of its topics and its range of voices would ensure that it would transcend any easy definition. For example, *The Bell* was the first to publish Stephen Hayes's account of his involvement and eventual kidnapping by the IRA. Hayes was acting chief officer of the IRA in southern Ireland during Seán Russell's absence in 1941. However, suffering under external pressure from the governments of both Northern Ireland and Éire, the organisation was almost a spent force. The northern IRA leadership decided that its failures had resulted because a spy had leaked information to the Fianna Fáil government, and the man they suspected was Hayes. As such, they issued an order for his arrest and trial. Under torture Hayes agreed to write his confession, but lax security allowed him to escape and turn himself in at a local Garda station.[34] The controversy surrounding Hayes's arrest and imprisonment continues to this day, and although he always maintained his innocence, the issue remains unresolved.[35]

Hayes's attempt to rehabilitate himself in the public eye and deny the charges of spying on the IRA for the Fianna Fáil government were first aired in *The Bell*: 'it never crossed my mind that my authority within the I.R.A. was being undermined, however much the I.R.A. might have lost control of the general political development. I had no whisper that a conspiracy was afoot: no whisper that in the feverish situation perfectly innocent happenings were being twisted by suspicion into a trap for honest men.'[36] This article was an unusual one for O'Donnell to publish, considering Hayes was a member of the physical-force men who sided against O'Donnell in his split from the IRA hierarchy in 1934. However, it was still a sensational story to be printed in 1951, after Hayes had served five years for his membership of the IRA in 1942. O'Donnell was much more magnanimous than O'Faoláin with those whom he disagreed with, and this is reflected in his editorial style, printing articles without comment from contentious political sources. O'Donnell's reputation as a man of principle allowed him to exploit these conflicting sources within the IRA for the benefit of *The Bell*. This morass of contradictory voices in *The Bell* was exactly the sort of cultural expression that O'Faoláin had hoped to promote. What was developing, for O'Faoláin, was an expression of the racial identity of the Irish in their artistic productions, an identity that was embodied in the magazine itself.

O'Faoláin's travels around Ireland in the years after the Civil War as a salesman for the Talbot Press showed him that different cultures imprinted individuals with distinctive identities. Despite an awareness of the constructed nature of national identity O'Faoláin still maintained a strong belief in the natural characteristics of different racial types. He firmly believed that racial identity was the result of an inherent disposition towards certain proclivities that were nurtured by external social forces. This belief is readily recognisable in his historical writings such as *The Irish* (1947) or *The Great O'Neill* (1942), where he identified the development of the Irish as a race, or where he traced the embodiment of a racial strain through Hugh O'Neill the Earl of Tyrone. In a 1948 letter to his friend John V. Kelleher, he was to remark:

I gather you are an anti-racialist also, and you ought to be ashamed of yourself if you are. the argument is simple: there are genetic differences, e.g. negroes, jews, chinks. More than that there are what Kalmus (Czech writer on, now in London) calls 'strains', e.g. Celtic strain. The genes partially produce the distinctions, and nurture (the two thongs are nature and nurture: environment etc.) develops others. I have before me a paper from Heredity, vol 1 part 3. Pages 269–286 dec 1947) on 'The Genetic Component of Language' by C D Darlington which sets out to show that the reason Cork and Kerrymen say dis and dat is blood gene distribution. The essential historical point is that when the 'celtic strain' got the seeds of civilisation (western european type) – they were, in my phrase, at the end of the queue; hence their abortive civilisation; but they were already natured and nurtured; they were distinct. There is no denying a racial character. The test is to ask 'Why didnt they turn the queue around?' Why didnt they do what the Greeks Syrians etc did, create and originate? Michael [Frank O'Connor] says impossible; the stream came from the west, science, maths, architecture. True. The bloody Chinese didnt get it from 'the west'. There ARE racial qualities; or call it qualities of 'strains', if you like.[37]

This belief in identifiable racial characteristics informed all of O'Faoláin's writings, from topics as diverse as the political to the aesthetic. O'Faoláin was not alone among the international literary elite in holding these views, although he was not tempted into eugenics, unlike some other notable Irish writers such as George Bernard Shaw or W.B. Yeats. Although his belief in inherent racial characteristics might seem at odds with his stated preference for a new Irish identity, it was to influence his editorial selections in *The Bell* as he sought to develop distinctive voices that would be representative of their racial origins. Because of his 'lethally mechanical, pedantic and dogmatic' Harvard training, he was too drawn to simple analogies: thesis, antithesis and synthesis.[38] Yet he was also capable of complex and oscillating opinions and of a duality of nature that would lead him to produce a variety of contradictory positions within his own work. He could express two conflicting opinions within his writing and expected such a tension as a normal part of the human condition; writing to his friend George Weller (Pulitzer winning journalist for the *New York Times*) in the winter of 1977 he was to claim, 'There MUST in the sacred name of sanity be at least two different sides to each of us. That is fair play. Accepted. Normal. Healthy. The way of the world.'[39] This literary schizophrenia is evident throughout all of O'Faoláin's writings and reflects better his desire to attack whatever target was currently in his sights, rather than his claims to a unified and complete aesthetic system. However, it was also to have a benefit in his editorship of *The Bell* in that he expected to view arguments from opposing sides. In the case of writings on Northern Ireland this would allow for a considerable contribution from Unionist voices.

The third special Ulster issue of *The Bell* contained the anonymous leader 'Conversation Piece' by a writer signing off as an Ulster Protestant.[40] The article was in the form of an interview, and its author was the poet W.R. Rodgers.[41] He was a Presbyterian minister from Belfast, whose first collection of poetry, *Awake! And Other Poems* was launched in the same year as *The Bell*. He never fulfilled his early potential despite being considered of the same quality as Louis MacNeice, with whom he was friends.[42] Rodgers published eight poems in *The Bell* throughout the course of its run and also was known personally to O'Faoláin and Frank O'Connor.[43] 'Conversation Piece' contained a note from O'Faoláin introducing it as 'one of the first attempts that has been made to put the case for Ulster from the intelligent, humanist point of view. We invite replies.' This open invitation indicated that O'Faoláin anticipated a reaction to *The Bell* carrying a leader written by a Protestant from Northern Ireland. It also offered an insightful look at O'Faoláin's own reading of the article, in that he believed it to encapsulate an 'intelligent' and 'humanist' position.

The piece is printed in a question and answer format and is relaxed and informal in tone. It nevertheless fails to accurately identify the sources of tension between Catholics and Protestants in Northern Ireland and reproduces familiar tropes in its analysis. In a time-worn fashion and adhering to a formula already established in *The Bell*, Rodgers locates the reasons for the conflict between Protestant and Catholic factions in an underdeveloped Irish historical tradition: 'but what you really mean is that in England and in America there is a stage of civilisation, the industrial stage, where the old religious patterns have broken down'. Rodgers shares with O'Faoláin a belief in inherent racial characteristics, and that a conception of racial distinction is vital to any understanding of the problems of Northern Ireland: 'The racial difference is, I think, fundamental to an understanding of Ulster.' He continued to develop his argument with this logic so that the opposition between Catholic and Protestant is not only presented as a matter of linguistic expression over rational analysis, but also a distinction between opposing internal and external world-views:

> The Protestant has a self-consciousness which the Catholic has not. The Protestant has an *inner* opposition, his conflict is, first and last, a private one: it forces self-awareness on him. The Catholic's oppositions and operations are *outside* of himself; his devils are public enemies, and his motions and emotions are excursive ones.

Rodgers's distinctions hid what could be seen as simple sectarian stereotyping, and his reasoned arguments acted as a shield to obfuscate his assumptions. He believed that the 'Orange Order *is* the expression of the feeling of Ulster', and although he is keen to distance himself from what he knows to be a sectarian emotion, he also feels it deeply enough to cross the boundaries of reasoned analysis: 'and you will notice how this racial memory – or prejudice, if you like – persists even in educated and intelligent Ulster people (who laugh at Orangeism), how it shines through all the rationalisations with which they clothe it'.[44] This prejudice was at the root of Rodgers's own feeling concerning Northern Ireland's racial tensions.

   In part, Rodgers's early regionalist style – he was writing in the mode before his younger compatriot John Hewitt defined the term – such as in the poem 'Ireland', can be seen as an attempt to validate Protestant insecurities about land rights in Northern Ireland by aestheticising their identity and realigning it with the landscape of Ulster itself.[45] Rodgers's argument tails off into metaphor and a more universal conception of identity. Although his work is complex and often resistant to simplistic interpretations, the difficulties that he faced as an Ulster poet are crystallised here. What is surprising is that O'Faoláin should have seen this argument as the 'intelligent, humanist point of view' without addressing its underlying assumptions. It is easy to see the allure of Rodgers's argument to O'Faoláin in that it offers a simplistic economic/racial account of Northern Irish tensions while allowing for a distinctive Ulster aesthetic. However, in light of his other writings on Northern Ireland, and his own perceptive criticism of identity politics in Éire, O'Faoláin's support of this article is confusing, unless it is considered as part of his attempt to provoke reaction from nationalist sympathisers within Éire. But even if one accepts that this was his intention, it still remains unclear why he would single out this article for special praise as balanced and rational, particularly when one considers that he had a low personal opinion of Rodgers.

In a 1949 letter to John Kelleher, O'Faoláin complained of W.R. Rodgers's inclination for drunken self-righteousness: '[s]o out came W.R. stochious, and said M's [Frank O'Connor] ma was fine when he left her and I still wondering was W.R. fobbed off on me after M. had endured his norrrth of Irrreland drunken sententiousness beyond screaming – point, and I must say I don't blame M if he did.'[46] Again with this submission O'Faoláin was to demonstrate his ability to court controversy and to put his personal feelings behind him when he came to selecting articles for *The Bell*, or when he strove to provoke a reaction from his readership. However, it also points to his desire to appear as thoughtful, intellectual and liberal, especially through the publication and support of articles he would have personally disagreed with. This technique was used to great effect in his writings on politics and political issues in Éire as well.

In 1937 the Irish people approved a new constitution which Eamon de Valera saw as a necessary step in restoring Irish sovereignty. However, the new-found state of Éire's policy towards the legal status of Northern Ireland, and its role in any potential future European war were yet to be resolved. As Diarmaid Ferriter has argued, there was a contradiction at the heart of this document that ensured 'the forthright claim ... of the legitimacy of the state's right to rule all of Ireland was immediately qualified by the reassurance that there would be no attempt to implement the claim'.[47] This new constitution empowered de Valera to the 'brilliant success of 1938' in his negotiation of the Anglo-Irish Trade Agreement, which ended the economic war and ensured the return of the treaty ports to Irish control.[48] It was in this period of radical change and future uncertainty that *The Bell* was formed.

In many ways, the existence of *The Bell* owed its vitality to the ambiguity of these difficult times leading up to, and including, the Second World War, as it acted as a running social commentary to the period. For a man who insisted on the artist's right to produce material outside of political influence, O'Faoláin was heavily involved personally in political action, and he published several biographies of political figures. His interest in writing political biographies stems from his time working with the Manchester-based newspaper, the *Sunday Chronicle*, where he produced a number of serialised sensationalist biographies on prominent Irish political figures. O'Faoláin's first work for the *Sunday Chronicle* was his 'de Valera's Life Story' published in 1932; he followed this with other serialised biographies of Michael Collins and Constance Markievicz.[49] It was this work that would form the basis for his two biographies, *The Life Story of Eamon de Valera* (1933) and *Constance Markievicz*

(1934), and point to O'Faoláin's ability to exploit his journalistic writing to its maximum potential, with a keen eye for opportunities in the markets of both England and Ireland.[50] Although money was perhaps the key motivating factor in many of O'Faoláin's biographies, they are worthy of further inspection for insight into the political pressures of the day.

O'Faoláin first developed the idea for a biography of Constance Markievicz in August of 1932; however, he initially wished for a collective effort, utilising some of the top writers of the day to offer their reminiscences of the countess. With this in mind he wrote to Sean O'Casey asking him to contribute: 'The present idea is that I am "editing" a series of articles on Countess Markievicz. I had originally undertaken to do a life myself but thought this a better scheme. The contributors would be (in my plan) yourself, Maeve or Stanislaus Markievicz, Miss Sheehy-Skeffington, Captain J.R. White and Derek Verschoyle of the Spectator – and myself. The paper is the Sunday Chronicle. The fee is £10 for 2000 odd words.' O'Faoláin continued to promote his request and even went as far as to suggest topics that O'Casey might write: 'I don't know if you've written before for the Sunday press but its very easy – done in a few hours. I hope you will commit? The second proposition is that you should do a series of say, 18,000 words, on some such subject as The Ireland I know – or Ireland as I knew it: a series of articles again consisting of memories, and pen-pictures of your Dublin.' O'Faoláin completed his hard sell to O'Casey by appealing to the financial rewards of the work: 'If I may say so it is an easy way to get a book done and to get paid twice for it; which is a commendation', before finishing with a declaration of his intentions to return home to Ireland: 'I am here now 3 years and am thoroughly fed up with London suburbia. I sigh for fields of buttercups. Often I plan madly for life in Ireland – but just now the bloody gunmen are out for my blood: And what a country it is anyway!'[51] This letter is instructive for several reasons, as it contextualises O'Faoláin's mindset before he returned to Ireland to write in a full-time capacity.

First, it demonstrates the matter-of-fact attitude O'Faoláin displayed to writing, and his willingness to put the pragmatics of fees as the condition on which any work would be undertaken. Second, it shows the dismissive attitude in which O'Faoláin held his own journalism, seeing it as worthy, but inferior, to his proper career as an artist. This insight goes some way to explaining why O'Faoláin would later be so dismissive of his achievements in *The Bell* and why he attempted to downplay their importance in relation to the rest of his corpus of writing. It also shows O'Faoláin's growing confidence in his ability as a writer, if he was willing to instruct an author of the reputation of O'Casey and make suggestions for article titles similar to those found in *The Bell* eight years later. This willingness to write sensationalist histories, and his enthusiasm for encouraging other writers to do the same, might indicate a possible source for Frank O'Connor's biography of Michael Collins, *The Big Fellow* (1937).

Perhaps most tantalising of all is O'Faoláin's suggestion that he was afraid to return home because of violent reprisals by the IRA. Such a flourish might be an example of the young O'Faoláin dramatising his republican past in front of the more established artist. However, it might also point to a genuine fear of republican reprisals. At this stage O'Faoláin was describing himself as the former Director of Propaganda to the IRA in advertisements for his series. It would not have been considered acceptable in Ireland to be cashing in on your IRA past by pandering to English newspapers. He was concerned enough about them to warn his editor at *Ireland To-Day*, Jim O'Donovan, of their danger as late as 1936: 'Don't you see the fellows who shot Somerville and Egan [the IRA] are the mush who are reducing Irish life to imbecility? You know these chaps. I know them. We worked and fought with them. They'd plug you or me in two seconds in a moment of hysteria.'[52]

It is difficult to know just how seriously to take O'Faoláin's concerns but worth noting that the Ireland he planned to return to was in a state of flux, and its political future remained uncertain. In light of this letter, O'Faoláin's decision to return home looked more like simple homesickness than the more romanticised explanation he gave in his autobiography, where he claimed he returned at Edward Garnett's suggestion to 'go home and write about the sort of things he really did know'.[53] There are also grounds to dismiss O'Faoláin's first biography of de Valera as unrepresentative of his true opinion of the leader, being an overly reductive picture of the man for a mind as congenitally bent to elaboration as O'Faoláin's. Yet even this laudatory biography was insufficient to impress one reviewer writing for de Valera's own *Irish Press*: 'Mr. O'Faoláin simply had not the materials for a biography nor does he pretend he has written one.'[54] For a more insightful view of his opinion of de Valera we must turn to his second biography, *De Valera* (1939), published specifically for Penguin's new series on political events and released in the same year as the outbreak of war. This biography was much more critical of de Valera and encapsulated some of the frustrations O'Faoláin felt with Irish society, which would lead to the formation of *The Bell*.

The publication of *De Valera* captures exactly the mood of the author living in an Ireland that was in danger of being dragged into a war over which it had no control. O'Faoláin's analysis of de Valera in this later biography is much more critical, although it still strives to achieve a reasonable balance. As with all of O'Faoláin's biographies, what is more important than the mere representation of historical fact is an analysis of what the subject represents to the historical movement of his people, that is to say what the subject represents as a symbol or a character. For O'Faoláin, de Valera was an unsatisfactory subject who was too detached and emotionally cold to offer worthwhile insight into his thinking. He was, for O'Faoláin, too embedded in the past to present a symbol readily available to the present; his main political drive was to sustain his policies by appealing to an idealised life, a life no longer possible within modern Ireland. The conditions of de Valera's Ireland were such that his model of a Gaelicised, nationalist, Catholic people was undermined by the realities of its citizens' lives. Such regressive idealisation, according to O'Faoláin, had practical implications for the present and the future. For a republican such as O'Faoláin, de Valera's policies were counterproductive and unworkable. For example, it was de Valera who was doing the most to reinforce partition by making no ideological or pragmatic concessions to the Protestant population of Northern Ireland: 'his difficulty is that the more he behaves as a Nationalist, Gaelic-revivalist, anti-British, the more does he estrange the north. It is not the north alone which is keeping itself distinct. The south is maintaining partition even more effectively by refusing to demonstrate a practical spirit of tolerance and broad-mindedness.'[55] De Valera's inaction on partition remained one of the most consistent criticisms which O'Faoláin levelled at him, claiming that his refusal to foster unity with the people of Northern Ireland was denying reconciliation between the two communities.

In this hope of reconciliation, O'Faoláin was in agreement with many other republicans. Although he had personal experience of Northern Ireland, he failed to acknowledge fully the extent to which northern Protestants felt alienated and threatened by the predominantly Catholic south. After the outbreak of war, the Prime Minister of Northern Ireland, Lord Craigavon, travelled to London to plead with the British government to introduce blanket conscription in the province as a means of ensuring unity through sacrifice.[56] In light of such commitment to separation, a policy of appeasement and conciliation seems doomed to failure, or at least misguided. However, O'Faoláin was also alert to the potential benefits that de Valera's policy entailed, and in concluding his biography decided that the jury remained out on de Valera as a political leader. Although he felt incapable of warming to him as a man, he thought that time would be the wisest judge of his abilities: 'as for his fame, that may be left to time, the only critic who does not lie. Meanwhile somebody like myself, a biographer or a novelist interested in the solid variety and warm colour of human nature, wrestles with him uneasily terrified lest at any moment he should vanish – as an abstraction.'[57]

By the time of *The Bell*'s inception in 1940, O'Faoláin's position had hardened and he was no longer concerned with capturing the nature of de Valera, rather the consistent reality of his political presence. This is the essential question of *The Bell* as a form of political opposition; the main constant throughout its fourteen-year lifespan was the presence of de Valera and his government. If *The Bell* opened a space for alternative political voices, that space was conceived against a political landscape dominated by de Valera. Peadar O'Donnell's political resistance to individual governments was much more complete than O'Faoláin's, considering he wished to overthrow the state entirely. But even

his radicalism had been tempered and focused by the political policy pio-
neered by O'Faoláin in the formative years of *The Bell*. Towards the end of
the war, another biography of Eamon de Valera appeared, this time written by
bibliophile and *Irish Press* journalist M.J. MacManus. His *Eamon De Valera:
A Biography* (1944) made no attempt to hide its admiration for its subject.
In fact, MacManus considered the biographer's task as being distinct from
that of a historian, in that objectivity was an unnecessary encumbrance: 'in a
biography written from the standpoint of an admirer, there is no possibility
of doing adequate justice to those who were de Valera's opponents'.[58] That
MacManus's text was considered hagiographical is unsurprising considering
that he finished his analysis of de Valera with a direct comparison to Abraham
Lincoln. Such uncritical reflection on de Valera's achievements caught the eye
of O'Faoláin, who used the opportunity to reassess his view of de Valera and
attack MacManus in the process.

O'Faoláin opened his analysis by suggesting that republicanism as espoused
by de Valera during the Civil War was a rejection of democratic consensus. On
reflection, in following de Valera, the anti-treatyites only succeeded in chasing
defeat: 'All of us Republicans who followed his lead in 1922 refused to accept
majority rule ... and we got licked.' For O'Faoláin, it was this capacity for the
triumph of idealism over pragmatism that characterised de Valera's personality
and politics, and while it was a powerful motivating factor in opposition, it
remained totally unsuitable to the practicalities of running the country: 'he has,
since his great days when he used to be a revolutionist, done very few wrong
things, though chiefly because since then he has done very few practical things
of any kind whatsoever'. Such an account of de Valera's achievements was a
marked change from O'Faoláin's open verdict, as espoused in his 1939 biography. After evaluating MacManus's analysis he now clearly saw de Valera as
deficient. By 1945, after six years of wartime isolation, and restricted financial
and cultural conditions, O'Faoláin felt that de Valera had not done enough, that
frustratingly simple solutions were available to him and yet he chose inaction
over dynamism. If de Valera's Ireland was the blank canvas on which *The Bell*
was drawn, five years of focusing on its problems and of struggling to build up
new cultural standards had left O'Faoláin embittered to the task. In summing
up de Valera's failures, O'Faoláin touched on the problems he had endlessly
enumerated over the previous five years in *The Bell*. Such was the focus on the
Fianna Fáil government and its leader that the entire project of the magazine
was a sustained political criticism of Ireland as it existed during the 1940s.
Ultimately, his final evaluation of de Valera is more insightful into the political
nature of *The Bell* itself than as a useful barometer of public feeling:

And so, we are constantly aware that thousands of our people have to be sent
abroad to work, that thousands of them are probably lost to us forever, that our

slum problem is hardly being touched, and if the poor were not kept alive by
doles of every kind many of them would simply starve to death, that it is only in
the thirteenth year of office that the present Government introduces legislation to
deal with tuberculosis, that our educational system is antediluvian, that we are in
many respects a despotism disguised as a democracy, that the dismemberment of
our country has been allowed to become a frozen problem, that our relations with
Great Britain are as ambiguously unsatisfactory as ever they were.[59]

This comprehensive list of de Valera's failings formed the core of *The Bell*'s
social policy and, supported by the theoretical underpinnings of the Mass
Observation movement, accounts for the particular realist flavour of articles
with which it became synonymous. Although ostensibly a literary journal, with
its republican heritage and overt criticism of state policy, *The Bell* was a magazine of strong political commitment.

In the November 1943 issue O'Faoláin re-launched his editorial under the
new title, 'One World'. Immediately he looked to situate Irish political identity
within a wider international context, opening with the lines:

> If there are any charges which we resent more sharply than others to-day they are
> the charges of being ignorant or indifferent about the war: especially the latter.
> For ignorance is at worst a fault, whereas indifference in the face of such wide-
> spread and terrible suffering would be the basest crime.

Such a direct address of what was as sensitive a political issue as the war was
risky in the face of the paranoid excesses of the Irish censorship board, especially in light of the government's fear of supposed media bias towards either
side.[60] However, it was also typical of O'Faoláin in that he attempted to address
explicitly a topic that was of huge significance to the whole of Ireland. O'Faoláin
strove to push his own concept of liberal republicanism, as inspired by the
French model, and his 'One World' series was an attempt to criticise domestic
policies and practices by drawing comparison with other countries. All in all,
the 'One World' series ran for fifteen articles over two years before culminating
in March 1946 with a detailed analysis of France's post-war political parties and
the sections of society from which they drew their support. His opening editorial looked to a perceived bias in the wartime media of United States and Great
Britain against Irish neutrality that sought to morally undermine the Irish right
to non-belligerence, stating of these accusations: 'The dishonesty of that [the
accusations] becomes apparent when we realise that these charges are not made
against other neutral countries, whose decision to stand apart from the conflict
is never twisted into the conclusion that they must be morally callous to it.'

O'Faoláin finished this editorial by making ameliorative suggestions with
regard to the Irish press, recommending that they should initiate a formalised
system of communication between political leaders and the fourth estate: 'that
weekly meeting between the President and the Press, in which questions are fired

at him from right and left, is a symbol of the rights of a democratic people which would be much appreciated here'.[61] This pattern of comparison and didactic suggestion was to dominate the format of 'One World' articles in *The Bell*.

O'Faoláin's next target for analysis was Yugoslavia, which was then undergoing a process of armed resistance to Nazi occupation. For O'Faoláin, Yugoslavia made an interesting point of reference for what was happening politically in Ireland. In a global environment where world powers were fighting for their lives, the fate of small nations was often pushed aside, leaving their destinies in the hands of external sources, forcing their governments into a position of political impotence: 'the small nations which again suffer all the agonies of war, of civil strife, of military occupation, can only look in dismay and bewilderment to their future as to their past'. For O'Faoláin, this state of helplessness in the face of external events greater than the fate of any nation left Ireland in an invidious position, unable to assert its independence without compromising political goodwill in a post-war Europe. O'Faoláin then anticipated the arrival of a political hierarchy in Europe that would form the model for later developments with the European Union, and asked what role Ireland would play in such a society. His speculation as to post-war Europe's political future was relevant to an Ireland questioning its place in a continent rocked by financial crises:

> All that one can see emerging is this suggestive idea of great blocs of federated states
> co-operating autonomously under some supra-national administrator, and some
> men dream of a day when these blocs will further federate into a vast European
> Federation. If that is to be the shape of the Europe of the future we need to think
> hard and long on Ireland's position in it: for whatever the solution of the problem
> of reconciling freedom with security it is obvious that isolationism is the groggiest
> of all 'solutions' in a world of air warfare, swift communications, and the *Diabolus
> ex Machina*. In addition there is that insistent magnet which, even as powerfully as
> physical security, drags all countries, from the great to the small, into participation
> in world-affairs, i.e., the economic pull. In this dilemma our Little Islanders offer
> us nothing but the exhaustion of their self-protective cynicism.

O'Faoláin's ideas here require further unpacking as he directly addressed the Irish public and asked what part it wished to play in the emergence of a new world order. His own preference is clear in that he saw that an Ireland isolated and apart from Europe was at a competitive disadvantage, unable to add its voice to any debates about the future of the nations around it. O'Faoláin was acutely aware that Ireland was in itself powerless to effect much politically on a world stage. However, as part of a collective in solidarity with other small nations it could enhance their reputation, articulating their right to sovereignty, and by extension its own.

O'Faoláin believed that the culture of political isolationism was adversely affecting Ireland economically. He wished to see Ireland abandon its policies of economic self-sufficiency, which he associated with cultural immaturity, and move to a more free market model that embraced the challenges of interaction at a political and economic level. O'Faoláin discussed the particular case of Danish farmers and their policy of borrowing heavily in order to reinvest directly into their own farms. Although such a significant overhead on a business might seem counterproductive, they more than made up for such a burden by modern farming methods and better productivity. Such progressive use of capital and the high gearing of mortgages on farms contrasted favourably with the situation in Ireland, whereby Irish farmers still viewed credit suspiciously as a form of usury, and were unable to maximise their potential:

> The fact that the Danish farmer is in debt, mainly in his own country, does not mean that he is in a poor way. On the contrary, he may be favourably contrasted with our farmers, with their slim incomes, long faces, and their idle money in the banks growing less valuable … Certainly it is a queer 'sovereign independence' that is not independent enough to use its own sovereigns.[62]

Such an account of the financial flexibility of Danish farmers gives an insight into the breadth of O'Faoláin's interests; it also highlights his impatience with the financial conservatism that he felt was prevalent in Irish society at that time and his willingness to push for market reforms in the context of the Irish economy. This article shows O'Faoláin as a free-market liberal, and even an early herald of globalisation. His interest in the seemingly obtuse example of Danish farmers' fiscal policy was probably inspired by his friend Francis Hackett's book, *I Chose Denmark* (1940).[63] Hackett was married to the Danish-born writer and editor Signe Toksvig; along with O'Faoláin he was prominent in his criticism of Irish literary censorship. Both Hackett and his wife had books banned in Ireland, and his article attacking state-censorship, 'A Muzzle Made in Ireland' (1936) remains a classic of its kind.[64] Another possible source for O'Faoláin, for the example of Denmark's farming industry, was AE's *The Irish Statesman* (1923–30) which, having its base in the Irish cooperative movement, often cited Denmark as an example to follow.

O'Faoláin, who had himself fought during the War of Independence and during the Civil War, was aware of the burning passions of nationalism. Although he had personally become deeply suspicious of unreflective nationalism, he was willing to acknowledge the strength of its ideals and even approved of its benefits when applied with sympathy and humility. As such, his own political outlook was one of liberal republicanism, drawn to the appeal of individual rights enshrined in the legislation of the state. He was at pains to emphasise the inclusive nature of republicanism, one that protected the rights of all minorities within the society that upheld it. Even though O'Faoláin's main concerns were aesthetic, he could not see how anyone could avoid participation in the political economy of wartime Europe. Such a position was an unforgivable naivety, and although the artist's role in such trying times was to remain committed to his art, he should be aware of external events or be in danger of being swept aside by them:

> We have but one reason for drawing attention to these ideas here. This is, the-
> oretically, a literary magazine; but for a long time – ever since Flaubert, and
> Balzac, and even so far back as Dryden – men of letters everywhere have realised
> that literature and politics are not two separated things. The man of letters who
> tries to avoid politics is trying to avoid life. We know that Ireland must be aware
> of world-trends, or, as in the past, she may be absorbed with local affairs, as in a
> sort of tribalistic preoccupation, that the world may come suddenly down on her
> like a whirlwind.

O'Faoláin was hopeful that a politically informed Ireland would be able to maximise its own interests in post-war Europe by showing solidarity with other small nations, and by expressing their own national agendas within an international forum. He believed that Ireland could not participate in any 'sort of plan which does not guarantee the essentials of absolute equality, and national distinctiveness'. O'Faoláin was concerned that during the rush to divide Europe into a coherent and stable political system after the war, the great powers would take insufficient heed of the voices of national identity.

This ignorance of individual nation's concerns would be inevitable on some level in Europe, but a systematic failure to address it correctly would leave a bitter legacy in the form of conflict and strife. This residual conflict was an experience of which O'Faoláin was only too aware, after his own demoralising participation in civil war in Ireland. However, he retained an optimism regarding the ability of small nations to offer a valuable contribution to any social reconstruction after the war, and was quick to warn against defeatism:

> To some, of course, all this may be no more than pious hopes and wishful think-
> ing. One may, to be sure, dismiss it all as theory and dream. One may pretend to
> be very 'realistic' and say that the Big Powers will, in the end, have their own way.
> That is folly and despair. It is anarchy and selfishness. And it is as far beneath the
> dignity of nationhood as remote from a sense of human responsibility.[65]

Such despair, for O'Faoláin, was beneath Ireland's true national stature, and he personally sensed it in the policies of de Valera's wartime government.

However, to O'Faoláin's credit, he was not beyond support for his own government when he felt that it had acted within the democratic spirit, and had resisted attempts to undermine its authority. To evidence such a case O'Faoláin cites an incident that occurred on 21 February 1944 where the US ambassador in Dublin handed the Irish government a note signed by Cordell Hull, the US Secretary for State, asking for a full recall of German and Japanese diplomatic representatives in Ireland on the grounds that all Axis diplomats in neutral countries were a veneer for the use of espionage against the United States.

Such an incident, as leaked to the press, was obviously cause for much concern in Ireland, as pressure from United States was difficult to resist, especially as it became clearer that the Allies were in a militarily dominant position. De Valera's reply was to equate such an action with a complete betrayal of democratic trust. O'Faoláin himself remained suspicious of de Valera's government but, in light of his experiences with censorship, he found that any accusations against it as a politically biased administration were absurdly unjust. He noted that the reason Britain had remained grudgingly supportive of Irish neutrality was because the Irish government was so efficient in removing any obstacle that might smack of favouritism or bias:

> Ireland's neutrality has been so scrupulous that many of us have girded time and again at the rigorous – the word is Mr. De Valera's in his reply to the American Note – Government measures to preserve it ... Mr. De Valera sometimes gets one's goat but one has to grant him that even if somebody has, not unfairly, compared him with Napoleon III, who was a sort of benevolent despot, he holds the midway gap better than any other Irish politician.[66]

This acknowledgement of de Valera's achievement in steering Irish neutrality throughout the course of the war is a credit to O'Faoláin as he later turned into one of his more established critics.

As the war drew closer to its end, O'Faoláin turned his attentions towards the difficulties to be faced by the victorious powers. Despite his previous concerns about their intentions, and a worry about riding roughshod over individual nations' rights, O'Faoláin was sensitive to the need to properly develop checks and balances in any political solution: 'there are, however, other questions involved in European reconstruction as important as class ideologies. There is the task of balancing nationalist claims and rights.' This difficult balancing act cannot but offend some element of the people, as in the problems faced with the future of Poland. O'Faoláin was suspicious of Russia, and its post-war intentions towards Poland, in particular the threat of a forced communism. He felt that Irish attitudes were unfair in their reactionary rejection of British suggestions, and that the balance of Irish political will was influenced by an inherited Anglophobia that perverted its interpretation of world events. For O'Faoláin, with regards to issues of Polish independence, it was a case of better the devil you know:

> Where the line between moral rights and possible agreements may lie has so far defeated everybody concerned – except the Russians, who are determined that Polish life, to quote the Lublin socialist paper *Robotnik*, must be 'cleansed of anti-democratic elements'. And yet in this I can only say that I would prefer to trust the British than the Russians.[67]

Contrary to many of his colleagues, such as O'Donnell, O'Faoláin's distrust of Russia stemmed from his desire to see a prosperous and developed society rise from the ashes of post-war Europe. He had previously spent time in America studying at Harvard and must have been impressed at the affluence of its society. As such, he was inclined to promote market reform, and saw the need to develop global growth as the solution to world problems. Restrictive isolationist fiscal policies were damaging in a world so politically and financially interdependent, because disparities in wealth were the seeds of international disharmony.

Seán O'Faoláin offered a voice of liberal democracy in the pages of *The Bell*. His excursion into the world of politics in the 'One World' series offered his readers a partisan, but rigorously argued, account of world events. He retained a healthy scepticism towards unbending ideological positions, and consistently strove to relate international events to their context in Irish society. As the choice for his title suggests, O'Faoláin was at pains to emphasise the interdependent nature of global politics. He also was aware of the impact of financial markets on world events and presciently argued 'We have long realised that a man in Wall Street scribbling his name on a cheque may be writing the first words of an epic of happiness or misery for your child or mine.'[68] Although the value of O'Faoláin's attempt to address politics head-on in a literary magazine may be questioned, its execution may not. *The Bell* remained a valuable source of political information and debate during the war years. However, O'Faoláin's was not the only active political voice in *The Bell*. Peadar O'Donnell was also committed to passing comment on political matters, although his style was typically more direct than O'Faoláin's.

On 9 November 1935, a boat of migrant workers set out from Burtonport in County Donegal for Arranmore Island on the last leg of their journey home from seasonal labour in the potato fields of Scotland. The boat struck a rock in the dark and nineteen of the twenty persons on board were drowned. The only survivor was a young boy called Gallaher, who lost his father, four brothers and two sisters in the disaster. He was found after sixteen hours at sea, clinging to the bodies of his father and brother.[69] Two years later, in September 1937, a fire in a bothy on a Kirkintilloch farm in Scotland killed ten seasonal workers from Achill, in County Mayo. The ten victims were all male, three were aged 15, two were 16, and the others were 13, 17, 18, 19, and 24. They worked a fifty-hour week over five and a half days, digging potatoes for around 35 shillings a week.[70] Such horror and devastation in small communities on the western coast of Ireland caused a national scandal. It was particularly galling for Peadar O'Donnell, who had also worked in the potato fields of Scotland in appalling conditions for a basic wage. O'Donnell was moved to publish a pamphlet *The Bothy Fire and All That* (1937) criticising the Irish government and attacking the lack of opportunity for rural workers in their own lands, which forced people to seek employment abroad. The dire need for social change was expressed in *The Bell*, and O'Donnell continually pushed his campaign to have the plight of the emigrant Irish highlighted within it.

O'Donnell's genuine sadness at the tragedy of these losses was compounded by the fact that he considered them totally unnecessary. For him, the losses were an inevitable result of capitalist forces which bound the worker as a wage slave, and maintained support for imperialist industry which dislocated labour in order to obfuscate their exploitation. According to O'Donnell, although the peasant farmers of Donegal were supportive of the de Valera government, the time for waiting for change had passed, and more immediate action was required. To complicate this picture, the Roman Catholic hierarchy had united with the forces of large cattle ranchers and industrialists to keep the truly democratic voice of Irish Catholicism suppressed. These combined forces, he argued in *The Bothy Fire*, had blocked the potential for change in the de Valera administration and rendered impotent the working poor, on whose support de Valera was elected: 'The Catholic Fascism of Cardinal McRory [*sic*] is the deadly enemy of the Catholic Democracy of which you made de Valera your symbol.'

For O'Donnell the answer was clear, de Valera should re-arm these urban and rural poor, to take by force what was their democratic right. Once a worker-led revolution was in place, proper planning organised around state farms would remove the necessity to travel for employment entirely: 'Could they [migrant labour] not be equally well employed on State farms at home?' O'Donnell sought the nationalisation of other industries as well as farming. In particular, he advocated state control for the peat, fishing and mining industries. He also believed that proper planning in civic amenities and in public buildings had the power to transform the quality of ordinary people's lives, and called for regulated state planning: 'it should be a co-operative village, with its hall, library, gymnasium, swimming pool, and all that'. The concerns raised in this pamphlet, the plight of the poor (particularly the rural workers of the west), the nationalisation of industry and the better planning and execution of building works were all issues that O'Donnell would bring with him into his work with *The Bell*.

O'Donnell never significantly changed the format which he inherited from O'Faoláin when he took over as the magazine's editor in 1946. The peculiar blend of social realism and high art suited his own disposition and complemented his commitment to socialism. Although *The Bell* is remembered for the artists who wrote for it, and O'Faoláin's criticisms of censorship, it might just as easily be remembered as a magazine of social justice. O'Donnell's commitment to ameliorate the plight of the working man and to improve the conditions of labour is a constant throughout the entire run. He had learned to curb his more overt expression of political opinion within *The Bell*, never actively calling for an armed struggle, yet his socialist vision is also the one consistent voice within its pages. O'Donnell's editorial style was also much more forthright than that of the capricious O'Faoláin, if perhaps less interesting because of it. Although his anger at the time of the bothy fire led him to publish his pamphlet in 1937, none of his political conviction had faded by the time of *The Bell*'s launch in 1940. Throughout his time writing for *The Bell* he remained hopeful for social change, even if, fearful of wartime legislation, he would never be bold enough to express his hopes so clearly as in 1937: 'If the Federated Irish Industries and de Valera lead the fight, the victory will come to rest in a thickening of the defences of capitalism in Ireland … If the Trade Unions lead and bring the rural battalions into step with the Trades Councils then the Republican and Democratic forces will win a victory which must place the working class in power.'[71]

Such a powerful commitment to social justice would compel O'Donnell to produce article after article of political agitation in *The Bell*, and he continued to return to issues close to his heart, namely rural depopulation, under-use of state industries and the poor living conditions of the working classes. These sentiments were reiterated in the same year in *Ireland To-Day*, a journal with much more overt republican credentials than *The Bell*. In it O'Donnell struck a stronger militant note:

> And it may seem strange, but I think *Ireland To-Day* could do a better service than any journal in Ireland. It rests on a tier of Republicans near enough to Ryan, Ruttledge, Aiken, Derrig and Co., to make them listen while they [the government] get told their little social flutterings are tiresome … But when in the face of such happenings as the tragedy of Kirkintilloch we lift our heads and see where these men who were of their Ireland yesterday have betaken themselves to-day, we realise we must cure them or blast them, and quickly.[72]

As late as 1965 he was still agitating for the west and its plight of depopulation and low wage conditions, producing pamphlets claiming that a radical reorganisation of society was still possible: 'The hope for a national movement rests in wage-earners gathering to them intellectuals, language enthusiasts, students, the youth in general, to link with the hard-pressed small farm countryside itself. It is an exciting prospect.'[73] In this respect and in light of the enthusiasm he displayed for socialism at such a late stage, it is better to see his involvement with *The Bell* as a continuation of his life's work, rather than a break from it into a distinct world of literature. For O'Donnell, the two remained intrinsically linked and were part of the same whole, namely the promotion of a new socialist vision of Irish society, although O'Donnell's own position was not unproblematic.

In an article from 1941 O'Donnell complained of the psychological scars that mass migration was imposing on Irish youth. For O'Donnell, the Irish youth living on smallholdings along the western seaboard were compelled to travel to the industrial centres in England and Scotland, drawn by the promise of decent wages and a new chance for a life with dignity. Those who remained at home were committed to imposed seasonal work outside of Ireland and the care of their parents on their subsistence farms. O'Donnell rallied to their cause, complaining that, until work could be found in Ireland for them, the seasonal migrant should have his passage eased and the bureaucracy reduced to facilitate travel: 'The problem of enabling the small farmer heads of households to stay at home is the problem of finding him seasonal work where his fifty pounds can be saved. Until that can be done there should be only one attitude towards the migrant – to smooth his going and coming, and make his journey cheap.' Such a decision was lamentable, but necessary, until a long-term plan could be put in place to facilitate the workers at home. For O'Donnell, the Irish turf industry was one of the country's best sources of hope in the development of native labour markets. However, he wished to see committed investment in the schemes to ensure the plans for turf cutting continued past the imposition of the war, and could be a sustainable industry in its own right: 'Is our turf effort a mere war-time fit, or is it the beginning of a scheme of long-term national development?'[74] O'Donnell's concern for the exiles did not only extend to their wages, he was also aware of the conditions under which they operated and their potential for exploitation at the hands of unscrupulous employers.

O'Donnell was alert to the appalling conditions endured in 'The Model' doss-houses and bothies in English towns and Scottish farms. He felt that the Irish worker endured these conditions through a stoic acceptance of fate, and a failure to organise to demand better conditions. He personally went to experience these hovels, ten years after first making the trip to a Scottish potato farm as a matter of necessity. His account is detailed and moving:

> Ten years later, and this time as an inquirer masquerading, I first entered the bothy of a potato squad. We scraped the dry cow-dung from the stalls, shook down clean straw and bedded ourselves down. The door – two doors on wheels meeting badly – had a great gap up the middle, and the straw rustled in the wind. The dung-hill was in front of the door. There was no separate accommodation for girls. I think our people took the bothies the way soldiers took the mud of the trenches – something to be endured because of the job a man was doing.

He also felt that there was an element of hypocrisy on the part of the Irish worker in Great Britain, and was critical of the workers themselves. He believed that they accepted sub-standard conditions abroad that would be rejected out of hand at home. Thus, physically degraded, the migrant worker underwent a moral degradation also, and behaved as if he was outside of the society in which he worked. Excessive drinking, fighting and anti-social behaviour were the result and O'Donnell felt that the key to restoring workers' dignity would be to appeal to their own standards and a sense of communal shame: 'For one thing alternative lodgings must be found. The Models themselves must come under fire: but the mainly men must be shamed out of these haunts.' The thrust of O'Donnell's criticism was reserved for the middleman of the operation, the potato merchant. He acted as a sort of gombeen man, excusing the farmer of any moral obligation to his workers by applying pressure directly to the workers' gaffer: 'the real villain of the piece, however, is the potato merchant, though he keeps well out of the picture, for he buys the growing crop from the farmer and arranges it that the farmer provides the housing. When the workers take a stand against bad housing, the merchant cracks his whip at the heels of the gaffer, and not over the head of the farmer.'[75]

Such open criticism of Irish emigration during the wartime conditions of Great Britain and Ireland was a brave move on behalf of O'Donnell. The experiences of those migrants contributed to a cultural legacy in Ireland, whereby emigration is viewed with a tinge of personal shame.[76] His campaign to highlight political awareness of these conditions broke an open taboo in Irish society by discussing the realities that parents were sending their children abroad to face. Almost every level of Irish society was touched by emigration, and the economy of entire communities depended on remittances from those abroad, especially in the congested districts, such as O'Donnell's own Rosses in County Donegal. His open commitment to their plight was admirable, and his own personal experience of those conditions gave him a moral authority which was difficult to dispute.

Towards the end of the Second World War, in February of 1945, O'Donnell was again calling on the government to alleviate the plight of the emigrant Irish. This time he worried that new peacetime conditions in Great Britain would lead to job losses on a mass scale that would affect the 250,000 Irish living there. O'Donnell was bleak about their prospects of a dignified return home where there were no decent jobs, and the de Valera administration had failed to deliver on the promises of the 1916 Rising:

> They [the migrants] blame everything and curse everybody. The Ireland they freed has failed them and it hurts. Yonder they are, the veterans of the Tan War and the youth who are near enough to those days to have caught their glow, frustrated, bewildered, ready to fly to Canada or Australia if the opportunity offers. If the way should open to the U.S.A. there would be a stampede. They ask one thing of God – not to be sent back home.[77]

At the very least, O'Donnell demanded that the Irish government introduce a minimum wage into the market, so that the employed should have the dignity and comfort which was their due. O'Donnell's concerns for Irish workers were not the platitudes of a left-wing writer who could safely throw plaudits on the working man from the comfort of his ivory tower. He lived and breathed political agitation and firmly believed that the role of the writer was to propagandise on behalf of the working classes. A writer should educate and agitate on behalf of his political cause, and those writers who romanticise their work are in danger of doing a disservice to the people as a whole. Regarding the idealisation of 'the West' in Irish society, O'Donnell apportioned some blame on the writers and artists of his day and was angered that their work had contributed to the political inertia surrounding the issue: 'It would be interesting to sort out the share of blame to be charged against Irish writers for the spread of the mischievous idea that the cottage-laden townlands of the coastal fringe have but to be duplicated across the country to make this a prosperous land.'[78] O'Donnell always emphasised the social responsibility of writers and intellectuals to the public in his own work, and although he lived a comfortable life personally, his commitment to communism remained undiminished.

A large part of O'Donnell's reputation lies in his accomplishments as an artist, yet he never saw art as anything other than an extension of the political arena; it was politics by other means. This idea is evident in his belief that a writer can only express the truth of his own community, and in doing so will awaken them to their political realities:

> For when the artist denies a Mussolini's or Hitler's claim to a corner in truth, he does not do so by making an opposing claim on his own behalf, but by preserving in himself a sense of the people breathing near him. At moments he sees himself, as night-watchman over qualities in man, without which his spiritual life must stifle. The artist may be a tradesman, working in the materials that excite his mind, but that material is the community in which he himself is set. He is the aspect of the imagination of the people which speaks to them through a representation of their own experiences.[79]

Such an idea would have been anathema to O'Faoláin, who was devoted to the freedom of artistic expression over any social consideration. He was shocked by O'Donnell's honesty in these matters, and could not comprehend his dismissive attitude to artistic work for its own sake. From very early in their relationship, O'Faoláin was left in no doubt that, for O'Donnell, politics and social change were the key motivating factors in his writing and not a love of art. Writing to their shared friend and patron, Edward Garnett, O'Faoláin complained in a letter of 1931:

> I said – 'what do you want to do? Write books or work at politics? – I don't give a damn about books, says he. – If you were given the choice, said I, never to be able to write a line or never to be able to take part in politics! – There wouldn't even be a conflict, said he, not a moment's hesitation. I wouldn't need to think.' So there you are. Next time he goes to jail he'll go for 5 years and I told him so.[80]

This letter offers a key insight into the success of *The Bell* in combining the force of these two men's personalities. O'Faoláin's writing became more politicised when working with O'Donnell, and O'Donnell wrote less stridently in working with O'Faoláin. The breadth of literary talent available to the editors was enhanced by O'Faoláin's concern with artistic excellence, and O'Donnell's committed social activism dovetailed with O'Faoláin's ideas about knowing the truth of Irish society through its faithful recording. When O'Donnell took over from O'Faoláin, he inherited a journal with a reputation for literary excellence which tempered its more political content and the subversive nature of its accurate, if depressing, descriptions of Irish life.

During the early decades following independence there was much crossover and consultation between political leaders and the Roman Catholic hierarchy, so that 'the values and culture of the major political parties in the 1920s and 1930s reflected the dominant Catholic ethos'.[81] In later life, O'Faoláin would see his contribution to Irish society in terms of a long struggle as a force for progressive change against a repressive establishment, as embodied by these two dominant social institutions, the Roman Catholic Church and the Irish state. O'Faoláin identified this as the case when he reflected on his six years as editor of *The Bell* between 1940 and 1946:

> In the days of *The Bell* I was fully integrated because I was on the attack. I had accepted responsibility as a citizen and thought of myself as speaking for a great silent majority ... I found a silent minority which in time became more numerous. Life in Ireland has changed completely since those days – not, to be sure, because of liberals like myself, but, inevitably, with the changing quality of life, the coming of radio and television which swept Ireland into the bosom of the twentieth century. Those were the forces which won the battle for us – as we had always known they would.[82]

Although, with hindsight, it can be alluring to see history as a linear struggle between competing agents, such a view is not unproblematic. O'Faoláin's relationship with the political establishment and, in particular, with the Catholic Church was much more nuanced and complicated than the simple case of binary opposition that he presents here. O'Faoláin's attitude towards religion, and particularly towards Roman Catholicism, is uniquely insightful as a means of evaluating the achievements of this versatile and multifaceted figure in Irish letters. Although he was a champion of civic freedom and a vocal opponent of perceived church influence in political affairs, particularly in *The Bell*, Catholicism is central to any understanding of O'Faoláin's work. That said, he also characterised Catholicism as open to different interpretations, and to him the manner of its expression was as important as adherence to its teachings. Even his own daughter Julia was unsure of the full extent of his commitment to the Irish Catholic Church, noting that 'if he was Catholic at all, he was no longer a full time one'. Yet she does recognise that he died 'yearning for a belief in an afterlife which had evaded him, and feeling the ire of a man who had paid his dues to a club [the Catholic Church] which welshes on commitments'.[83]

O'Faoláin's stated rebellion against Catholicism was never as one-dimensional as now perceived, and through a review of the omissions and contradictions in his own writing a much more rounded picture of this elusive writer can be formed. O'Faoláin's recollection of himself as a 'citizen' speaking for the 'great silent majority' is easy to accept when we weigh up the aggregate of his writings in *The Bell*, especially when we consider his attacks on conservative nationalism and hypocritical piety. Writing to Edward Garnett, eleven years before the establishment of *The Bell*, he confessed to having lost his faith, an experience which left him with little optimism for the future:

> My religious beliefs are gone by the board long since, though that was merely under stress of a more implacable idealism still: now I am in the backwash of that event and I am rather terrified by all I see around me – everyone struggling in the sea after leaving the drowning ship. Unless I find some unity in myself to recompense me for what I have lost – I *am* lost. All these I consider lost – Mr. Eliot and the Sitwells and Joyce and those other worser rebels. No hope there. It seems that each one must henceforth be his own universe and hope for nothing from his contemporaries, for nothing from the social world about him, from religions or morals or society.[84]

The 'implacable idealism' to which he was referring consisted of his republican values, which were condemned by the church hierarchy. O'Faoláin later confirmed the republican basis for this great loss of faith in his *A Summer in Italy* (1949). Also in this book he describes his return to faith in dramatic terms, and it demonstrates his attempt to position republican nationalism in direct opposition to Roman Catholicism.

O'Faoláin travelled to Italy in the summer of 1947 where he had 'been invited by Graham Greene', another Catholic writer, to 'share in, and to describe the life-ways and the traditions of one of the most civilised countries in history'.[85] This tour of Italy was to spark a lifelong obsession. *A Summer in Italy* describes his return to Catholicism through a chance encounter with an old Italian man called Cipolla. The simple way in which Cipolla viewed the Roman Catholic Church as a human institution accountable for its actions, but also how he maintained a deep and moving faith, inspired O'Faoláin. This led him to rush to confession in Saint Peter's where his return to Catholicism was consecrated:

> Under the vast dome, in that great town of Saint Peter's, I felt as minute as a Lilliputian. And then I realised the infinite kindness of the man and I was overcome with emotion ... In those seconds I knew that I was caught, and caught for ever. I was lost or saved, according as you happen to look at it. People approached the altar. The Light of the World became flesh of their flesh, I was present at the greatest drama in all the world, in all eternity. *Ecce Agnus Dei ...*

O'Faoláin implied that this re-conversion was necessary as he felt isolated from the Catholic Church after republican volunteers during the Irish Civil War had been threatened with excommunication for their activities. Imagining that he would have to explain his absence from the Church during his confession he practised his lines with an account of his experience during the Civil War,

"'You see Father, when we took up arms to defend the Republic the Church pronounced us virtually excommunicate" ... For what could he possibly know about the intricacies of Irish revolutionary politics?'[86] However, such a romanticised account of his 'conversion' during that summer in 1947 needs to be scrutinised and it should be compared with the other writings that he produced between the long period of his youthful republican activity and his summer of religious exaltation in post-war Italy.

Despite this self-affirmed lack of faith, O'Faoláin was interested enough in Catholicism to see it as no less than the saviour of the modern novel. In July 1935 he wrote 'The Modern Novel: A Catholic Point of View', where he advanced on his artistic criticisms in earlier articles and made a direct plea for the creation of a new Catholic-inspired novel. This new type of novel would return dignity and artistic credibility to the genre which had been lost to it in English since its destruction at the hands of proponents of naturalism. Acting directly under the influence of the French and later Russian realists, the novel in English had turned towards a sceptical and bitter disposition where life was analysed and dissected without any reference to the wonder and imagination it could contain. This movement ran in line with the change in social conditions that marked the turn of the century, and the transition into late-capitalist society. According to O'Faoláin, scientific modernism accelerated from the beginning of the century, and life began to intrude more forcibly in art, precipitating the development of the psychological novel: 'in a sentence, the world is accepted with a bad grace and the universe and all creation is faced with an endless outpouring of questions ... To the modern novelist life is evil and it is, apparently, his self-chosen task to prove it.'

Although, for O'Faoláin, such a movement was valid and inspirational in its time, it had now become stale and conventional, resulting in a false note for modern society whereby artists labour under the conventions and rules of an outmoded, restrictive format. O'Faoláin also was, if anything, a harsher critic of contemporary Catholic novelists for their failure to execute their duty as artists, if not their duty as Catholics:

> But in the Catholic novelists one knows, there is, so far, little or no improvement on unethical naturalism as we now know it. I find in all of them a painful self-consciousness, as if they could not forget they were Catholics, a timidity evident in their fear of the senses, a priggishness and a solemnity which has nothing to do with religion and for which there is no excuse, a lack of humour, and a tendency to underwrite about the emotions as if they feared to raise a storm they could not ride, and as by way of recompense for this slowness of the drama an overlyrical quality that verges on the sentimental and the neurotic.[87]

This reading of the Catholic novelist, for O'Faoláin, points to some core problems for them as artists. It illustrates the difficulty that Catholic novelists face when dealing with life, in all its impurity. Such distaste for life can lead the Catholic artist to force morality into art where none is called for. This rejection of the seedier aspects of human experience is the imposition of a false moral doctrine on life for O'Faoláin.

Any artist who tries to recreate a moral balance within their work by compensating for the lack of morality in life is acting in bad faith. This conflict cannot be resolved by 'pretending that art can be a charwoman for religion, cleaning up life with her broom'. To do so is to make a mockery of the delights of sin, and to deny their powerful allure; it is tantamount to avoiding reality, and sacrifices truth on the altar of moral prudery. Such was O'Faoláin's faith in this doctrine of the transcendent powers of Catholic art that he had been planning to write such a novel as early as 1933. Again, writing to Edward Garnett, O'Faoláin confided that he was conceiving of a novel with the trials of faith at its core:

> I am lying fallow for a novel. I am compiling dossiers. I have one germinating. I feel interested in Irish religious types and I think that an interesting novel could deal with the strange Irish mentality about religion – the contradictions, the deep piety, the absence of any real morality, the clash between desire and religion – the odd types, the Augustinian who finds *faith*, the Thomist who reasons towards belief, the Franciscan filled with love & softness & charity – but it must be all seen in character. I have 2 men in mind. It is only a seed yet. I must observe and ponder. There must be a clash in it, and some terror (of the grave and hell) and pity of it all. We'll see.[88]

The novel he was planning would be published as *Bird Alone* in 1936, and it stands as a testament to O'Faoláin's commitment to Catholic art.[89] Yet he was also aware of the way in which Catholicism was being exploited in an Irish context, and felt its appropriation in the hands of conservative zealots. O'Faoláin's own journalistic career in Ireland was honed during his spell as the books editor for *Ireland To-Day* and it was here that he would first argue in defence of the right to self-expression against the political establishment. However, O'Faoláin's ire was directed less at the Church itself and more towards those who would assume its moral authority and use it to attack others as anti-clerical when they wished to discredit them. Such accusations, he contended, had been made against *Ireland To-Day* itself and he saw this as evidence that his own political views were not complacent: 'Any man who holds, to-day, unpopular opinions on social or political matters may, I think, feel almost complimented by being called "anti-clerical" by such people.' O'Faoláin also saw the Church's position in Ireland as dependent on a social contract with the laity. This contract is based on broad support for Church initiatives by the people in return for its support of popular political movements.

However, this agreement is threatened by the Church's opposition to left-wing nationalism. Officially, the Catholic Church remains politically neutral, but it informally activates secular agents to act on its behalf. Such actions are ultimately self-defeating, according to O'Faoláin, as they undermine support for the Church from its members. This grand bargain has left the Church in a very strong position in which it has become, in O'Faoláin's words, 'independent of political control. It is sufficiently endowed financially. It exerts just as much influence (in Ireland, only, I agree) as if it held direct political power. But all three aspects depend, for effectiveness, on the moral influence of the Church on the people.' O'Faoláin believed that social development in Ireland was dependent on a happy marriage between the two, with a sensitive response to the needs of the people on behalf of the Church and respect for the traditions and moral guidance of Roman Catholicism by the people. Any organisation that attacked the expression of national sentiment as anti-clerical was likely to be rebuffed by the people and would ultimately be against the interests of the Church itself:

> If deliberate they are scandalous attacks. If they are unpremeditated and unconsidered, most foolish. In either case they are most dangerous to that harmony that ought to exist between priests and people and to the ascendency of religion, which can only be achieved and maintained by both – either working together, or working separately in a condition of mutual respect.[90]

This article is typical of the kind that O'Faoláin would later write in *The Bell* in that it never overtly rejected the Church itself, instead attempting to subvert its political influence and struggle to maintain a healthy balance between social development and Catholic dogma.

For O'Faoláin, the Church's attitude in Ireland was not one of malicious intention and political opportunism; rather it was one of misguided paternalism, an inherent conservatism and a culture of suspicion of secular movements inspired by French Jansenistic thinking. In a book review for the *Irish Times* in 1943 he revealed an admiration for something that approached his ideal relationship between a Church and its people. 'A Neglected Autobiography' is a review of the autobiography of George Tyrrell, Irish Jesuit priest and theological modernist. O'Faoláin saw modernism (an attempt to reconcile the Catholic faith with modern life and, in particular, the threat posed by science) as 'one of the greatest of all modern schisms' whose influence has 'spread over the whole world, and whose reverberations have not yet wholly died away'.[91] Tyrrell was a leader in this theological movement and was eventually excommunicated, while the movement itself provoked the publication of an oath against modernism on the 1 September 1910 by Pope St Pius X, which was required to be taken by all clergy.[92] Tyrrell was also of interest to O'Faoláin because he was a convert to Roman Catholicism. Like Cardinal Newman, Tyrrell was a rationalist, and O'Faoláin was drawn to intellectualised accounts of conversion, accounts where reason had taken men to the zenith of their beliefs and still left them dissatisfied.

What was required by these converts as the next step towards God was a blind leap of faith. The rationale behind conversion on behalf of educated and conscientious men was of great interest to O'Faoláin who emulated their thinking in his own justification of religious faith. Newman's intellectual approach appealed enough to him that he was drawn to write an account of it, and he found that Tyrrell had 'in addition to and inspiring his deep sensibility and latent intelligence ... an almost Dostoievskian power of self-immolation. I have read several books by and about converts, but in none is there this amazing selflessness.'[93] O'Faoláin's faith in Roman Catholicism allowed for a mother Church so large as to encompass all opposites, one in which contradictions were inherent and change was necessarily incremental. In a Church of such eternal ambitions change was always resisted and slow to be implemented, heresy becoming orthodoxy only after its threat to centralised power had passed. It is typical of O'Faoláin that he could remain resistant to the Church's interference with secular politics and yet maintain his empathy for those in religious life who were deeply concerned with men's actions for the sake of their souls. Of Tyrrell's autobiography he asked that only those who could empathise with a man whose conscience was that of the intellectual convert should read it. This tension in O'Faoláin's thinking points to someone who was sympathetic to a wide variety of human experience and was capable of a deep empathy with those in whom spirituality and religious sentiment were real and moving. He also felt culturally Catholic, a condition that was inescapable for the generation of working-class Catholics who grew up to feed Ireland's revolutionary zeal: 'One who has once submitted to the symbolism of Catholicism, in childhood, seen all things through the stained-glass window – death and birth and the tales of the Prophets – all highly histrionic and idealised – can never really have the objectivity of a non-believer.'[94]

Despite the evidence that O'Faoláin was deeply concerned with Catholicism, scholarship tends to focus unreflectively on his resistance to Church interference and on his moment of Pauline 'conversion' in Rome.[95] He remains a favourite with historians as a voice of counterculture resistance in Ireland against the hegemonic weight of state and Church authority, as one critic saw it: 'O'Faoláin launched attack after attack on these romantic conceptions [of Ireland] in the name of pragmatic realism.'[96] However, O'Faoláin's opinions of the Roman Catholic Church in Ireland are nuanced. On the whole, they avoid direct criticism of the Church and its members and prefer to stress the mistakes made in the application of its power rather than in questioning its right to that power. An interesting example of O'Faoláin's attitude to the role the Catholic Church should play in Ireland came after the scandal caused by Dr Noel Browne's Mother and Child scheme, proposed in 1950.

This scheme was an attempt by the then minister for health to introduce free health care to pregnant mothers and to develop a system of postnatal care for mothers and children. This caused consternation among the Catholic hierarchy in Ireland as the first steps towards the socialisation of health care, and their opposition to it put an end to any chance of it becoming law. The political fallout from this crisis led to the eventual dismissal of Dr Browne from his post, and was widely regarded as evidence of undue Church influence in Irish politics. O'Faoláin documented his personal views of this event through a series of articles in *The Bell*, hoping that:

> Now that the excitement aroused by the sudden demise of the Mother and Child Scheme has died away, and we can detach our emotions and our thoughts from the accidents and personalities involved, the issue becomes a bit easier to define. The issue is that no country can be ruled 'democratically' by two parliaments; or at least not as the world understands that word. Here in the Republic, as the crisis has revealed to us, we have two parliaments: a parliament at Maynooth and a Parliament in Dublin.

O'Faoláin's response was forceful but measured and he stated explicitly that the Church had been wrong in its handling of the case and had been using its position unfairly to force home its advantage. In reviewing this affair, O'Faoláin pointed out that no one was questioning the Catholic Church's right to comment or advise Parliament on its position, nor did he feel that it was wrong to do so. What he objected to was the Church in an Irish context acting as a direct political entity and issuing decrees that it expected to be followed by the elected secular Parliament: 'In practice, the Hierarchy does much more than "comment" or "advise". It commands.'

What made this political interference particularly galling according to O'Faoláin was the special relationship that the Catholic Church had with its members. Unlike other religions, Catholics operate under a unique set of constraints, tied to the edicts of the Church through the ritual of the blessed sacraments. Under Catholicism, anyone who is denied the sacraments is in danger of threatening their immortal soul, rather than simply evoking the ire of their Church. This threat, argued O'Faoláin, was unfairly wielded in Ireland by the Church hierarchy: 'The Maynooth Parliament holds a weapon which none of the other institutions mentioned holds: the weapon of the Sacraments ... when the Catholic Church, through its representatives, speaks, he realises, and the Roman Catholic public realises, that if they disobey they may draw on themselves this weapon whose touch means death.'[97] O'Faoláin's concern here is not just academic; rather it reveals one who considers this threat to his soul as a serious matter and who takes the issue of papal comment as a real and concrete issue.

O'Faoláin clearly understood and sympathised with the majority of Irish

Catholics at that time, who would have taken the word of the Church hierarchy
as vital as catechism itself. However, his concern with Church interference
in the political sphere was not as antagonistic as some of his contemporaries.
For example, Owen Sheehy Skeffington, O'Faoláin's erstwhile colleague at
Ireland To-Day had already caused a public dispute with the Church which
was covered by O'Faoláin in *The Bell*. Skeffington had invited to a meeting
of the International Affairs Association in Dublin another regular contributor
to *The Bell*, Hubert Butler. At that meeting, Butler had insulted the papal
nuncio by implying that the Roman Catholic Church had been complicit in the
Nazi occupation of Yugoslavia during the Second World War. The chairman
stopped Butler from continuing his point because he was worried that the
authority of Church had been compromised:

> His Excellency, the Papal Nuncio, who was present, had risen from his seat
> and walked out in protest at Mr. Butler's opinion. The next day two members
> of the Committee called on the Nuncio to apologise to him. Subsequently Mr.
> Butler was forced to resign from his honorary post as Secretary of the Kilkenny
> Archaeological Society. Later, under obscure circumstances, but with the great-
> est publicity, Dr. Sheehy-Skeffington was banned from a public debate in Dublin
> – controlled, or controllable by the Dublin Vocational Committee.[98]

Despite O'Faoláin's protestations at excessive church influence on political
issues, he did not believe in a total separation of church and State. On the
contrary, O'Faoláin saw Church activism in the political sphere as right and
proper. Nationally, he felt it was right that there existed tension between secular powers and the Church, as the distinction between how a Catholic society
chooses to live, and how it ought to live, are inseparable. There can be no divide
between life as it is lived and the moral guidance as dictated by the Church with
regards to how it ought to be lived. For O'Faoláin, the difficulty that arose with
regard to the Mother and Child Scheme was a matter of degree rather than
kind. This tension should play itself out in the public sphere and allow some
element of synthesis between the Church authorities and the laity: 'Nobody has
ever defined the just limits of the Church's power in politics; nobody ever will.
The relation of Church and State is, must be, and should be one of constant tussle.
That is the essence of the whole matter.'

One of O'Faoláin's main concerns following this crisis was that the relationship between Church and state should be symbiotic, and as the Church forages
deeper into the realm of politics, so too will politics follow deeper into Church
affairs. If the Church unbalances this relationship by gaining undue power
and, by extension, commensurate responsibility, then it is in danger of losing
its eternal spiritual authority, and becoming embroiled in the worldly affairs
of man: 'In that state of affairs the Church will be blamed, and rightly blamed,
for such things as infant mortality, slums, and poverty, and the State will be

hamstrung.' O'Faoláin was concerned here with what might result from a politically unrestrained Church, seeing the anti-clerical violence of the Spanish Civil War as a direct result of political meddling: 'that is the way things came slowly to a head there, and sooner or later, if undue intervention by the Church is not resisted by the State, must be the way things happen in every country, including this'. The real issue with Church interference in the politics of the Irish State in this case was its own suspicion of its lay members.

According to O'Faoláin, an organisation of faith with no faith in its members is dehumanising and authoritarian. The Irish Church is guilty of a politics of negation, having the luxury to criticise things as they are without being forced to offer an alternative as to how they should be. O'Faoláin contrasts the Church in Ireland with rather starry-eyed and effusive praise of the Church as it is operated in Rome: 'who would object if the Vatican stood where Maynooth stands: with all its ancient culture, its human wisdom, its political intelligence, its immense tolerance, its rich traditions, its prestige and its panoply?' In the end, O'Faoláin is more disappointed than bitter with the Church in Ireland, he still sees hope in a radicalised Catholic political ethic, something approaching Newman's idealism married with O'Connell's pragmatism. Such a political movement could be formed within the ranks of the Catholic laity to pursue a positive and progressive political agenda: 'The only possible triumphant movement of the future will, whatever it calls itself, be far removed from all that. It will be a Christian Radical Movement; which ... was what O'Connell tried gropingly to adumbrate for Ireland and the world.'[99] Seen as such, O'Faoláin's position could equally be interpreted as pushing for stronger secular liberalisation of Irish politics, or, contrastingly, a reinvigoration of the Catholic body politic in Ireland with a new progressive Catholicism. This deeply Catholic aspect of O'Faoláin's thinking and his attitude to the Church as a whole, as opposed to its specifically Irish embodiment, is often ignored at the cost of emphasising his liberal credentials.

Two of O'Faoláin's short stories published in *The Bell*, but not present in any of his collected short stories, offer an illustration of his attitude to the Church in Ireland and to Roman Catholicism in general. 'Eden' and 'Imaginary Conversation' both deal with Catholicism in different ways, but both reveal the threads of O'Faoláin's thought with regards to Church authority.[100] 'Eden' is a short story about an Irish bishop who is staying with gentrified friends in their landed estate. He is a kindly old man from humble origins sitting comfortably in the guest room of the house overlooking the gardens and the bay. He is a picture of assured, self-confident contentment: 'He leaned back and let his eyes wander to the ocean's vast dishes of sunlight. A yacht, miles out, was becalmed in the dead centre of one of those circles of sun. His eyes sank to the rocks off-shore, pale as pearls. On the second terrace the gardener was softly raking the gravel. "Eden!" he said to himself, "Eden".' This scene and the bishop's

demeanour combine to give him an other-worldly appearance, someone who is
outside of life as it is lived, aware of its vicissitudes only when the gardener's
gentle raking of a gravel path intrudes on his reverie. He is interrupted in his
attempts to write a sermon by the daughter of the host family, through whom
the dramatic tension is played out. She intends to marry a Protestant against
her parents' wishes. This girl is wilful and determined, representing the new
youth of Ireland; she is frustrated by the rules of her parish, set by the bishop
himself, that forbid her the right to marry outside of her religion. She com-
plains that 'in England Catholics are allowed to marry Protestants under dispensation'. Although he humanly sympathises with her position, and can see
her difficulty, the bishop fails to accept the need for change; rather he lectures
her on the necessity of rules in all social clubs and reminds her that the Church
is no different.

   Frustrated by his off-hand patriarchal rejection of her concerns, she feels
isolated and rejected by her Church. The bishop finally dismisses her, telling
her that he will pray for her, and he sees her frustrations as symptomatic of her
generation, unable to understand the wisdom and benevolence with which the
Church treats its flock: 'this spirit of rebellion is sometimes no more than the
headstrong impatience of youth and the Church will gently and kindly guide
them from this wayward path back to those sane and wise precepts which the
experience of centuries has tested and not found wanting'. The story ends with
the bishop resuming his pastoral letter on the duties of children to their parents,
while simultaneously thinking of the love and respect in which he held his own
dead mother. He feels as detached and remote from his own community as if
he were trying to communicate with the dead. O'Faoláin finishes the story with
lines which echo James Joyce's often-quoted closing paragraph in 'The Dead':

> He resumed his pastoral letter and now it began to flow quietly and simply,
> though as he wrote it he felt little joy or pride in it, no more than if this, too, were
> a letter, not to the young and the living but to a generation that was dying, or a
> generation that was dead.[101]

O'Faoláin's rather didactic message is clear, that there is a failure to trust and
understand its flock by the Catholic hierarchy in Ireland and they are trapped
in a discourse with an Ireland long since passed.

   This story (appearing in December 1951, just seven months after his article
'The Dáil and the Bishops') is O'Faoláin's attempt to respond artistically to the
reaction of the Irish Catholic hierarchy to the Mother and Child Scheme. Here
O'Faoláin depicts a kindly, but out of touch, bishop who cannot comprehend
the changes in Irish society, nor feel the impositions that such high-handed
dismissal of the laity's needs generate. Importantly, O'Faoláin portrays this as
a failure to communicate by both sides. He evokes sympathy for the bishop by
offering us an insight into his thinking, from his rationale for diocesan law, to

the pathos of his thoughts for his lost mother. It is typical of O'Faoláin that he would try to understand both sides of this debate and would maintain a strong sympathy for the Church's position while simultaneously arguing for change. Politically, O'Faoláin's ideal response would be a Catholic-driven radical movement that would push for change from within the Church and not in direct opposition to it, something that would emulate the example set by Cardinal Newman in an intellectual embrace of Church thinking: 'anti-liberals seem, to a man, to imagine that if you cannot be a tolerant liberal your only alternative is to be a smug Conservative. Newman's alternative has not occurred to them at all'.[102] O'Faoláin's sympathy for the difficult balancing act that Roman Catholicism must maintain in order to survive is also illustrated in 'Imaginary Conversation' where two different interpretations of Catholic identity collide.

Set in the papal apartments of the Borgian Pope, Alexander VI, 'Imaginary Conversation' depicts a discussion between Alexander and the Dominican friar, Savonarola. These two historical figures are remembered for their corrupt savagery and devout holiness respectively. In 1498 Alexander browbeat the Florentines into having Savonarola 'arrested, tortured, hanged and burned in Florence … as a traitor and a heretic'. Fifty-six years later a papal commission declared his complete doctrinal orthodoxy, and his views became accepted across the Church. O'Faoláin has picked on this topic to show his opinion of Catholicism and of the Church as an institution, simultaneously trying to prompt change within the Catholic hierarchy in Ireland. Published in 1952, 'Imaginary Conversation' builds on O'Faoláin's understanding of Catholicism as depicted in *Newman's Way*, published the same year, and offers us an insight into his religious views. For O'Faoláin, the debate between Savonarola and Alexander was the debate between a puritan mind and a life-affirming mind. The puritan or ascetic as represented by Savonarola denies life and seeks to suppress it in favour of the spirit, an idealisation of the mind that prevents man from accepting life in an imperfect world:

> Savonarola: It is you who blaspheme! For when you talk of ruling the world, as if it were for God's glory, you are taking Christ up to the pinnacle of the temple to tempt him with the world's vanities. The Kingdom of God is within us. It is not in this wretched world outside us. Alexander: This world is God's world! To be enjoyed, to be ruled, to be won in God's name![103]

The debate here is one of a difference between a mind of a fundamentally Protestant or puritan bent, that of an idealist, and between a more humanist Catholic view.

According to O'Faoláin, puritans have traditionally dealt with life in one of two ways, through flight from life to abstract idealism, or through social reform. This is contrasted in the story with a mother Church, as represented by Alexander, that must preach transcendent morality and yet make its way using the political and social tools open to humanity, to strive to protect its position in the world of men: 'The Puritan has always resolved this dichotomy in one of two ways: the way of the ascetic who flies from the wicked world entirely; or the way of the reformer who fights this disgusting clod of earth to conquer it for God. One thinks of the desert hermits; one thinks of the zealots of the Inquisition, of Savonarola, or Cromwell, of hosts of well-meaning and utterly objectionable minor reformers whose main urge is hatred of the very fact of life.'[104] For O'Faoláin, proselytising Protestantism is essentially anti-life, a force that emphasises the corrupt and fallible aspects of human life over its divine potential.

Hatred of life and all its impurities is the main driving force behind Savonarola's criticisms of the Church and his attack on Alexander, his suggestion is to remove all the physical trappings of prestige and wealth that can block the way to Christ's light: 'I will tell you what must come to happen if the Church is to be purified. You must put away your pomps and powers, your politics and stagecraft, your pagan palaces and paunchy prelates, stepping proudly, spitting gravely, plotting hourly in every court in Europe, draining the poor with taxes.' However, Alexander will not agree with him, and knows that 'without a strong Church religion would become a vague misty feeling, a disembodied ghost, seen by a few, heard by a few, believed in by a few, wandering the world like an evening wind'.[105] O'Faoláin himself has a strong sympathy with Alexander's position, seeing the need for a strong Church, involved in the world and the workings of men, resistant to the strains of life-denying Jansenism that he detected in Irish Catholicism, and broad enough to understand the realities of human existence:

> So it has been with Christianity. Its original documents do not determine it; for the ideas of Christianity are in the reader and writer of revelation, not in the written text, and only in time can they hope to be clarified; just as Christianity, in its external or political framework, must expect to conform to the general methods by which the course of things is always carried forward in this mortal world. We only have to open the text of Scripture to see that this is true. '*The Word became flesh.*'[106]

The mother Church was right to burn Savonarola because it was protecting its temporal interests and position in the world, his criticism was a threat to its existence and had to be repressed: 'The reason Savonarola was burned was not because he was a heretic – it has long been conceded that he was not – but that he encouraged the French King to invade Italy, and because he defied the Papal League formed against him.' O'Faoláin here is acting as an apologist for the Roman Catholic Church, seeing her actions as necessary evils for an institution that holds global power and influence, one that is forced to operate in this world of men, so that it may better account for the saviour of their souls in the next.

O'Faoláin's compassion for both Savonarola and Alexander points to a pre-dilection for thinking in binarisms; he could empathise with both of these men for their differing logic, but his own sympathy is clearly on the side of the Church. In a remarkable extract from *A Summer in Italy*, O'Faoláin, talking to a local cabbie, states his case for special consideration for the Church in full:

> 'I once met a bishop in a railway train,' I said, 'who believed that the three marks of the Church should be that she be poor, unprivileged and free. I disagree. She should be immune … privileged on every count and exempt on every count; an enclave recognised by all men as something separated from this fleshy world. She should therefore be celestial; that is she should only have to do with heavenly order, and though she must, since this is the world and not the otherworld, have to do with temporal things she should employ no temporal weapons. She should be rich, the richest of all mortal institutions, so that she would be able to influence the thoughts of men by all these same things, and more.[107]

It seems O'Faoláin was able to see the influence of the Church in secular affairs as right and justified. His complaint with Church interference in an Irish context was that it was not properly resisted by the state, or that the Irish Church failed to provide reformers from within its own ranks to promote a new Catholic humanism. He felt it was the responsibility of all members of the Church to try to change it for the better: 'As Paddy Browne [Pádriag de Brún] says, "Humanise the Church." Humanise what we have. Humanise it as far as it is humanised in Britain. And that's not very far. Give us an enclave. A Catholic enclave. A bold, free, intelligent Catholic enclave. Even a free and intelligent one. It's the only way. It's a pity so many Irish writers have been anti-Catholic. It's our only European link.'[108]

The details of O'Faoláin's attitude to the Roman Catholic Church as published in *The Bell* and his other writings paint a different picture to his own depiction of himself as a secular liberal. They must also cast doubt on the account of his 'conversion' to Catholicism as recalled in *A Summer in Italy*. This account forms the basis for much of the criticism of his work and his relationship to Catholicism at a cost to his earlier writings and the nuances of his own position.[109] Although it is tempting to give O'Faoláin the benefit of the doubt when reading his own account of religious experience in his autobiography, at least one of his contemporaries was also suspicious of this version of events:

> All this daft stuff about O'Faoláin being reconciled with the Church makes me laugh and go wild at the same time. The bloody stupidity of it! O'Faoláin was never anything else than a Catholic. He may have shown ignorance of things or he may have barked at a few clerics, but he was never anything but what he was baptised. This reconciliation story is all the result of a bit of self-dramatisation which he concocted in his book about Italy. Being in the middle

of a description of St. Peter's, he couldn't resist staging a confession scene. Unless he's a liar, it's not thirty or even five years or even a few since he said bless-me-father-for-I-have-sinned.[110]

Such deliberately misleading information is typical of O'Faoláin in his auto-biography. This duality of nature and deliberate obfuscation of the truth are also evident the downplaying of his achievements in *The Bell*, his attitude to republicanism, and accounts of his love affairs. It is difficult to chart a man's relationship to religion over the course of a life as long and as eventful as O'Faoláin's, perhaps it is best defined as one of sceptical belief, or as a vague comfort:

> It's no trouble to me to fall in love three times a year with the fullest realisation it's all nonsense, just as it is no trouble to me to be a Catholic and go to confession once a year and take the Body of the Young God, and see it all as a vast poetic metaphorical nonsense which is nonetheless the essential Truth.[111]

Such an attitude is not inconsistent with O'Faoláin's professed liberalism, especially in light of his own conception of Catholicism and the Catholic Church. As has been pointed out elsewhere, it was not that the Catholic Church was opposed to art or even modernist art; at times it even embraced it. But it was opposed to subjective artistic visions that opposed its view of a fundamental Christian truth.[112] At any rate, O'Faoláin accepted inconsistency as part of the human condition. Inconsistency is also present when we look at his attitude to literature, in particular, at his changing views on the role of the artist and his relationship to society.

Notes

1 Seán O'Faoláin, 'One World', *The Bell*, 7:6 (March 1944), p. 471.
2 See Margaret Ward, *Hanna Sheehy Skeffington: A Life* (Cork: Cork University Press, 1997), pp. 336–337.
3 For an account of this, see J. Bowyer Bell, *The Secret Army: The IRA* (Piscataway, NJ: Transaction Publishers, 1997), p. 81.
4 Richard A. Furze Jr is the first to suggest this in 1974, although it is repeated as late as 2006 by Caleb Wood Richardson. See Richard A. Furze, Jr, *A Desirable Vision of Life: A Study of The Bell, 1940–1954* (Dublin: National University of Ireland, University College Dublin, 1974), p. 39, or Caleb Wood Richardson, *That is Only War: Irish Writers and the Emergency* (Stanford: Stanford University, 2006), p. 167.
5 Walsh is interviewed by H.L. Morrow (writing under the pseudonym of The Bellman) in an early edition. See The Bellman, 'Meet Maurice Walsh', *The Bell*, 4:2 (May 1942). Luke Gibbons provides an insightful history of the transformation of Walsh's story into the film, see Luke Gibbons, *The Quiet Man* (Cork: Cork University Press, 2002).

6 For a full history of *The Bell*'s publication dates see Kelly Matthews, *The Bell Magazine and the Representation of Irish Identity* (Dublin: Four Courts Press, 2012), pp. 179–182.

7 For a brief description of Róisín Walsh's life, see her obituary in Kenneth Reddin, 'Roisin Walsh', *Irish Times* (12 July 1949), p. 5.

8 Seán O'Faoláin to Sean O'Casey (6 November 1917), O'Casey, MS38, 129.

9 Seán O'Faoláin, *Vive Moi! An Autobiography* (London: Rupert Hart-Davis, 1965), pp. 94–171.

10 Seán O'Faoláin to the British Broadcasting Corporation, Merton House, Teddington, Middlesex (11 November 1932), Correspondence with Seán O'Faoláin, The British Broadcasting Corporation's Written Word Archive Centre, Reading.

11 Bureau of Military History 1913–21, Statement by Witness, Document no. W.S. 779 (Section 3), p. 725.

12 For more on these two incidents, see Julia O'Faoláin, *Trespassers: A Memoir* (London: Faber & Faber, 2013), pp. 8, 44.

13 For an account of its formation, see Peter Hegarty, *Peadar O'Donnell* (Cork: Mercier Press, 1999), pp. 217–226.

14 Ernie O'Malley to Molly Childers (5–7 December 1923), in Cormac K.H. O'Malley and Anne Dolan, *'No Surrender Here!': The Civil War Papers of Ernie O'Malley 1922–1924* (Dublin: The Lilliput Press, 2007), pp. 457–458.

15 See Hegarty, *Peadar O'Donnell*, pp. 173–183.

16 James Hogan, *Could Ireland Become Communist?* (Dublin: Cahill and Co., 1935).

17 Peadar O'Donnell, *Monkeys in the Superstructure: Reminiscences of Peadar O'Donell* (Galway: Salmon Publishing, 1986), p. 7.

18 Hogan, *Could Ireland Become Communist?*, p. 20.

19 See Brendan Behan, 'I Become a Borstal Boy', *The Bell*, 4:3 (June 1942).

20 See Michael O'Sullivan, *Brendan Behan: A Life* (Colorado: Roberts Rinehart Publishers, 1999), p. 94.

21 See Brian Hanley, *The IRA, 1926–1936* (Dublin: Four Courts Press, 2002), pp. 104–109.

22 For an account of these men, see Geoffrey Elborn, *Francis Stuart: A Life* (Dublin: Raven Arts Press, 1990); Seán Cronin, *Frank Ryan: The Search for the Republic* (Dublin: Repsol Press, 1980).

23 Francis Stuart, 'Frank Ryan in Germany', *The Bell*, 16:2 (November 1950), p. 40.

24 Francis Stuart was elected a member of Aosdána in 1997, and his appointment caused much controversy due to anti-Semitic remarks made by him on a Channel 4 documentary and his work with the Nazi administration in Germany. Among those to complain were Val Mulkerns, Louis le Brocquy and Andreas Roth. See Mulkerns, le Brocquy and Roth, 'Francis Stuart and Aosdána', *Irish Times* (1 December 1997), p. 15.

25 Peadar O'Donnell, 'German Spies in Ireland', *Irish Times* (14 June 1958), p. 7.

26 See Monk Gibbon's introduction in: Michael Farrell, *Thy Tears Might Cease* (London: Arena Books, 1984), p. 11.

27 For a contemporary reference which sees Farrell as important, see Diarmaid

Ferriter, 'The Not so Swinging Sixties', *Irish Times* (15 September 2009), p. 17.

28 Shea Murphy, 'The Saddest Sight', *The Bell*, 13: 6 (March 1947).

29 For more on the camps, see Bryce Evans, *Ireland During the Second World War: Farewell to Plato's Cave* (Manchester: Manchester University Press, 2014), pp. 159–163.

30 Peadar O'Donnell to Sean O'Casey (26 August 1946), O'Casey, MS 37, 998.

31 See Seán O'Faoláin, 'Don Quixote O'Flaherty', *The London Mercury*, 37:218 (December 1937), pp. 170–175.

32 Liam O'Flaherty to Edward Garnett (29 February 1932), in A.A. Kelly (ed.), *The Letters of Liam O'Flaherty* (Dublin: The Wolfhound Press, 1996), p. 256.

33 Liam O'Flaherty to Edward Garnett (21 June 1927), p. 188.

34 For an account of Hayes's arrest and trial, see *Irish Times* (20 June 1942), p. 3.

35 See Brian Girvin, *The Emergency, Neutral Ireland 1939–45* (London: Macmillan, 2006), pp. 83–84.

36 Stephen Hayes, 'My Strange Story', *The Bell*, 17:4 (July 1951), p. 16.

37 O'Faoláin to John V. Kelleher (31 August 1948), UCC, BL/JVK/25.

38 Seán O'Faoláin, *Vive Moi! An Autobiography* (London: Sinclair-Stevenson, 1993), p. 214.

39 O'Faoláin to George Weller (26 November 1977), George Weller/Seán O'Faoláin Letters, Boole Library, University College Cork, BL/L/GW/6.

40 An Ulster Protestant (W.R. Rodgers), 'Conversation Piece', *The Bell*, 4:5 (August 1942), p. 305.

41 Gillian McIntosh, *The Force of Culture: Unionist Identities in Twentieth-Century Ireland* (Cork: Cork University Press 1999), p. 193.

42 See Edna Longley, 'Rodgers, William Robert (1909–1969)', *Oxford Dictionary of National Biography* (Oxford University Press, 2004; online edn, 2008). www.oxforddnb.com/view/article/62958 (accessed 15 November 2010).

43 For a brief description of his life, see James McGuire and James Quinn (eds), *The Dictionary of Irish Biography from the Earliest Times to the Year 2002*, vol. 8, *Patterson – Stagg* (Cambridge: Cambridge University Press, 2009), pp. 581–582.

44 An Ulster Protestant, 'Conversation Piece', pp. 305–314.

45 W.R. Rodgers, 'Ireland', *The Bell*, 2:4 (July 1941), p. 12.

46 O'Faoláin to John V. Kelleher (24 January 1949), UCC, BL/L/JVK 29.

47 Diarmaid Ferriter, *Judging Dev: A Reassessment of the Life and Legacy of Eamon de Valera* (Dublin: Royal Irish Academy, 2007), p. 149.

48 R.F. Foster, *Modern Ireland 1600–1972* (London: Penguin, 1988), p. 554.

49 Seán O'Faoláin, 'de Valera's Life Story', *Sunday Chronicle* (13 March 1932): Seán O'Faoláin, 'The True Story of Michael Collins', *Sunday Chronicle* (15 May 1932): Seán O'Faoláin, 'The Countess Markievicz', *Sunday Chronicle* (27 November 1932). The holdings at the British Library contain no such articles, so it is likely that O'Faoláin was published in a regional variant for Ireland, although the National Library of Ireland has no such holdings either. Piaras Béaslaí sued the *Sunday Chronicle* to prevent further publication of the O'Faoláin article and this

may explain its absence in the British Library and the National Library of Ireland holdings. A copy of the article exists still in Béaslaí's personal papers, see Piaras Béaslaí Papers, the National Library of Ireland, Manuscript Collection List 44, MS 33,937 (6).

50 Seán O'Faoláin, *The Life Story of Eamon de Valera* (Dublin: Talbot Press, 1933); Seán O'Faoláin, *Constance Markievicz* (London: Jonathan Cape, 1934).

51 Seán O'Faoláin to Sean O'Casey (4 August 1932), O'Casey, MS 38,129.

52 Quoted in Frank Shovlin, *The Irish Literary Periodical 1923–1958* (Oxford: Clarendon Press, 2003), p. 79.

53 O'Faoláin, *Vive Moi!* (1993), p. 266.

54 Henry O'Neill, 'Another "Life-Story" of Eamon de Valera', *Irish Press* (27 March 1933).

55 Seán O'Faoláin, *De Valera* (London: Penguin, 1939), p. 156.

56 See John Bowman, *De Valera and the Ulster Question 1917–1973* (Oxford: Oxford University Press, 1989), pp. 203–205.

57 O'Faoláin, *De Valera*, p. 181.

58 M.J. MacManus, *Eamon De Valera: A Biography* (Dublin: The Talbot Press, 1944), p. 7.

59 Seán O'Faoláin, 'Eamon De Valera', *The Bell*, 10:1 (April 1945), pp. 3–18.

60 For an insightful analysis of Irish censorship during the Second World War, see Donal Ó Drisceoil, *Censorship in Ireland 1939–1945: Neutrality, Politics and Society* (Cork: Cork University Press, 1996); for a comprehensive list of banned authors, see Donal Ó Drisceoil, 'Appendix A: Irish Books Banned under the Censorship of Publications Acts 1929–67', in Clare Hutton and Patrick Walsh (eds), *The Oxford History of the Irish Book Volume V: The Irish Book in English 1891–2000* (Oxford: Oxford University Press, 2011), pp. 644–649.

61 Seán O'Faoláin, 'One World', *The Bell*, 7:4 (January 1944), pp. 281–284.

62 O'Faoláin, 'One World', *The Bell*, 7:5 (February 1944), pp. 376–381.

63 Francis Hackett, *I Chose Denmark* (New York: Doubleday, Doran and Co., 1940).

64 See Francis Hackett, 'A Muzzle Made in Ireland', *Dublin Magazine* (October–December 1936), pp. 8–17. On the banning of his wife, see Lis Pihl, '"A Muzzle Made in Ireland": Irish Censorship and Signe Toksvig', *Studies: An Irish Quarterly Review*, 88:352 (Winter 1999), pp. 448–457.

65 O'Faoláin, 'One World', *The Bell*, 7:6 (March 1944), pp. 471–474.

66 O'Faoláin, 'One World', *The Bell*, 8:2 (May 1944), p. 102.

67 O'Faoláin, 'One World', *The Bell*, 9:4 (January 1945), pp. 279–281.

68 Seán O'Faoláin, 'One World: The Next Geneva?', 10:2 (May 1945), p. 97.

69 Anon., 'Arranmore Disaster', *Irish Times* (28 November 1935), p. 7.

70 Anon., 'The Bothy Fire Victims', *Irish Times* (12 November 1937), p. 8.

71 Peadar O'Donnell, *The Bothy Fire and All That* (Dublin: Irish People Publications, 1937), pp. 10–17.

72 Peadar O'Donnell, 'Achill, Arranmore and Kirkintilloch', *Ireland To-Day*, 2:10 (October 1937), p. 50.

73 Peadar O'Donnell, *The Role of the Industrial Workers in the Problems of the West* (Dublin: Dochas Co-Operative Society, 1965), p. 8.

74 Peadar O'Donnell, 'Migration is a Way of Keeping a Grip', *The Bell*, 3:2 (November 1941), pp. 116–118.
75 Peadar O'Donnell, 'The Irish in Britain', *The Bell*, 6:5 (August 1943), pp. 358–369.
76 See 'Ireland's Crash: After the Race', *The Economist* (17 February 2011).
77 Peadar O'Donnell, 'Call the Exiles Home', *The Bell*, 9:5 (February 1945), p. 383.
78 Peadar O'Donnell, 'At the Sign of the Donkey Cart', *The Bell*, 12:2 (May 1946), p. 93.
79 Peadar O'Donnell, 'Under the Writer's Torch', *The Bell*, 12:6 (September 1946), p. 462.
80 Seán O'Faoláin to Edward Garnett (14 August 1931), Boston, MS 89–14 (Box 2, Folder 11).
81 Dermot Keogh, *The Vatican, the Irish Bishops and Irish Politics* (Cambridge: Cambridge University Press, 1986), p. 227.
82 Quoted in Julia O'Faoláin, 'O Faoláin at Eighty and Post Mortem', *The Cork Review* (Cork: Triskel Arts Centre, 1991), p. 9.
83 Julia O'Faoláin, *Trespassers*, pp. 73, 237.
84 Seán O'Faoláin to Edward Garnett (4 February 1929), Garnett. MS 1542.
85 O'Faoláin, *Vive Moi!* (1993), p. 334.
86 Seán O'Faoláin, *A Summer in Italy* (London: Eyre & Spottiswoode, 1949), pp. 165, 164.
87 Seán O'Faoláin, 'The Modern Novel: A Catholic Point of View', *The Virginia Quarterly Review*, 11:3 (July 1935), pp. 341–350.
88 Seán O'Faoláin to Edward Garnett (n.d. but posted 1933), Boston, MS 89–14 (Box 2, Folder 11).
89 Seán O'Faoláin, *Bird Alone* (London: Jonathan Cape, 1936).
90 Seán O'Faoláin, 'The Priests and the People', *Ireland To-Day*, 2:7 (July 1937), pp. 36–38.
91 Seán O'Faoláin, 'A Neglected Autobiography', *Irish Times* (3 April 1943), p. 2.
92 This oath is reproduced in full at www.franciscan-archive.org/bullarium/oath.html (accessed on 10 May 2010).
93 O'Faoláin, 'A Neglected Autobiography', p. 2.
94 Seán O'Faoláin to John V. Kelleher (5 July 1943), UCC, BL/L/JVK/2.
95 For examples, see Fergus O'Ferrall, 'Christian Sensibility and Intelligence: the Witness of Seán O'Faoláin', *The Cork Review* (Cork: Triskel Arts Centre, 1991); or Hilary Jenkins, 'Newman's Way and O'Faoláin's Way', *The Irish University Review*, 6:1 (Spring 1976).
96 Terence Brown, *Ireland: A Social and Cultural History 1922–2002* (London: Harper Perennial, 2004), p. 189.
97 Seán O'Faoláin, 'The Dail and the Bishops', *The Bell*, 17:3 (June 1951), pp. 5–7.
98 Seán O'Faoláin, 'The Liberal Ethic', *The Bell*, 16:5 (February 1951), p. 517.
99 O'Faoláin, 'The Dail and the Bishops', pp. 8–13.
100 Seán O'Faoláin, 'Eden', *The Bell*, 17:9 (December 1951), p. 18 and Seán O'Faoláin, 'Imaginary Conversation', *The Bell*, 18:5 (October 1952), p. 261.
101 O'Faoláin, 'Eden', pp. 18–26.
102 O'Faoláin, 'The Liberal Ethic', p. 10.

103 Seán O'Faoláin, 'Imaginary Conversation', pp. 273, 270.
104 Seán O'Faoláin, *Newman's Way* (London: Longmans, 1952, p. 103.
105 O'Faoláin, 'Imaginary Conversation', pp. 271–272.
106 O'Faoláin, *Newman's Way*, p. 241.
107 O'Faoláin, *A Summer in Italy*, pp. 224, 166.
108 Seán O'Faoláin to John V. Kelleher (31 August 1948), UCC, BL/L/JVK/25.
109 For examples, see Daniel Murphy, 'Religion and Realism in Seán O'Faolain's Prose', *Imagination & Religion in Anglo-Irish Literature 1930–1980* (Dublin: Irish Academic Press, 1987); O'Ferrall, 'Christian Sensibility and Intelligence'; and Jenkins, 'Newman's Way and O'Faoláin's Way'.
110 Frank MacManus to Sean O'Casey (11 February 1950), O'Casey, MS 38,126.
111 Séan O'Faoláin to John V. Kelleher (September [1948]?), UCC, BL/L/JVK/26.
112 Dublin Municipal Gallery had rejected George Rouault's expressionist painting *Christ and the Soldier* in 1942, but it was happily accepted by St Patrick's seminary in Maynooth. The Church was less sympathetic to the artists of the White Stag Group that were supported in *The Bell*. See Róisín Kennedy, 'Experimentalism or Mere Chaos? The White Stag Group and the Reception of Subjective Art in Ireland', in Edwina Keown and Carole Taaffe (eds), *Irish Modernism: Origins, Contexts, Publics (Reimagining Ireland)* (London: Peter Lang, 2009), pp. 179–194.

4

The mart of ideas:
O'Faoláin and literature

In keeping with its professed commitment to a wide and inclusive audience, the first edition of *The Bell* contained an eclectic list of contributors, and Elizabeth Bowen was not the only writer of note to grace its pages. Articles in that edition were drawn from a diverse section of Irish society and artists. No mention of the editorial board was made but, interestingly, Frank O'Connor's column 'The Belfry' is clearly delineated, marking his contribution as integral to the magazine's identity. Flann O'Brien is also a notable contributor to the first pages, publishing a humorous article called 'Going to the Dogs', which describes in painstaking detail the experiences of losing a bet on dog racing in Shelbourne Park.[1] His presence in *The Bell* and the publication dates are also noteworthy as this was the month which saw the launch of his 'Cruiskeen Lawn' column for the *Irish Times*, wherein he wryly commented on the lack of Irish language words to discuss the war, and imagined the 'stormy philological breakfasts that obtain in the household of the Gael' which deal with this pressing problem.[2] O'Brien's inclusion is puzzling for another reason, namely that he had launched a spiteful personal attack on Seán O'Faoláin in a letter to the *Irish Times* two years earlier, criticising him for his commitment to realism and questioning his authority in a typical mock-heroic manner. It was signed 'Flann O'Brien' and it formed part of a long-running debate between O'Faoláin and the younger artist.

On 4 November 1938 Seán O'Faoláin addressed a symposium held by the Dublin Literary Society on the question, 'Are Modern Novels Telling the Truth?' O'Faoláin's speech was based on his theory of the novel as charted by his scholarly essays written throughout the 1930s and, in particular, on the proletarian novel and its brutalising tendencies.[3] This speech was reported in the *Irish Times* and O'Brien took exception to O'Faoláin's position.[4] O'Brien opened his letter to the editor, 'Sir, – I see that tremendous cerebrite, Mr. Seán O'Faoláin has been at it again. He announces that Irish novelists are in a bad way thanks to the "venom of provincialism and nationalist and religious obscurantism."' O'Brien's response was to attack O'Faoláin for his criticisms of Irish society by inverting the high rhetoric of his speech, turning his words into a critique of O'Faoláin's own realist writings: 'What Mr. O'Faoláin did not mention was the spiritual amortisation of the realist (as distinct from the naturalistic) novel as a result of the decadent vogue of representationalism.' O'Faoláin's serious point was that Irish writers are forced by society to write defensively, protecting themselves against the barbs of criticism and censorship within the country. As a result, Irish writing and the novel suffer a lack a balance wherein the vagaries of life impinge on the writers' work. As such, exile remained an attractive option for the writer, and O'Faoláin's suggestion that it is a real threat is mocked at length by O'Brien, as is the stuffy seriousness of the literary societies of which he was a member. The letter is remarkable for its sarcasm and fantastical humour:

> I notice a very ominous hint in the remarks of Mr. O'Faoláin made about the peacefulness of London and the crazy whirl of life in Connemara. Like everything he says, his words have no meaning at all (in the naturalistic sense). But, thanks to my highly developed conservation of spirit, I think I can detect a threat that soon another little window will light up in the high attics of the Rue St. Valentin. If Mr. O'Faoláin must go to live in a civilised country may I implore him to do something for the poor Irish before he sails. Why not send the Abbey on circuit and establish branches of the Dublin Literary Society or the P.E.N. Club in every town and village, each branch to be in charge of a genuine pallid spirit-deficient novelist of either the naturalist, representationalist or realist schools? The branch could be occupied with decontaminating provincialism, dispersing obscurantism and promoting the ballet, verse-speaking and *Weltanschauung*. If this plan is adopted I must utter a word of caution. It is well known that some of the members of these organisations are remarkably like cows. When they take up their positions down the country they would want to keep a sharp look-out for warble-fly inspectors.[5]

It is hard to see why O'Brien would want to be published in any journal associated with O'Faoláin after this letter, especially one, in a noticeably prescient reading of O'Faoláin's editorial predilections, which actually went on to carry articles promoting ballet and verse-speaking.

Anthony Cronin, who would later work in *The Bell* himself, identified a further intensive literary spat between O'Brien and O'Faoláin carried out in the pages of the *Irish Times* a year later, when Frank O'Connor had seen Flann O'Brien as one of his enemies.[6] O'Brien was so incensed by this exchange that he refused to allow a copy of his *At Swim-Two-Birds* (1939) to be sent to O'Faoláin.[7] O'Brien was a difficult character by nature, and even as late as 1954 he still was holding up O'Connor and O'Faoláin as examples of poseurs, peddling sentimental nostalgia about an Ireland that did not exist. For all his humorous language, this was a serious charge against O'Faoláin who was generally clear-eyed on Irish social pretensions: 'Not to be left out of the picture are Seán O'Faoláin and Frank O'Connor, with stories about wee Anne going to her first confession, stuff about country funerals, old men in chimney nooks after 50 years in America, will-making, match-making – just one long blush for many an innocent man like me.'[8]

This enmity being the case, it is difficult to see why O'Faoláin would want to publish anything by Flann O'Brien. It suggests that, to his credit, O'Faoláin's had a keen eye for literary talent, and the good grace to publish people whom he found personally disagreeable. Certainly, O'Faoláin was dismissive of aspects of literary society in Dublin. In particular, he disliked the backbiting and petty politics of the Dublin literary pub scene of which O'Brien was an intimate part. Writing to a friend in a disconsolate mood, O'Faoláin was critical of the Pearl Bar, a haunt of literary Dublin in the post-war period: 'Life here is rarefied and remote – for me at any rate on my hill-top. I went to Dublin to-day (fog) and wandered lonely as a cloud and met literally nobody I knew – I felt as remote as James Joyce (sans the pubs) for if I went into the Pearl bar I'd meet the low-brows and be infuriated.'[9] O'Faoláin's distance from the grittier sides of Irish literary culture was perhaps what made him a target for a younger generation of writers, but it also provided him with a degree of critical distance which allowed him to edit *The Bell* in a composed and even-handed manner. In his dealings with O'Brien, it was a coup for O'Faoláin to get him to write for *The Bell* at all, and a testimony to his judgement as an editor, even if O'Brien would only submit two further articles and one short story.

If O'Brien's presence in the first volume of *The Bell* is something of a surprise, then another prominent figure in the Irish literary landscape is not. Patrick Kavanagh submitted two poems for the opening edition, including perhaps his most famous 'O Stony Grey Soil'. *The Bell*'s existence is central to Kavanagh's development as a writer, and the core of authors who ghosted in and out of its offices played both major and minor parts in his life. By the time of *The Bell*'s establishment in October 1940, Kavanagh had been living in Dublin for less than a year, having moved there following his ill-planned sojourn in London. Before he left for London he had met and befriended Frank O'Connor through literary evenings at George Russell's (AE). His friendship with O'Connor would prove vital in introducing him to Dublin's literary circles and establishing his relationship with Seán O'Faoláin, Peadar O'Donnell and Róisín Walsh.[10] She was to remain a committed friend to Kavanagh throughout his life, and helped him whenever she could. At this stage of his development Kavanagh was still in awe of the literary elite of Dublin and he counted O'Connor and O'Faoláin among his closest literary friends, finding in them patrons and role models for his burgeoning talent. O'Faoláin was himself familiar with Kavanagh's small farm background from the long summers he spent at his maternal grandparents' farm in Rathkeale in County Limerick, although even as teenager he maintained a disdain for the uncultured rural life.[11] In recognition of the debt of gratitude which he felt to O'Faoláin, Kavanagh dedicated 'O Stony Grey Soil' to him in *The Bell*.[12]

Kavanagh's anti-pastoral lament for his misspent youth is in line with the cultural project that O'Faoláin was pushing in *The Bell*, by reflexively turning towards what was considered a given about Irish identity and reinterpreting it, often in a negative light. In this specific instance, Kavanagh looked towards an Irish country childhood and felt resentful of the limitations of such an upbringing. This was in direct contrast to much revival writing, which held the rural farmer as the ideal for Irish society to emulate. Kavanagh was initially very happy to be associated with *The Bell* and to have access and encouragement from writers of the calibre of O'Faoláin, O'Donnell and O'Connor. O'Connor remained committed to his poetic work, and recognised his ability immediately. However, Kavanagh was a contrarian and lacked the good grace of others. He was famously dismissive and heavy-handed in his assessment of other writers, and when dealing with an author as thin-skinned as O'Connor it was only a matter of time before tension would arise between the two.

In the December 1947 edition of *The Bell* Kavanagh submitted an article entitled 'Coloured Balloons: A Study of Frank O'Connor'. It was an extraordinary essay, and its publication by O'Donnell even more extraordinary, considering the severity of criticism it contained. Kavanagh began his review of O'Connor's work by claiming that he was at his best when writing short stories, yet even these he found to be flawed. For Kavanagh, O'Connor's work had become too imitative, it was superficial and rarely touched on the truths which Kavanagh associated with emotional contact with one's material in the soil. O'Connor, argued Kavanagh, was struggling to find a real sense of artistic purpose: 'O'Connor has a poor sense of direction, and a very dim consciousness of purpose ... The sum of his travels in the active cultural life of this country has been futility.' Kavanagh went on to further develop his theory that O'Connor's work rarely was great art. This, according to Kavanagh, was because O'Connor was always at a distance emotionally from his characters, and, what is worse, he sneered at them for conforming to type and thus becomes complicit himself in their difficulties. Reflecting on O'Connor's career, Kavanagh found him to be merely 'a purveyor of emotional entertainment, and that he has surrendered to this minor role'.[13] The presence of such a forceful condemnation of O'Connor's work in *The Bell* is unusual, and it would have been unlikely under O'Faoláin's editorship, as he was always quick to defend his old friend in public.

O'Donnell's judgement must be questioned for choosing to go ahead with its publication, and it probably reflects the greater distance between O'Donnell and O'Connor than existed between O'Faoláin and his old friend. Although O'Connor often tested his patience, O'Faoláin remained fiercely loyal to him. Typically, he rushed to O'Connor's defence in the next issue. He was incensed by Kavanagh's ungratefulness towards a fellow writer who had guided

Kavanagh's development and who had lauded his genius from the very start. O'Faoláin's own inability to understand Kavanagh's work came to the fore here, and his retort demeaned Kavanagh's subversive pastoral aesthetic. Although O'Faoláin published him often, ironically, he was blind to the true radical voice in Kavanagh's poetry, and its revolutionary challenge to hegemonic discourses surrounding poetic expression. Even though O'Faoláin was an excellent critic of prose writing, and demonstrated his skill as an editor, he was a much less insightful reader of poetry, a trait John Montague also identified in him: 'the emphasis in Irish Literature at that time was changing back to poetry which was something Seán did not quite understand'.[14] Writing to O'Connor he would complain of the young Monaghan poet: 'Oh the hell with it. One wants civilisation. Kavanagh doesn't wash his poetry's ears.'[15]

This aloof and haughty judgement is typical of O'Faoláin, in retaining an attraction to the more civilised elements in his life and in his preference for writers. There is something also in this judgement of a Cork city snob in his dismissal of Kavanagh's work and O'Faoláin's lifelong attraction to the affluent and refined, which may go some way to explaining his attraction to Elizabeth Bowen and the Big House. O'Faoláin rejected Kavanagh's rural poetic because it lacked the urbane sophistication which he was drawn to by inclination, and in spite of his pleading with Irish writers to write of what they knew. However, it was also characteristic of O'Faoláin to maintain a united public front with Frank O'Connor, even while disagreeing with him behind closed doors.

When his Welsh wife Evelyn was critical of their work in *The Bell* O'Faoláin was keen to point out to O'Connor that she could never understand the pressures and pleasures of their shared Cork background in revolutionary Ireland, 'God damn you is there nothing here but non-cooperating Celts? As for Evelyn [Bowen] drown her. She knows nothing about Blarney Street or Half Moon [street]. And THEY are Ireland, and us.'[16] Their own sense of being Corkmen under siege from a dismissive Dublin literary set forced them ever closer on issues of public disagreement, and O'Faoláin was keen to rush to his friend's defence. O'Connor instantaneously recognised Kavanagh's genius and championed him throughout the early years of his career, becoming a 'close friend as well as advisor', and O'Faoláin would have deferred to his judgement as poetry editor for *The Bell*.[17] Kavanagh's relationship with *The Bell* and its circle of principal actors is as long and varied as the magazine itself. He was involved with the magazine in some capacity from the very first volume under O'Faoláin until the last in December of 1954, when Anthony Cronin was doing most of the editorial work. Fittingly, as one great Irish literary institution was dying in *The Bell*, another was being born in Bloomsday, first celebrated in June 1954. In another coincidence, both Flann O'Brien and Patrick Kavanagh were the primary figures at this inaugural Bloomsday celebration, and their experiences there have been memorably captured by Anthony Cronin in his autobiographical *Dead as Doornails* (1976).[18]

When O'Faoláin did respond, he did so in a controlled and sharp analysis of Kavanagh's essay, and saw that, as a piece of literary criticism, it was found wanting. For O'Faoláin, Kavanagh's main criticism of O'Connor was that he did not write more like Kavanagh himself, and even in this Kavanagh failed to define the elusive qualities which he found so edifying in good literature: 'instead of describing what Frank O'Connor is trying to do he finds fault with him for not being down to Mr. Kavanagh's idea of reality, which he makes no attempt to define ... All of this is merely Mr Kavanagh, as usual, roaring contentedly at his own face in the mirror of everything he reads.' O'Faoláin's response then descends into personal attack, his criticism betrays his lack of sympathy with the radical nature of Kavanagh's work: 'Patrick Kavanagh never writes about the life of the aristocracy, or factories, or scientific discovery', complained O'Faoláin, 'his great weakness is that he cannot rise an inch above the small farm. He couldn't write about a painted fan to save his life.' It was here that O'Faoláin's criticism escalated to personal invective: 'always stuck in the old mud. Reality, reality, reality from start to finish. Dung from morning to night! With an occasional rush to the chapel, a bit of slobber about the sunlight on the Blessed Sacrament. Then a glaum at a girl, which never comes to anything – dreadful sentimentality mixed up with bits about his ma forking the old manure-heap.'[19] O'Faoláin's criticisms say more about his own elitist preferences in literature than they do about Kavanagh's writing, turning as they do the more poignant aspects of his work into a subject of ridicule, yet O'Faoláin's sense of hurt at Kavanagh's attack on his old friend is also palpable. This incident finished O'Faoláin and Kavanagh, and he even sought to prevent the poet from getting further work; writing in 1949 to John Ryan on the opening of the journal *Envoy*, O'Faoláin advised, 'Kavanagh is APPALLING. Drop him *at once*. He is shame-making.'[20] O'Faoláin's loyalty to O'Connor was noticeable to others, despite their frequent public and private disagreements; Sean O'Casey felt they were a 'curious pair. Always together (or were), yet never, seemingly, at one.'[21] This was especially true when criticism came from someone whom O'Faoláin would have regarded as lacking the professional attainment of both himself and O'Connor in a magazine which offered Kavanagh an early break.

O'Connor's reaction was more muted, considering that he could be as sensitive to criticism as Kavanagh. When O'Connor next met Kavanagh after the publication of 'Coloured Balloons' at a party held by Macmillan in London, he greeted him warmly and dismissed the article as a thing of inconsequence, yet privately he was very hurt.[22] However, O'Connor was not at that stage in a position to start any public debates, having become emotionally drained through his work and personal life.[23] O'Faoláin later recalled that Kavanagh had unsuccessfully sued *The Bell* in 1944, but his frequent contributions to the magazine would seem to contradict this. Perhaps this attempted litigation came at a subsequent date, in response to O'Faoláin's personal attack in 'Coloured Balloons'.[24] Kavanagh's ingratitude towards O'Connor was typical of the type of spats he became involved in within the tight confines of literary Dublin; he also maintained a long-running dispute with Roibéard Ó Farachain [Robert Farren], another regular contributor to *The Bell* and someone who was equally hated by O'Connor.

However, Kavanagh owed a great debt to *The Bell* both under O'Faoláin and O'Donnell, as they published him throughout difficult times, and O'Donnell was particularly supportive financially, being known as a soft touch among Dublin's hard-up literary set. At least one writer saw his generosity within *The Bell* as a 'one-man Arts Council, functioning tangentially to the real one'. On O'Donnell's side, his contribution to Kavanagh's promotion was very important, and the offices of *The Bell* when it moved to No. 14 Upper O'Connell Street were a refuge for the young writer, whose large frame could often be seen 'bellowing for his free copy'.[25] O'Donnell's serialisation of Kavanagh's novel *Tarry Flynn* (1948) between May and September 1947 represented what he later claimed to be 'the only useful thing that I did on *The Bell*'.[26] To his credit, he identified it at the time as the work of a great talent, calling Kavanagh 'the outstanding Irish novelist to-day; the most authentic voice rural Ireland has yet achieved'.[27] Perhaps O'Donnell saw in Kavanagh the realisation of his earlier call for distinctive working-class Irish voices in *The Commonweal*. It has been suggested that Kavanagh even worked for a time as an 'assistant editor' at *The Bell*.[28] This followed his promotion by O'Donnell from the agreement whereby he received the substantial sum of '£5 per published poem'.[29] This figure stands well above the average rate given to other authors, including those of international repute.

Initially, *The Bell* could only afford to make an 'exiguous gesture of £1.1.0 per 1,000 words' and nothing for reviews, even to poets as established as Austin Clarke.[30] However, Kavanagh's name does not appear anywhere at this time as an editor in *The Bell*, although his contributions indicated a closer level of collaboration with O'Donnell. Kavanagh was supposed to guest edit an edition of *The Bell* under O'Faoláin as early as 1943, but considering their difficult relationship it is no surprise that he did not. O'Faoláin wrote to Frank O'Connor to complain: 'I do not know if Kavanagh is going to produce his Guest Editor edition in January.'[31] After O'Donnell published his 'Suggestions for a Fighting Wake' editorial in July of 1947, which criticised official government censorship, Kavanagh responded with his poem 'The Wake of the Books'. This poem sets out Kavanagh's own peculiar views on censorship and echoes some of the concerns with which O'Donnell was preoccupied. Kavanagh even makes a reference to rural depopulation, a theme close to O'Donnell's heart and often mentioned in *The Bell*:

In my parish for twenty years
There isn't a marriage to sneer at.
The old unmarried people sneer at life,
While every writer has at least one wife.[32]

Although Séan O'Faoláin, Frank O'Connor and Austin Clarke all appear as characters in this poem, it is arguably Peadar O'Donnell's influence that most clearly informs Kavanagh's new-found political social conscience. Even if O'Donnell and O'Faoláin were not particularly well suited to evaluate poetry, they were ably assisted by a cast of poetry editors in *The Bell*, and perhaps chief among these was Geoffrey Taylor.

Geoffrey Taylor was born Geoffrey Phibbs in Norfolk, England in 1900, the eldest son of Basil Phibbs and Rebekah Wilberham Taylor, into a well-to-do Anglo-Irish landowner family whose country seat was in Lisheen, County Sligo.[33] The young Geoffrey began his schooling at Haileybury public school in Hertfordshire, where his passion for natural history was first inculcated. On leaving school, Phibbs served in the Officer Training Corps at Queens University Belfast, before leaving for Dublin to work as a demonstrator at the Royal College of Science. He also spent some time working with the Dublin Drama League, acting in Arthur Schnitzler's play *The Festival of Bacchus* at the Abbey Theatre in 1922.[34] It was during his time in Dublin that Phibbs began to receive recognition as a poet, having his early verses published by George Russell (AE) in *The Irish Statesman*. As with O'Faoláin, O'Connor and Kavanagh, Phibbs's relationship with AE was to prove the foundation on which his later literary success was built. It was around this time that Phibbs also switched profession, working instead for the newly founded (1913) Carnegie Trust Libraries in Ireland, under the directorship of Lennox Robinson.[35] During his time at the Carnegie Libraries Trust, Phibbs was based in several different locations across Ireland, including Enniskillen, Kilkenny and Wicklow. It was while at Wicklow in 1924 that Phibbs first met his new assistant Frank O'Connor. O'Connor had obtained his position in the library under Lennox Robinson's recommendation (whom he had known from his theatre days in Cork), and later that year both aspiring writers would have reason to fear for their positions after the dismissal of Lennox Robinson from his post for the publication of 'The Madonna of Slieve Dun' in *To-Morrow*. Phibbs and O'Connor were instantly drawn together by a shared love of poetry and through a rejection of what they perceived as the stifling atmosphere of reactionary Catholicism pervasive in Irish society.

O'Connor later remembered that he and Phibbs had called on AE to protest against the dismissal of their youthful manifesto against Yeats in *The Irish Statesman*. While there, O'Connor felt a growing sense of kinship with AE who 'put his arm around my shoulder and said, "send me something for the paper."'

I did, and he printed it.'[36] However, O'Connor was already being supported in his bid to become a writer by Phibbs who campaigned on his behalf with AE, as this letter of 1925 testifies: 'I like your verses on October Night and hope to get them into the Statesman. I think I have another one or two of yours which I hope to get in also. I would like to put in more verse, but the Irish Statesman is not a poetry magazine. I liked your friend O'Donovan's [Frank O'Connor] poem and will look forward to his book of stories.'[37] AE would later promote O'Connor to Macmillan where the young writer published his first collection *Guests of the Nation* in 1931. He wrote to them to say, 'He is a young man of very great talent, an admirable poet and something of a scholar ... I have come across no young Irish writer since in whose future I have more confidence.'[38]

Phibbs was also married on 15 April 1925 to a talented young Derry painter, Norah McGuinness, whom he met while she was at the Dublin Metropolitan School of Art. In 1924 Norah first exhibited at the Royal Hibernian Academy, and she was thought of highly enough to receive a personal telegram of congratulations from W.B. Yeats.[39] Yeats was sufficiently taken by Norah's talent to commission her to illustrate his *Stories of Red Hanrahan and the Secret Rose* (1927) and to design the set and costumes for his Abbey production of *Deirdre* in 1926.[40] Nora was being promoted within W.B. Yeats's selected circle and was present when O'Faoláin was first invited to the Yeats's Dublin home in 1927.[41] Phibbs and Norah lived together in a small cottage in Wicklow town 'with a garden and a fine view of the sea', where he was, remembered O'Connor, 'happier, more contented, than I had known him, and very proud of Norah'.[42] Their private and personal lives seemed to be going from strength to strength, with Phibbs finally negotiating the publication of his first collection of poems with the prestigious Hogarth Press.

Phibbs's initial collection, *The Withering of the Fig Leaf* (1927), was published by Leonard Woolf. However, at the last moment and under advice from AE, Phibbs requested that the book be suppressed because of its anti-Catholic sentiment, and the danger its publication would pose to his work for the Carnegie Library Trust.[43] Although the book was published, Woolf had it removed from the circulating libraries, thus denying it any chance of a wider audience. Phibbs published his next collection *It Was Not Jones* (1928) under the pseudonym of R. Fitzurse, one of the assassins of Catholic martyr St Thomas Becket. Leonard Woolf was sufficiently impressed by Phibbs's writing to publish this collection at Hogarth's own cost if Phibbs would agree to exchange five poems in the initial collection for five he had written at a later date:

> I can at last make you a definite proposition with regards to your poems. We would publish the book in our series at our expense and pay you a royalty of 10 per cent of the published price of all copies sold, provided that you would agree to the five poems which you sent me with your last letter being substituted for the five following poems

ENTERTAINMENT
TO MY FRIEND
REQUIRED ON THE ROAD TO PONTOON
   RED BANK GRILL ROOM
   ROMANTIC SURVIVAL.

Will you let me know what you think of this?
      Yours Sincerely
         Leonard Woolf.[44]

Norah's career was also going well, and she had been commissioned to do book illustrations with her London-based publishers. It was on one of her trips to London to see her publisher that Norah wrote to David Garnett, the son of Edward Garnett and a prominent member of the Bloomsbury group, promoting her husband's recent poems. Garnett responded to Norah and suggested they meet, and he expressed his delight at Phibbs's new work: 'I shall be in town to-morrow + Friday – free for lunch to-morrow ... But perhaps you will ring me up some time to-morrow morning after 11 o'clock + we could arrange to meet. I liked your husband's poems very much indeed. Some are very good indeed. I am rather excited about him.'[45] This meeting would prove fateful, as what followed was one of the most bizarre and controversial events involving an Irish author during the 1920s, and would eventually cost Norah her marriage.[46] It was during this trip to London that Norah began an affair with Garnett. Garnett who was 37 and older than Norah at 28, was also much more experienced – his lovers included, among others, the painter Duncan Grant, who was an influential member of the Bloomsbury group. At any rate, Norah was drawn to this bohemian figure, with impeccable credentials within the English literary firmament. However, his own insecurities drove him to compel Norah to tell Geoffrey of their affair. As chance would have it, on the day that Geoffrey received the terrible news of his wife's infidelity, he also received a letter from an American poet who was living in London and eager to make his acquaintance.

   This poet was Laura Riding, who was, by 1929, living with the poet, translator and novelist, Robert Graves. Graves and Riding were living together, along with Graves's wife Nancy Nicholson and their four children in a *ménage à trois* at their apartment in south-west London. Phibbs, flattered by the attention of a fellow writer and devastated by the news of his wife's infidelity, insisted on travelling to London that night to see Riding. Laura Riding was a troubled young woman, a talented poet with a mesmeric power over Graves who had been associated with the Fugitives, a literary movement in America.[47] Phibbs was accepted by Riding with enthusiasm, but Norah was pushed to one side. Riding would continue this pattern of destructive behaviour throughout her life with people who did not fit her immediate needs. Norah was left in a hotel

room by herself for three days, until she decided she could take no more isolation and departed for Wicklow: 'Geoffrey was received with open arms – I was
unimportant, an outsider and must be got rid off [*sic*].' Norah's rejection cul-
minated in the ritualised burning of all of Phibbs's effects to rid them of their
association with her. Phibbs stayed on with Graves, Riding and Nancy working
on a new poetic project together. At this time 'Robert Graves shared a bed with
Geoffrey and Laura – Nancy (Mrs. Graves) having been safely put on a barge
on the Thames with Robert's four children'.

   This unconventional new relationship lasted until Phibbs tired of Riding's
domineering personality and delusions of divinity. Riding insisted on being
made love to, turn by turn, by Graves and Phibbs in the same bed, above
which hung a sky blue tapestry embroidered with the words 'WOMAN IS GOD'.
Phibbs found this experience particularly disconcerting and it affected his ability to perform sexually.[48] Perhaps because of such demanding pressures Phibbs
fled from their company and decided to collect Norah to see if they could
redeem their marriage and escape to Rouen in France on a second honeymoon.
However, Riding was distressed at the loss of Phibbs and duped an aged old
aunt into betraying his whereabouts. Laura, Graves and Nancy arrived at the
hotel where Geoffrey and Norah were staying in order to convince them to
return to London. Norah would have nothing to do with Laura, and refused to
go outright. However, she could see that Geoffrey was torn, and on their return
to Ireland, she was aware that their marriage was doomed. According to Norah,
it was Phibbs's attraction to Hellenism that led to their split; he was forever
promoting the ideals of a sexually open marriage, but was unable to accept it in
actuality. He certainly felt that Christianity had to some degree destroyed society's ability to enjoy sex. In an early letter to Norah he was to declare that: 'Oh
Lord I wish we could get back to the Greeks when sex was known to be beautiful and recognised as clean.'[49] Frank O'Connor identified a trait in Phibbs's
personality that meant he was forever torn between his rational beliefs and his
true feelings: 'he was a man trapped by his own nature ... because in him the
gap between instinct and judgement was wider than it is in most of us, and he
simply could not jump it. With the two-thirds of him that was air and fire he
adopted new attitudes and new ideas, without ever realising how they contradicted conventions that were fundamental to himself.'[50] Phibbs acknowledged
this trait when he claimed that, 'at times I "thank God I am not as other men
are", but at times I rebel against my nature and would give a lot to be a little
more ordinary'.[51]

   On returning to Ireland they stayed at Geoffrey's parents' house in Lisheen,
where Geoffrey was taken ill with flu. However, Riding was not to be easily
dismissed and sent Nancy to convince him to return. Her arrival proved the
final straw for Norah, and for Geoffrey's father, for whom the shame was too
much to bear. He confronted them in the garden and 'shouted "Get out of my

grounds you scarlet woman"! Geoffrey then said he was so ashamed that, from that moment, he was changing his name from Phibbs to Taylor (his mother's name).' Geoffrey and Norah stayed together for a further three weeks before Norah told him she was returning to Paris to continue her studies. Phibbs went back to London, where, unusually for a cuckold, he stayed with David Garnett, and later returned to Riding, Graves and Nancy. Phibbs remained remarkably magnanimous about this whole period in his life and would even later go on to write a very supportive review of Graves, a man who hated him bitterly for interfering in his relationship with Riding.[52]

What followed was a bizarre and nearly fatal event which caused a great scandal among the London literary set. Phibbs decided that he could no longer live with Laura and Graves, and that he would instead live with Graves's wife Nancy and her four children, who had, at this stage, fallen in love with him. When this was announced and in a fit of dramatic hysterics, Riding drank a bottle of detergent and threw herself from a fourth storey window. Graves, distraught, ran to assist her and during his descent of the stairs decided he could no longer live without her, and threw himself from the third storey. Riding was nearly killed, and was able to walk only because of the intervention of a new technique for spinal surgery, Graves landed unharmed in the back garden. Phibbs, fearing for his life, fled the scene, but was picked up by the police later before being finally cleared of suspicion. According to Norah: 'Geoffrey and Nancy then hitched up for many years. Geoffrey told me "platonically". They lived in Wiltshire until Nancy told Geoffrey he should get married and produced a Welsh girl [Mary Dillwyn] whom he did marry and they came to live in Dublin when the war started.'[53] The somewhat unbelievable course of events that led to Phibbs's return to Ireland is of interest to scholars of *The Bell*. His literary connections and the path of his reading, led him to develop his tastes as an authority on English poetry.

Although this episode in Phibbs's life is dramatic, what is as important in any history of *The Bell* is his time in Ireland between the outbreak of war and his premature death in 1956 from a second heart attack. His close friend John Betjeman was saddened to hear of his illness, and wrote to him to sympathise: 'I am so sad to hear of your heart attack, it is a most unexpected thing in one so lithe [at the time of his first marriage Geoffrey was 6 foot 2 inches and 11 stone 2 pounds] and spare and calm as you.' Betjeman was devastated by his death, and one of Phibbs's last literary actions was to approve the preface to *English Love Poems* (1957), a book he co-edited with Betjeman.[54] This collection and his selections in *The Bell* demonstrate his traditional and conservative tastes in poetry (as distinct from his more unconventional love life), although he was capable of supporting more experimental works, such as Nick Nichols's 'The Bone and Flower'. His real strength lay in his encyclopaedic knowledge of obscure or minor poets from the eighteenth and nineteenth centuries, doing much to recover authors such as William Allingham, for example. The years of *The Bell* were ones of exceptional productivity for Phibbs, and after his turbulent time in London show him as a mature and settled author.[55] Phibbs took over O'Connor's role as poetry editor for *The Bell* in the summer of 1941.[56] It was also a period where he was able to exploit his prestige as a writer of the Bloomsbury set, to attract poets of considerable quality to the magazine. However, his involvement with *The Bell* came to an abrupt close over a controversy involving another Irish author of considerable stature, Austin Clarke.

Clarke was O'Faoláin's senior by four years and had already published a substantial body of work by the time *The Bell* first appeared in 1940. As an established literary figure in Ireland in that period, he is conspicuous by his relative obscurity in the pages of *The Bell*, having only published one poem, two articles and three book reviews over the course of its life. Clarke's absence can be explained by the imperious attitude with which O'Faoláin dominated the magazine in its early years. Vivian Mercier noted this contradiction with O'Faoláin's editorial style in his own analysis of *The Bell* printed as part of the series 'The Fourth Estate': 'I lack the moral courage to tell the Editor all those dreadful things I've been thinking about him. For Seán O'Faoláin *is* The Bell. He is not just a figurehead – he is the magazine as you find out after, or before, you have written one article for it.'[57] Of course, an article in *The Bell* criticising its editorial methods demonstrates the success of those methods to some extent, but it also tells us something about how O'Faoláin was perceived by other writers. His total control over what was Ireland's most established and influential literary journal was not unnoticed by his peers and raised resentment towards him, often with some degree of merit, as Austin Clarke was to discover.

In the build-up to Christmas 1936, O'Faoláin was busy working from his home in County Wicklow trying to organise 'an anthology of Irish verse, chiefly for the use of schools here'. With this in mind, he approached Clarke asking if it were possible to 'print three of your poems', but forewarning him that the fee was small and copyright was to be paid by him directly: 'I am allotted the usual small fee for editing AND payment of copyright fees, so be gentle with me, but, of course, I must pay something.'[58] O'Faoláin was also sorry to hear of Clarke's resignation from the Irish Academy of Letters and placed more emphasis on this than on the formality of asking Clarke for the use of his poems. However, Clarke's response was not as straightforward as O'Faoláin would have wished. Instead, Clarke interrogated him on the specifics of the volume and the exact details of the fees involved, wishing to know what other writers had accepted and which publisher had agreed to his terms. O'Faoláin was recognisably piqued by this request, but wished to reassure Clarke that he was not profiting excessively from the collection, so he replied giving a full breakdown of the contents layout and the financial details of his contract. To demonstrate his goodwill he also conceded to Clarke the fee of three guineas, which he refused to grant to any other poet, and, as if to demonstrate the insignificance of his request, listed those who had already agreed: 'I have so far received permission from Yeats, Gogarty, Joyce, Strong, Higgins, O'Connor, O'Sullivan, Monk Gibbon, Kavanagh, MacNeice, MacGreevy, – and others living and dead; all, without exception, on the terms I have stated. So to be persistent ... May I have something of yours, the selection I am quite content to leave to yourself, at any fee up to even the three guineas I would not give to [Joe] Campbell? And there is NO mystery about the book, as you see.'[59] However, Clarke was not convinced, instead seeing this proposed schools anthology as an operation in political one-upmanship and a transgression of his artistic integrity.

O'Faoláin was shocked by Clarke's reticence and again wrote to explain his terms by the end of the letter appealing to Clarke's sense of duty towards a fellow writer and to Irish letters in general:

> we are trying to find a modus vivendi between rank individualism and going with the mob. So don't be so bloody uppish and insulting. You can save your soul any damn way you like but it's not the only way, and we (or I) must find our own ways. I'm fed up with people who can't realise that in a critical period we simply HAVE TO find a common ground of agreement by accommodating our own egos to one another – so don't lord it over me, blast you. Let's pull together, for God's sake, and not all living on mountain tops, I'm as Irish as you so go to hell. Meanwhile, do say what about those poems. Yours more or less amicably, Seán O'Faoláin.[60]

This letter is important for reasons outside the relationship between Clarke and O'Faoláin, in that it touches on some of the themes which would become so significant in *The Bell*. O'Faoláin's claim that he was as Irish as Clarke articulates a sense of the restrictive identities which he felt were limiting the Irish writer. It also demonstrates a genuine belief in fraternity and goodwill towards other writers who were struggling to make their way through their craft. *The Bell* strove to be inclusive, opening a new market in domestic writing, and trying to find common ground with a vast selection of different writers. This policy led the magazine to be far more eclectic and catholic in its tastes than other literary magazines and also accounts for its popularity and endurance within the Irish literary psyche. Despite O'Faoláin's appeals for solidarity, Clarke could not resist the opportunity of refusing his request, citing seemingly spurious concerns about the danger to his artistic integrity posed by what was supposed to be a simple Irish school book, celebrating the best of Irish writers. Its tone of self-aggrandising importance is notable:

> I am afraid that you have not really considered my point of view in this matter. I am recognised as an antoity [authority] on Irish verse and in particular its Gaelic aspects, both in this country and elsewhere ... In plain words you are asking me

to stand aside, while you, as a novelist, place contemporary Irish poets in their proper rank and air your opinions at length. It has not even occurred to you that later on I might find myself, as a critic, in the absurd position of having to condemn the main argument to which I had lent my name. I realise that my complete refusal to allow you to quote my work must injure the validity of the book, since my Collected Poems spans the years 1917 to 1936. But you should have foreseen all this, before you decided to rush in where we poets fear to tread. The trouble about Dublin is that everyone wants to do the other fellows [*sic*] job instead of their own. We are all waiting for the present generation to produce the really big novel so why not make that your ambition. I regret that I cannot accede to your wishes and as far as I am concerned the matter is entirely closed.[61]

Clarke's letter, even now, seems highly confrontational and condescending, considering his own evaluation of himself as the foremost authority on Irish poetry, and that any collection of Irish poetry would be impossible without his inclusion.

O'Faoláin was understandably incensed; he had been writing successfully for many years by 1936, and was an established author with an international reputation. If anything, this whole series of correspondence demonstrates why O'Faoláin excelled where others faltered. His earlier quip about J.J. O'Leary at Cahill's Press having: 'the flair for spotting the urgency of a public need, and his salesman's skill in simultaneously promoting himself as the best man to fulfil it' could as easily be applied to his own character.[62] He worked incredibly hard and was continuously engaging other writers and advising them on opportunities to publish, as he did with Clarke. Clarke's rejection of an opportunity to appear in a school book, with its captive audience and high publication numbers, must have seemed utterly incomprehensible to the even-tempered and pragmatic O'Faoláin. However, Clarke's condescending tone, to a man as proud of his achievements and as socially conscious as O'Faoláin, would have been too much to bear. His reply was delivered in a typically cool manner, although it cannot but betray O'Faoláin's disgust:

It has been a painful experience for me to offer you ordinary friendliness and to be met with a mixture of highfalutin nonsense, and toploftical contempt. I cannot finish, however, without saying that whatever personal objection you may have to me your tone, and attitude is not that of a common literary esprit de corps – if you understand the term at all.

O'Faoláin then took exception to Clarke's suggestion that he should stick to what he knew best and write novels:

had there been an airing of views am I to be told by you, who have written novels, and criticised novels, and no doubt lectured on novels, that I may not criticise poetry? Have I trained myself in three universities, taken three degrees, two fellowships, and lectured in three countries on literature to be now confined by you to one kind of thing only? You would move me to improper repartee if I did not control a most natural irritation at your insolence.[63]

This rift may go some way to explaining the championing of Patrick Kavanagh as the pre-eminent Irish poet in *The Bell* at a cost to Clarke. However, O'Faoláin's anger had subsided by the time that *The Bell* opened, four years later. Although their relationship remained tentative O'Faoláin was still willing to let Clarke publish in *The Bell*, and felt that Clarke's talent would enhance the publication sufficiently to ask him directly for contributions: 'I wrote you; but a certain timidity kept the letter around for so long that I cannot tell if it has been lost or is posted … Would you let us, at any rate, see the poems?'[64] However, Clarke's presence in *The Bell* should not be read as evidence of a clear reconciliation between the two writers. Rather, it speaks to that duality of mind that allowed O'Faoláin to differentiate between his role as an editor and his work as a writer. If O'Faoláin was initially reluctant to publish Clarke, there are clear reasons why none of his poetry was present while Frank O'Connor was poetry editor. O'Connor reserved a deep dislike for Clarke, and believed his caustic personality was affecting his writing: 'Forgive my comments on Clarke. They were not intended seriously. The truth is I loathe and detest the man and that stems from the Yeats days when he pursued the Old Man with his hatred and spleen. I have the good attitude to literature; it's written by good guys and the better the guy the better it's likely to be for the literature.'[65] Despite O'Connor's strong feelings, O'Faoláin was capable at times of temporarily putting pragmatics before principles when it came to running his magazine and of publishing quality as his first concern.

Although O'Faoláin wanted submissions of Clarke's quality, he could also be insistent on suiting his own particular tastes. Naturally, this led to some degree of resentment among writers who had submitted work to *The Bell*. The strength of its articles and the names associated with it meant it was the prestige journal of letters in Ireland during its print run. O'Faoláin had no difficulty in rejecting those whom he felt were not suitable for publication, even if they were also writers of some repute, as this rejection letter to Brinsley MacNamara shows:

> I know perfectly well that you will be not merely angry with me but disgusted when I say that I did not re-act perfectly to THE HOTEL. It has a lovely theme, and the last line is of a poignancy that sums up the whole subject. But, with my frail, and possibly erring judgement, I feel that the journey is not in itself interesting enough. What can I do? I must rely on my own re-action. Another's may be different … I am very grateful for being given first refusal – if that doesn't sound like a Cork compliment: double-edged.[66]

The rejection of a writer as established as MacNamara on artistic grounds may seem a little fickle on behalf of O'Faoláin. Perhaps there is even an element of irony in the fact that an editor who would campaign so vociferously on

MacNamara's behalf in his fight against censorship would deny him a voice in his own magazine. O'Faoláin's rejection letter is not unlike Clarke's refusal, in appealing to a nebulous set of artistic criteria that are never sufficiently defined. Obviously, in O'Faoláin's case, *The Bell* must have rejected good writers as a matter of course and such incidences should be expected. Austin Clarke seems to have been one of the prime movers in a group that felt itself scorned by O'Faoláin. However, he was not the only one to feel that O'Faoláin was acting like a self-appointed censor for Irish artists, as Frank MacManus was to complain to Sean O'Casey: 'Frank O'Connor reminds me of Seán O'Faoláin, who also helps visiting journalists to compile lists of writers, [always] the same lists. O'Connor and O'Faoláin first, and then the inevitable Paddy Kavanagh, with his two little books, and [Valentin] Iremonger. Nobody else.'[67] O'Faoláin's high-handed editorial style, coupled with his own obvious personal success and foreign recognition was perhaps too much for many of Dublin's writers. This also would not be the last time O'Faoláin's personality would be cited as the cause of a rupture among *The Bell*'s writers.

If this exchange between Clarke and O'Faoláin left the latter feeling that Clarke was not showing artistic solidarity, it would leave Clarke feeling as if he were being persecuted. On 30 May 1945, Geoffrey (Phibbs) Taylor wrote to Clarke asking him for a poem to include in the next edition of *The Bell*. The July issue was to be a special international number and, for Taylor, Clarke represented 'the only established Irish poet whose work is comparable to that of established English or American poets (one can't really count Robert Graves)'.[68] Clarke sent his poem 'The Lucky Coin', and it was published alongside a review, 'Irish Literature To-Day' by Seán O'Faoláin's friend Professor John V. Kelleher of Harvard University.[69] After its publication, Clarke wrote to Taylor complaining that his poem had been misprinted and that O'Faoláin had deliberately suppressed a positive reference to him in Professor Kelleher's article, which had originally been published in the *Atlantic Monthly*. For Taylor, O'Faoláin's actions had compromised him and his ability to act as a fair critic of Irish poetry. O'Faoláin had also suppressed a footnote explaining who Clarke was, which was present for all other contributors in the issue. Taylor wrote to Clarke immediately to apologise: 'I think the misprint in your poem must have been a genuine mistake. Certainly I am technically responsible, and needn't tell you that I am exceedingly sorry … To your poem I had simply written this footnote: – "Austin Clarke is the most distinguished living Irish poet". I was surprised and slightly irritated to find that this had not been printed. Combined with what you now tell me about suppressing the reference to you in Kelleher's article, it seems that I must be rather more than irritated.'[70] Taylor decided that his position at *The Bell* no longer remained tenable, and determined to resign with effect from the September issue (he would later take up the position of poetry editor for *Time and Tide* between 1954–56).

He wrote to O'Faoláin to indicate his intent, and posted a copy to Clarke as well:

> Beyond the increasing lack of sympathy on my side the fact that determines my resignation at this particular moment is your treatment of Austin Clarke in the July 'International' Number. I was mildly irritated that you should have dropped my note about A.C. being the most distinguished living Irish poet – but then, I have stopped worrying about occasions of mild irritation. I now hear, however, that you deleted a laudatory reference to Austin Clarke which appeared in Kelleher's original article in the Atlantic Monthly. The combination of these two deletions makes something which is really inexplicable on any grounds that I should think excusable.[71]

It seemed that for O'Faoláin revenge was a dish best served cold, and the suppression of Clarke in *The Bell* was something he actively pursued. Clarke's bad experience with *The Bell* continued under O'Donnell's editorship when he was involved with the retirement of another of its editors. Hubert Butler, Anglo-Irish writer, intellectual and regular contributor to the journal was books editor from May 1951 to December 1952 when he also resigned because a submission by Clarke was omitted from the journal. He wrote to Clarke to explain that he was ending his association with the magazine because of O'Donnell's haphazard editorial style: 'I am sorry that your review was not published in this issue of THE BELL. It was sent up weeks ago with nine others for inclusion. I disclaim all responsibility for the current book section which appears under my name … I do not know when your review will be now published as my connection with THE BELL ends with this issue.'[72] This series of letters demonstrates that although the proximity of this core of writers to each other could prove a strength, it also had its drawbacks.

O'Faoláin's active suppression of Clarke shows that he was less averse to censorship than he is remembered for; it also shows Clarke at his most contentious. Geoffrey Taylor's thanks for resigning in his honour was a dismissive review of his work *Irish Poets of the Nineteenth Century* (1951) by Clarke in the *Irish Times*.[73] This review began a series of public exchanges that degenerated into complete farce when the two poets ended up debating the historical precedents for rhyming 'shove' with 'love'.[74] Such intellectual vanity and public debate over personal scores was commonplace among the writers of the time, both in *The Bell* itself, and in other publications. Although these debates denigrated the work of the artist by reducing it to the level of the petty, it was also exactly the type of material on which journal culture thrived and showed the level of interdependence between journals, newspaper publications and books.[75] A large section of *The Bell* was devoted to book reviews, and the debates that appear in its pages were informed by other public fora, such as lectures, public debates and print media. Although these private and public exchanges are petty in the extreme, they do help to depict the atmosphere in which O'Faoláin and other writers of his generation were operating. The sense of isolation and frustration is palpable within them, and it manifests itself in these pathetic squabbles.

The *Bell*'s literary achievements are real. However, it must be remembered that its legacy is often evaluated through the prism of the younger writers who published in its pages. As a result, the thrust of their reminiscences is often about the difficulties created by state censorship of publishing, and on the various literary personalities that collected around the journal. Its political legacy has faded into the background as a result of this viewpoint, even though many of its readers must have enjoyed the insightful political arguments within its pages. O'Donnell's contribution to this is vitally important. Although O'Faoláin wrote his most outwardly political works in *The Bell*, and the spirit of the Mass Observation movement he endorsed was also a form of political statement, it is O'Donnell whose convictions provide the foundation for *The Bell*'s political writings. Censorship became a cause célèbre among the writers and critics of *The Bell*, yet there are as many articles arguing about turf-cutting, emigration or land reform. These articles, along with descriptions of occupations, family budgets and criticism of the government form a large part of *The Bell*'s identity, and must account for some of its appeal.

Accounts of the Irish experience of censorship during the build-up to, and during, the Second World War often emphasise the draconian nature of the Censorship of Publications Bill 1928 and the avid zeal with which the Censorship of Publications Board executed its duties. However, the censorship of immoral or obscene publications was an issue of concern for most sovereign nations at that time, and Irish censorship should be seen in this wider international context rather than as an issue of isolated intolerance. Some of the more recent scholarship has gone some way to redressing this imbalance and attempts to situate Irish censorship in a world where *Lady Chatterley's Lover* (1928) could remain banned in Great Britain until 1960, or Australia would ban 5,000 books between 1929 and 1936.[76] Nor was it the case that history moved continuously from a conservative and censorious past to a liberal and secular future. In 1954 the cartoonist Donald McGill was successfully charged under the 1857 Obscene Publications Act for his saucy seaside postcards in a vice crackdown by Winston Churchill's post-war Conservative government; he had been producing these cards for fifty years at the time of his prosecution.[77] As a correlation to this narrow focus on the excesses of Irish censorship, the principal figures involved have become polarised into champions of civil liberty or reactionary conservatives. It is in this light that O'Faoláin and *The Bell* become so important to the historiography surrounding Irish censorship.[78] *The Bell*, and O'Faoláin in particular, have come to represent the vanguard of a liberal civic consciousness, battling oppressive state control. However, O'Faoláin's attitude to censorship, and his role in challenging it, are much more complex than such a simple reading would imply. Literary censorship, specifically, was not a major issue for the majority of the Irish population during this time, and it is hard to gauge just how much impact it had on the lives of ordinary working men and women, especially considering the centrality of other media such as newspapers and the cinema to the Irish cultural scene. Similarly, O'Faoláin's own attitude to censorship is much more layered than simple direct opposition, and the arguments he developed against it deserve closer attention.

From today's perspective, censorship in Ireland can seem extremely harsh, or frustratingly inane. Books were banned that would hardly have caused a stir in their own day, let alone to our more jaded modern perspective, while novels like James Joyce's *Ulysses* (1922) would pass unnoticed. However, it is important to remember that the need for censorship was, on the whole, broadly accepted and there were as many intellectuals arguing for its enforcement as against it. In November of 1935 O'Faoláin attended a meeting of the PEN Club at Jury's Hotel in Dublin.[79] During this meeting O'Faoláin put forth the proposition that: 'This meeting is of the opinion that the Censorship Board has exceeded its powers.' He wanted to point out that Irish artists and many members of PEN had suffered unnecessarily under censorship, and that 'a number of books of literary and artistic value had been banned without it being made plain that the writer was conniving at evil for its own sake, and they had been censored without regard to their literary and artistic merit'. It is noticeable that O'Faoláin's argument never directly questioned the validity of state censorship, just its application, and the disregard for the effect on authors' lives and the artistic value of the work when considered as a whole.

O'Faoláin was opposed by University College Cork's Professor James Hogan, who made a barbed reference to O'Faoláin's abandonment of his roots by claiming that 'living in Cork, of course, he had not been in touch with the books that had been banned by the censorship board'. Hogan, who in the same year published his attack on Peadar O'Donnell, *Could Ireland Become Communist?* (1935), denied that artistic freedom was any criterion for the production of literature. For him, society had always needed some form of restraint akin to censorship and he claimed that most indecent books were written with the intention of increasing sales. Hogan's argument was based on a strong Catholic ethic, and his logic is sound if one accepts its first principles: 'Salvation was the most important thing in the world, and no person who accepted the Catholic point of view would place the claims of Art above those of morality, truth and goodness.' The incident then led to a series of claims and counterclaims from the members, and O'Faoláin was forced to withdraw the motion before PEN settled on a compromise agreement which recognised that: 'various and contrary views were held regarding the principles involved in the Censorship of Publications Act, [but PEN] would express no collective judgement'.[80]

What this incident demonstrated was that there was no clear-cut consensus on censorship, even among a group whose livelihood it directly threatened in a writers' organisation like PEN, and that there was no shortage of educated intellectual support for censorship. The meeting also highlighted the Roman Catholic morality which informed decisions about what was, on the whole, 'indecent' and how this morality framed the lives of the majority of Ireland's inhabitants. There was in the Ireland of this period a popular intellectual Catholic avant-garde which has been largely ignored by historians in preference to the liberal political outlook as favoured by *The Bell*. This movement of Catholic revivalism was at the time competing equally with other discourses about the direction which Irish society should take.[81]

Two months after the banning of *Bird Alone* (1936) O'Faoláin published 'The Dangers of Censorship' in *Ireland To-Day*. This article does not criticise censorship in itself, but rather its execution: 'We do not (apart from the disgraceful absence of any machinery of appeal) object to the Censorship Act. We object to the censors who have exploited it with a stupidity amounting to malevolence.' For O'Faoláin, this stupid, indifferent trend in the Censorship Board was due to the conflation of two reactionary forces, nationalism and unreflective Catholicism: 'the combination of forces which is at present most active here in supporting such prohibitory ordinances as the Censorship Act is a combination of the Gaelic Revivalist which fears the influences of a European, and especially English, Literature (for nationalistic reasons) and the Catholic Actionist which fears the same influences (for pious reasons). Their motives are the best. Their methods are the worst.' The forces which drove this censorship were willing conspirators in sustaining ignorance among the population, which denied them the education to 'live and choose wisely' in their morality.[82] So, for O'Faoláin, the crux of his argument came not in criticism of the idea of censorship, but on the deadening effect that it imposed on society. This distinction would form the main thrust of his subsequent attacks in *The Bell*, and are in line with his thinking on a 'thinly-composed' society. What was being retarded by censorship was not the individual's right to free speech, but the development of society as a whole.

O'Faoláin was even, on rare occasions, capable of demonstrating his support of censorship, as when Frank O'Connor attacked him for describing it as 'natural' and 'easy to forgive'.[83] O'Faoláin also chose to support the banning of a particular edition of Daniel Defoe's *Roxana* by an American publisher. In December of 1957 O'Faoláin wrote to the *Irish Times* explaining the nature of the ban. The book had not been banned entirely, but one 'cheap, luridly-presented, American, Paper-back' edition had been prohibited because its publishers were not 'selling literature. They are insulting it by trying to make it look like pornography. These people are confusing the whole issue for all those of us who are honestly concerned with the difficult problem of reconciling individual liberty, the dignity of letters, public taste and morality and respect for the law of the land.'[84] Although O'Faoláin's appeals to the edification of the populace by a reduction in the severity of censorship and protection from pornography are justifiable in their own terms, they are not unproblematic.

O'Faoláin's own work is a good case in point. In the title story from his first collection *Midsummer Night Madness* (1932), O'Faoláin tells the tale of a young republican gunman sent into the countryside to see why one of the IRA battalions, headed by his friend Stevie Long, had been inactive for so long. The story unfolds, about a young girl named Gypsy who is pregnant by Stevie but living in the gate-house on a landed estate owned by an old Anglo-Irish man called Henn. Henn has being paying visits to Gypsy and proposing to marry her, even though she is in love with Stevie. When Stevie hears of Gypsy's pregnancy he gathers his battalion and threatens to burn the estate to the ground unless Henn marries her and claims the child for his own. Such a story would have been controversial in Ireland of 1932 because of its depiction of an IRA battalion leader in a cowardly and vicious light. Yet what is really remarkable is a passage in the text that is explicitly voyeuristic in its descriptions of a sexual act. In it, the narrator follows old man Henn down to the gatehouse as he attempts to solicit sexual favours from Gypsy, despite his impotence. O'Faoláin describes the development of the scene in graphic detail, as the narrator watches silently through the window as Henn masturbates the weeping young girl:

> To which of these men, I wondered, had this girl given herself? For now with her hair dragged on the ridge of her chair and her head falling lower and lower on her bosom until her eyes caught in the embers of the fire, she permitted him to move aside her skirt, ever so little, from her bare knee, and caress it with his withered hand as softly as if it were swans-down, caress it even after the glow of the fire shone on her eyes drowned in tears, caress it while she sat rigid with misery, her moans breaking out in trembling waves to the whispering night outside. And yet not a stir or word from Henn, but as if hoping that his old hand could quiet her childlike sobs, he caressed and caressed and looked and looked dog-like into her face. Alas! each exhausted sigh was but a prelude to a new shuddering burst of tears like waves that are silent for a while and then burst suddenly and inevitably on the shore.[85]

Although distinct from the rest of the collection, this passage raises concerns for O'Faolain's writing as a whole. O'Faoláin was a shrewd reader of the Irish political atmosphere, and under a censorship which would later famously ban Kate O'Brien's *The Land of Spices* (1941) for one sentence alluding to homosexuality, he must have known a passage so vividly descriptive would be noticed and viewed unsympathetically by the censors. It is difficult to accept O'Faoláin's denunciation of 'pornography', as distinct from literature, in such light, or give credence to his claims that he was balancing a 'respect for the laws of the land', as this passage would clearly have been considered 'indecent' by any member of the censorship board. Its foreword by Edward Garnett, which explicitly, and incorrectly, attacked Irish censorship and Ireland as 'the most backward nation in Europe', makes *Midsummer Night Madness* all the more provocative, and would suggest that O'Faoláin was trying to get banned.[86] O'Faoláin's principled rejection of pornography is also a little difficult to accept as entirely honest, considering he began an eleven-year association when he wrote for *Playboy* magazine in January 1969, while the rest of the country would have to wait twenty-seven more years to see it even stacked on their shelves.[87]

Midsummer Night Madness must also be seen in the light of developments within the American and European novel. O'Faoláin must have felt that he was being quite constrained in his depiction of sex, considering that Henry Miller's *Tropic of Cancer* (1934) was published just two years later. However, O'Faoláin felt that such openly expressive sexual aggression was an artistic dead end.[88] As such, the sexual descriptions in *Midsummer Night Madness* can also be read as a response to the advanced levels of sexually explicit material already available in European literature. Yet, despite these inconsistencies, O'Faoláin's denunciations of state censorship in *The Bell* were frequent and insightful. O'Faoláin also encouraged other writers to express themselves clearly on their interpretation of censorship and its value to Irish society. C.B. Murphy wrote an article in September 1941 that started a debate which continued in *The Bell* over the next year. Murphy was writing because he was incensed by a review of Kate O'Brien's *Without My Cloak* (1931) in an unnamed Irish Catholic periodical, that condemned it on the grounds that it 'flaunts sexual sin, in all its seductive details', despite the fact that the book had already been reviewed by an English priest in a reputable Catholic journal as a welcome contribution to Catholic literature. Murphy explicitly disagreed with O'Faoláin's assertion that the values of society needed to be built from the bottom up; he felt that existing Catholic doctrine on indecent literature was a sufficient guide through what should be censored. What he objected to was the hijacking of Catholic teaching by pious lay advocates who conflated sex in all forms with a type of immorality. Murphy was keen to point out an irony that the native Catholic class, which was so zealous in denying literature as foreign to Irish ways and indecent in tendency, was expressing a particular form of English Victorian morality which carried over from English rule in Ireland. For him, 'the modern Irish tendency to evade sex in speech and writing is merely a hang-over from the Victorianism which is bound up with English at the time when it became the common language of Ireland'.

This inversion of the argument for censorship was the most consistent form of attack against it in *The Bell*. O'Faoláin's line of reasoning was to demonstrate that Catholics in other countries often found the material edifying, and that Roman Catholic doctrine already had mechanisms for dealing with such literature. This analysis, along with his assertion that censorship numbed the public consciousness, offered a more subtle break from the previous charges against censorship on grounds of artistic freedom, and demonstrated O'Faoláin's attempt to use the weapons of the Catholic actionists against themselves. Murphy's article showed that there were no good Catholic arguments against the disparagement, let alone banning of Kate O'Brien's work. For him: 'no Irish priest, who knows his theology, can insist that the censorship binds Catholics in conscience, and we know that legal obligations divorced from conscience get a thin time of it in Ireland'.[89]

Closely following Murphy's article was O'Faoláin's editorial, 'Beginnings and Blind Alleys' (October 1941). This article shows how O'Faoláin's attitude to his own role within Irish society was developing, and how he was beginning to see himself as a grand old man of Irish letters whose objective was to attack the false pieties of the middle classes. In this capacity O'Faoláin once again inserted himself among esteemed companions within the European tradition:

> As for the Middle Classes, if once they become consolidated here nothing can be done for them. Every country in Europe has, in time, found that out. A Flaubert will spend his life excoriating them; a Balzac fill volumes with their pathetic fol-lies; a Shaw will mock them without rest: ossified by an innate dread of insecurity – their hall-mark everywhere – they remain immovable until some cataclysm scatters them utterly, when they as assuredly slowly gather together again around that old nucleus of their Fear.[90]

O'Faoláin was obviously eager to see himself as directly part of this esteemed lineage and he filled his own journal with accounts of their pathetic follies, as his resignation letter to *The Bell* makes clear: 'I have, I confess, grown a little weary of abusing our bourgeoisie, Little Islanders, chauvinists, puritans, stuffed-shirts, pietists, Tartuffes, Anglophobes, Celtophiles, *et alii hujus gen-eris*.'[91] This conviction that O'Faoláin should fill the public role as a moral authority in line with a European ideal is at least as strong an impulse in his campaign against censorship as his own experience of its effects on Irish writers and their public. It is also the reason why O'Faoláin would use increasingly sophisticated arguments in his attacks, in an attempt to gather a liberal and pro-gressive body of work around his own position in *The Bell*, forming a consensus of 'correct' attitudes to censorship. That the debates surrounding censorship in *The Bell* were allowed to flourish shows that the Act was focused on sexually explicit material and discussions of the war, especially considering that *The Bell* itself had to submit draft copies to the censor. O'Faoláin complained to O'Connor that, 'two copies of everything goes to him before publication', thus demonstrating that if certain topics were off limits then criticism of the Act itself was not.[92]

To counteract this bias towards articles critical of censorship, O'Faoláin solicited the poet and author Monk Gibbon to write in defence of the princi-ple, if not its application in an Irish context. Gibbon captured the antagonism towards censorship among a certain class of intellectuals at that time. When he told his friends he was writing an article on censorship they exposed their bias by claiming: 'But it's useless. It has been attacked so often already.' For Gibbon, this unexamined antagonism was a form of 'intellectual anaemia', and any serious debate about censorship deserved clear critical attention. Gibbon began by laying out his terms for discussion; he assumed that books and ideas can influence society, despite the lack of a definitive causal link between the two. He suggested that societies were capable of degeneration, with a gradual lowering of their vital energy through a breakdown of their values. Gibbon claimed that, historically, societies had always fought to maintain their values and for him this was a universal truth. The attitude of two institutions, in particular, demonstrated the link between writing's influence and the need for censorship:

> If we can see that social deterioration is a historical fact certain relevant questions follow. Do writers cause or contribute to such deterioration, does youth accept its conception of things from them and have they the power to mould a new generation? Two realistic institutions, the U.S.S.R. and the Roman Catholic Church, have both consistently made it plain that in their opinion certain authors and certain books are better left unread. That writers influence current mentality, if not current morality, seems to me proved to the hilt.

Gibbon followed this assertion by claiming that the modern novel had lost its way, and its only guiding morality was the destruction of all morality. Such nihilistic tendencies in contemporary art debase the human experience and do no service to art itself: 'Just as the militant communist deprecates the use of force in any hands but his own, denouncing it as tyranny, so a certain type of modern novelist who would pour scorn on the "goody-goody" novel of the last century, never ceases to preach, indirectly, the doctrine of boredom, the principle of having no principle.' This lack of morality is coupled with a case of special pleading in the modern novel that undermines the artist's claims to be persecuted by censorship.

For Gibbon, the modern novel is scarcely more than a social pamphlet, and with a nod to the Auden generation he claimed: 'Writers are not artists, they are propagandists for a particular point of view. Poets tend to be communist firstly and poets, if at all, secondly. Novelists preach psycho-analysis, or cynicism, or promiscuity, and the artist in them, if he ever existed, is overwhelmed by the preacher. The threat of censorship to the work of art is certainly no greater than the threat from sophistication.'[93] For Gibbon, the modern novel was in a similar precarious position to the one O'Faoláin had articulated in his 'Pigeon-Holing The Modern Novel' in 1935.[94] Both authors felt the modern novel was under threat from a new materialism, yet they drew different conclusions as to what could be done about it. O'Faoláin hoped a new spiritual or Catholic morality could reinvigorate the novel and Gibbon felt censorship was necessary to protect society from the worst effects of artistic cynicism. For Gibbon, as with O'Donnell before him, when deciding between life and art, one should err on the side of life: 'but to regard virgins and boys as a negligible consideration, and a single novel or novelist as a matter of supreme importance, would show that we are losing our sense of proportion'.[95] Despite a strong similarity between Gibbon's and O'Faoláin's pessimistic outlook, this article proved the perfect straw man for O'Faoláin and he seems to have led Gibbon astray in asking for an article in defence of censorship. He commissioned several of the most famous names in literature to criticise Gibbon's position, and he started with a reply from George Bernard Shaw.

Shaw's presence in *The Bell* is perhaps something of a surprise. He had written to O'Faoláin saying he would be willing to subscribe to *The Bell*, but was prevented from sending money to Ireland without justifying his purposes to the British government. In a postcard to O'Faoláin he wrote:

> I should be very willing to subscribe to The Bell for the period of my expectation of life – say thirty shillings non-returnable in case The Bell should cease to ring within that period – but the British Government will not permit me to export money to Eire without an investigation of my purposes for which I cannot spare the time. Will you therefore put me on a free list as a fellow journalist and distinguished Eirishman, and pray that you may presently be rewarded by Providence.[96]

Shaw's request seemed reasonable, considering a war had started and he was an old man of 84 in 1940. However, O'Faoláin used Shaw's reputation as a literary giant to promote *The Bell*, and published a facsimile copy of the letter as a handout in December of 1940. Such shameless use of Shaw's reputation is understandable in a start-up journal which purported to be something new, and there is a healthy irreverence towards Shaw and his achievements. Yet the abridged version that O'Faoláin chose to publish points to an irritation with Shaw's request for a subscription gratis, and attempts to portray him in a mean-spirited light. As such, it is surprising that Shaw would agree to publish a reply to Gibbon in *The Bell*, but this indicates that perhaps his request for a free subscription was granted.

Shaw began his analysis by arguing that all societies are, in ways, proscribed against individual liberty. In fact, society itself is a form of contract between individuals and its other members to restrict certain freedoms. For Shaw this was natural, but caused a major difficulty in that 'civilisation obstructs and penalises all changes; and without change there can be no development. What we call progress depends on the toleration of novel and unexpected behaviour and doctrine.' Shaw's Fabianism is evident here, as he sees history as a progression towards a better society. Shaw's solution to censorship was to trust to the licensing system used in control of the professions, such as the doctors' register and publicans' licences. This system Shaw saw as flawed, and a great number of abuses had been executed in its name, yet it was a human solution in a human world. For Shaw, censorship caused more problems than it resolved, but he was grateful that most censorship happened in the human mind instinctively, rather than through official channels: 'civilised official censorship raises a hundred problems instead of one, and it would be impossible were it not that the great mass of its work is done by the human conscience spontaneously, and never comes into court at all'.[97] This article was Shaw's only contribution to *The Bell*, and it is more insightful about Shaw's own world-view than it is about the particulars of Irish censorship. However, it does demonstrate the reputation which *The Bell* had developed after its first five years in operation that it could draw writers of this calibre. As further evidence of this, and of the contentious nature of Gibbon's article, Sean O'Casey also published a reply.

O'Casey was much more irritated by Gibbon's defence of censorship. For him, the argument was 'a comic medley of fright, fear, superstition, faint piety, greek fire, and a cool desire to keep on the lee side of the counts, knights, and esquires of the Holy Roman Empire'. O'Casey's anger is palpable throughout his criticism of Gibbon. Like Shaw before him, O'Casey's politics were evident in his reply, but the gradual Fabianism of Shaw had been replaced by the more strident communism of O'Casey, who felt that each step in history had been a progression and that capitalism was now changing to communism in the world around them: 'the change from feudalism to capitalism wasn't deterioration; it was a step forward; and so, too, will the change – taking place now – from the control of the means of life by the few, to the ownership of these things by the people who created them'. O'Casey also took umbrage at Gibbon's coupling of censorship in the USSR and the Roman Catholic Church, and although he conceded the Church to be unrelenting in its suppression of literature, he could find no such evidence in the USSR: 'I have never yet heard a whisper of the banning of play, poem, or novel by the officials of the USSR, good, bad, or indifferent.' This claim, printed towards the end of the war, seems absurd in light of the atrocities committed under Stalin in the USSR, but O'Casey was a committed communist and the horrors of post-war Russia were yet to be revealed.

In a final flourish, O'Casey denounced Gibbon as a propagandist for the Church, and rejected anyone's right to decide what books were indecent, especially considering Gibbon's suspicion of Strindberg: 'Mr. Gibbon has a perfect right to banish Strindberg out of his own life, but none whatever to banish him from the life of others.'[98] Also included in this article were responses from T.C. Kingsmill Moore, who would later become a Supreme Justice on the Irish circuit and a strangely muted response from Professor James Hogan of University

College Cork, who had defended censorship, but wanted to see it implemented by jury trial. Gibbon's article proved invaluable for O'Faoláin as it defended censorship on two counts, both in theory and in practice. This allowed for the publication of rebuttals from the Irish, and in the case of Shaw and O'Casey the European, cultural elite. However, these articles were not the end of the debate. O'Faoláin followed this up with further attacks from other authors, although he allowed Monk Gibbon the right of reply. Both Margaret Barrington, whose works would feature much more frequently under O'Donnell's patronage, and Hubert Butler attacked Gibbon's position. Gibbon's reply was to concede that his position was untenable in parts, and he sought to take the sting from the attacks by playing down the remarks. He tried to suggest that his article had 'largely [been] in the interests of controversy', and he finished by trying to curry favour by making the tame suggestion that Professor Hogan's idea of censorship by jury was so 'monstrous' as to 'almost make me fall off the fence on Mr O'Casey's side'.[99]

This exchange between differing positions on censorship was typical of coverage in *The Bell*. With Gibbon's defence being comprehensively undermined, he had effectively been set up by O'Faoláin for a damaging attack on his reputation. O'Faoláin's influence as an editor can be hard to interpret in *The Bell* as the articles are often introduced without comment. However, in the case of Gibbon's article a letter to O'Casey shows how O'Faoláin primed potential contributors by articulating the magazine's position in explicit detail, thus framing their expected response in line with the journal's own:

> We have repeatedly criticised the present literary censorship in Eire. We have taken up the implicit position that censorship is a principle which may be sound in theory but is almost always unsound in practice, and should therefore be left (as far as the written word is concerned) to the attentions of the police and then only for <u>obviously</u> <u>commercial</u> pornography. For a change we are printing the attached article [Gibbon's]. I am asking for 6 comments – from you, G.B.S. [George Bernard Shaw], a K.C. [Kings Council], Jim Larkin Jnr., a professor, and a senator. If the article interests you I would be very grateful to hear your comments.[100]

O'Faoláin was also keen to praise contributors, especially ones as famous as O'Casey, despite the imbalance in his reply and its uncritical support of the USSR. Although O'Faoláin would have found this position personally disagreeable, he praised it directly to O'Casey: 'Thank you ever so much for your prompt comment on Monk Gibbon on censorship. It is at once incisive and cool, vigorous and restrained … Shaw also promises a comment, so we are going to have a bumper number and a most effective counter from our two most distinguished exiles. Bless you!'[101]

However, it is important to remember that censorship was supported by a large section of the population, and there was a vibrant Catholic intellectual movement in support of it in principle. The historiography of censorship has left us with the impression that Ireland under censorship was 'in the grip of cultural isolationism, anti-intellectualism, and sexual repressiveness. Beyond the personal hurt and economic loss being banned in Ireland has meant for the writers interviewed, and for many others, is the cautionary tale of a public that failed to come to their defence and that spurned their creative achievement.'[102] Such an account misreads the relationship between artist and society, implying that society owes a debt to artistic excellence, and ought to change its moral outlook to match that of a generation of writers keen to point out the hypocrisy of Irish cultural conservatism. A more accurate reading would be to suggest that censorship was acknowledged as necessary by the majority of the population who were happy to take their moral instruction from a conservative Catholic clergy. That society's values have shifted to favour those of these writers is a matter of historical accident, and not evidence of their inherent truthfulness. This, however, is not to deny the excesses of censorship as it was applied in Ireland, nor the hurt and distress it caused many of the writers who suffered under it.

Yet such a position should be expected from a magazine whose primary purpose was the publication of radical new writing and political opinion. Throughout its entire print run *The Bell* challenged censorship in a variety of ways, but, with O'Faoláin in particular, one should not correlate his editorials with his private feelings. O'Faoláin was a consummate builder of his own legacy, and continuously developed narratives of self-progression that were at odds with his own actions. This is why O'Faoláin was so dismissive of his achievements in *The Bell* in later years – his role as a political agitator was at odds with the cultivation of his identity as an established figure in Irish letters. For O'Faoláin, his own prejudices were inescapable, and even journalism of the most exquisite quality was to be held in distinction from his real work in 'literature' for fear it should corrupt his legacy. Ironically, *The Bell* is perhaps O'Faoláin's most enduring literary contribution, or second only to some of his masterful short stories. In the cultural debate around what shape society should take in post-independence Ireland, O'Faoláin kept faith with his beliefs, and promoted the artist's right to free expression. To achieve this goal, however, he had to take up the alternating roles of domineering editor and pleading supplicant in order to negotiate the extraordinary posturing and egos of the artistic community in 1940s Ireland. Fortunately for O'Faoláin he was ideally suited to such a position, having the authority to command respect while also being pragmatic enough to work with what he was given.

Notes

1 Flann O'Brien, 'Going to the Dogs', *The Bell*, 1:1 (October 1940), pp. 19–24.
2 Anon. Correspondent, 'Cruiskeen Lawn', *Irish Times* (4 October 1940), p. 4.

3 For an example of this, see Seán O'Faoláin, 'The Modern Novel: A Catholic Point of View', *The Virginia Quarterly Review*, 11:3 (July 1935), pp. 339–351.
4 'Modern Novels Criticised', *Irish Times* (5 November 1938), p. 10.
5 Flann O'Brien, 'Letters to the Editor', *Irish Times* (8 November 1938), p. 5.
6 See Anthony Cronin, *No Laughing Matter: The Life and Times of Flann O'Brien* (London: Paladin, 1990), and James Matthews, *Voices: A Life of Frank O'Connor* (New York: Atheneum, 1983).
7 See Anne Clissmann, *Flann O'Brien: A Critical Introduction to his Writings* (Dublin: Gill & Macmillan, 1975), p. 19.
8 Myles Na Gopaleen, 'Cruiskeen Lawn', *Irish Times* (4 October 1954), p. 4.
9 Seán O'Faoláin to John V. Kelleher (6 November 1946), UCC, BL/L/JVk/2.
10 Antoinette Quinn, *Patrick Kavanagh: A Biography* (Dublin: Gill & Macmillan, 2001), p. 73.
11 See Maurice Harmon, *Sean O'Faolain: A Life* (London: Constable, 1994), p. 34. For a fictionalised account of life on a Rathkeale farm, see Seán O'Faoláin, *Come Back to Erin* (New York: The Viking Press, 1940).
12 Patrick Kavanagh, 'O Stony Grey Soil', *The Bell*, 1:1 (October 1940), p. 42.
13 Patrick Kavanagh, 'Coloured Balloons: A Study of Frank O'Connor', *The Bell*, 15:3 (December 1947), pp. 17–21.
14 John Montague, 'A Literary Gentleman', *The Cork Review* (Cork: Triskel Arts Centre, 1991), p. 54.
15 Quoted in Quinn, *Patrick Kavanagh: A Biography*, p. 155.
16 Seán O'Faoláin to Frank O'Connor (n.d.), Gotlieb (Box 3, Folder 6).
17 Quinn, *Patrick Kavanagh: A Biography*, p. 73.
18 Anthony Cronin, *Dead As Doornails* (Dublin: Dolmen Press, 1976).
19 Seán O'Faoláin, 'Public Opinion: Coloured Balloons', *The Bell*, 15:4 (January 1948), p. 61.
20 Quoted in Frank Shovlin, *The Irish Literary Periodical 1923–1958* (Oxford: Clarendon Press, 2003), p. 141.
21 Sean O'Casey to Francis MacManus (8 February 1950), O'Casey, MS 38, 126.
22 O'Faoláin alludes to this incident in a letter to their mutual friend John V. Kelleher, see Seán O'Faoláin to John V. Kelleher (14 December 1947), UCC, BL/L/JVK/19.
23 For an account of this incident, see Matthews, *Voices*, p. 238.
24 See Richard A. Furze, Jr, *A Desirable Vision of Life: A Study of The Bell, 1940–1954*. p. 42.
25 Val Mulkerns, '"Did You Once See Shelley Plain?" Dublin, *The Bell*, the Fifties', *New Hibernia Review*, 10:3 (Autumn, 2006), pp. 13–15.
26 Fintan O'Toole, 'A Portrait of Peadar O'Donnell As an Old Soldier', *Magill*, 6:5 (February 1983), p. 28.
27 Peadar O'Donnell, 'Commentary', 'Tarry Flynn', *The Bell*, 14:2 (May 1947), p. 5
28 Quinn, *Patrick Kavanagh: A Biography*, p. 262.
29 Peter Hegarty, *Peadar O'Donnell* (Dublin: Mercier Press, 1999), p. 265.
30 Seán O'Faoláin to Austin Clarke (2 March 1941), Austin Clarke Papers 1913–1974,

The National Library of Ireland. MS Collection List 83. Hereafter referred to as Clarke.

31 O'Faoláin to O'Connor (3 November 1943), Gotlieb (Box 3, Folder 6).

32 Patrick Kavanagh, 'The Wake of Books: A Mummery', *The Bell*, 15:2 (November 1947).

33 Unless otherwise stated, all information on Geoffrey Phibbs and his wife Norah McGuinness is taken from the Norah McGuinness archive at the Dublin Writers Museum. Hereafter referred to as McGuinness.

34 See *Irish Times* (30 January 1922), p. 4.

35 For an account of the formation of the Carnegie Libraries, see Lennox Robinson, 'How the County Libraries Began', *The Bell*, 1:1 (October 1940), pp. 24–32.

36 Frank O'Connor, *My Father's Son* (Belfast: The Blackstaff Press, 1994), p. 29.

37 AE to Geoffrey Phibbs (3 March 1925), McGuinness, MS 1035.

38 AE (George Russell) to Macmillan and Co (30 August 1930), in Alan Denson (ed), *Letters from AE* (London: Abelard-Schuman, 1961), p. 189.

39 For information on Norah's success as an artist, see Theo Snoddy, *Dictionary of Irish Artists 20th Century* (Dublin: Wolfhound Press, 1996), pp. 294–296.

40 Marianne Hartigan, 'The Commercial Design Career of Norah McGuinness', *Irish Arts Review*, 3:3 (Autumn 1986), pp. 23–25.

41 See R.F. Foster, *W. B. Yeats: A Life II: The Arch-Poet 1915–1939* (Oxford: Oxford University Press, 2003), p. 721.

42 Frank O'Connor, *My Father's Son*, p. 67.

43 See J. Howard Woolmer, *A Checklist of The Hogarth Press 1917–1946* (Pennsylvania: Woolmer/Brotherson, 1986), p. 55.

44 Leonard Woolf to Geoffrey Phibbs (4 January 1928), McGuinness, MS 1082.

45 David Garnett to Norah McGuinness (n.d.), McGuinness, MS 1033.

46 All information from what follows is taken from a letter from Norah McGuinness to T.S. Mathews (6 March 1978), McGuinness, MS 1038. This letter came too late for Mathews to include it in his biography or collected reminiscences of Robert Graves, and he apologised to Norah for being unable to include it. It is Norah's version of the events surrounding the breakdown of her marriage to Geoffrey Phibbs.

47 For a full biography of Laura Riding, see Deborah Baker, *In Extremis: The Life of Laura Riding* (London: Hamish Hamilton, 1993).

48 See Richard Murphy, *The Kick: A Life Among Writers* (London: Granta Books, 2002), pp. 165–170.

49 Geoffrey Phibbs to Norah McGuinness (n.d.), MS 1033, McGuinness.

50 Frank O'Connor, *My Father's Son*, p. 68.

51 Phibbs to McGuinness (n.d.), MS 1033, McGuinness.

52 See Geoffrey Taylor, 'The Quality', *Irish Times* (12 January 1952), p. 6.

53 The veracity of Norah's account of these events is confirmed by Graves's nephew and biographer, Richard Perceval Graves, *Robert Graves: The Years With Laura Riding 1926–1940* (London: Weidenfeld & Nicolson, 1990), pp. 71–100. Richard Graves seems to have had access to Norah's letter from T.S. Mathews and supports this with the Graves family archive.

54 See Candida Lycett Green (ed.), *John Betjeman: Letters Volume Two: 1951–1984* (London: Methuen, 1995), pp. 91, 59.
55 For an introduction to Phibbs's life and work, see Terence Brown, 'Geoffrey Taylor: A Portrait', in *Ireland's Literature: Selected Essays* (Mullingar: The Lilliput Press, 1988), pp. 141–151.
56 See *The Bell*, 2:4 (July 1941).
57 Vivian Mercier, 'The Fourth Estate – Verdict on The Bell', *The Bell*, 10:2 (May 1945).
58 Seán O'Faoláin to Austin Clarke (1 December 1936), Clarke, MS 38,655/4.
59 O'Faoláin to Clarke (20 December 1936), Clarke, MS 38,655/4.
60 O'Faoláin to Clarke (n.d. January 1937?), Clarke, MS 38,655/4.
61 Austin Clarke to Seán O'Faoláin (n.d. January 1937?), Clarke, MS 38,655/4.
62 O'Faoláin, *Vive Moi!: An Autobiography*, p. 322.
63 O'Faoláin to Clarke (n.d. January 1937?), Clarke, MS 38,655/4.
64 O'Faoláin to Clarke (2 March 1941), Clarke, MS 38,655/4.
65 Frank O'Connor to John V. Kelleher (January 1947), UCC, BL/L/JVK/151.
66 Seán O'Faoláin to Brinsley MacNamara (n.d.), Boston, MS 86–180 (Box 2, Folder 1).
67 Frank MacManus to Sean O'Casey (22 February 1948), O'Casey, MS 38, 126.
68 Geoffrey Taylor to Austin Clarke (30 May 1945), Clarke, MS 38,655/4.
69 See *The Bell*, 10:4 (July 1945).
70 Taylor to Clarke (27 July 1945), Clarke, MS 38,655/4.
71 Geoffrey Taylor to Seán O'Faoláin (1 September 1945), Clarke, MS 38,655/4.
72 Hubert Butler to Austin Clarke (6 March 1952), Clarke, MS 38,655/4.
73 Austin Clarke, 'The Green Helicon', *Irish Times* (24 February 1951), p. 6.
74 Austin Clarke, 'Letters to the Editor', *Irish Times* (21 November 1951), p. 5.
75 Seamus Deane has written on the centrality of boredom to Irish writing, see Seamus Deane, 'Boredom and the Apocalypse: A National Paradigm', *Strange Country: Modernity and Nationhood in Irish Writing Since 1790* (Oxford: Clarendon Press, 1997), pp. 145–197.
76 Peter Martin, *Censorship in the Two Irelands 1922–1939* (Dublin: Irish Academic Press, 2006), p. 99.
77 See Alan Travis, 'Postcard Wars', *Index on Censorship*, 29:6 (November–December 2000), pp. 102–105.
78 Bruce Stewart claimed that 'in the 1940s the only voice raised against the Gaelic, Catholic Orthodoxy of the state … was Seán O'Faoláin's'. Bruce Stewart, 'On the Necessity of De-Hydifying Irish Cultural Criticism', *New Hibernia Review/Iris Éireannach Nua*, 4:1 (Spring 2000), p. 26.
79 For a list of banned books, see Michael Adams, *Censorship: The Irish Experience* (Tuscaloosa: University of Alabama Press, 1968), p. 242.
80 For an account of this incident, see *Irish Times* (14 November 1935), p. 8.
81 Susannah Riordan, 'The Unpopular Front: Catholic Revival and Irish Cultural Identity, 1932–48', in Mike Cronin and John M. Regan (eds), *Ireland: the Politics of Independence, 1922–49* (London: Macmillan, 2000), pp. 98–120.

82 Seán O'Faoláin, 'The Dangers of Censorship', *Ireland To-Day*, 1:6 (November 1936), pp. 60–61.

83 Seán O'Faoláin, '1916–1941: Tradition and Creation', *The Bell*, 2:1 (April 1941), pp. 5–12.

84 Seán O'Faoláin, 'Roxana', *Irish Times* (23 December 1957), p. 5.

85 Seán O'Faoláin, 'Midsummer Night Madness', *The Collected Stories of Sean O'Faolain Volume 1* (London: Constable, 1980), p. 31.

86 Edward Garnett, 'Foreword', in Seán O'Faoláin, *Midsummer Night Madness and Other Stories* (London: Jonathan Cape, 1932), p. 11.

87 Seán O'Faoláin, 'The Talking Trees', *Playboy* (January 1969). This is the first appearance of the title story from his collection of the same name published two years later. Seán O'Faoláin, *The Talking Trees* (London: Jonathan Cape, 1971).

88 For more on O'Faoláin and Miller, see Seán O'Faoláin, 'Pigeon-Holing the Modern Novel', *The London Mercury*, 33:194 (December 1935).

89 C.B. Murphy, 'Sex, Censorship and The Church', *The Bell*, 2:6 (September 1941), p. 68–74.

90 Seán O'Faoláin, 'Beginnings and Blind Alleys', *The Bell*, 3:1 (October 1941), p. 3.

91 Seán O'Faoláin, 'Signing Off', *The Bell*, 12:1 (April 1946), p. 1.

92 O'Faoláin to O'Connor (n.d.), Gotlieb (Box 3, Folder 6).

93 Monk Gibbon, 'In Defence of Censorship', *The Bell*, 9:4 (January 1945), pp. 313–21.

94 O'Faoláin, 'Pigeon-Holing The Modern Novel', pp. 159–164.

95 Gibbon, 'In Defence of Censorship', p. 322.

96 George Bernard Shaw to Sean O'Faoláin (3 November 1940), Boston, MS 89–14 (Box 2, Folder 1).

97 George Bernard Shaw, 'Censorship', *The Bell*, 9:5 (February 1945), pp. 396–401.

98 Sean O'Casey, 'Censorship', *The Bell*, 9:5 (February 1945), pp. 401–405.

99 Monk Gibbon, 'Public Opinion', *The Bell*, 9:6 (March 1945), pp. 533–35.

100 Seán O'Faoláin to Sean O'Casey (8 December 1944), O'Casey, MS 38, 129.

101 O'Faoláin to O'Casey (n.d.), O'Casey, MS 38, 129.

102 Julia Carlson (ed.), *Banned in Ireland: Censorship and the Irish Writer* (Athens: University of Georgia Press, 1990), p. vii.

5

The thin society:
O'Faoláin and the descent of *The Bell*

Scholars will yet study *The Bell* with the intentness of archaeologists turning over a few shards, flints and bones to discern a culture! (Francis McManus)[1]

On 12 May 1937, George VI and his wife Elizabeth were crowned King and Queen of Great Britain and Ireland. George VI was the last king to hold this title, dissolved under the Republic of Ireland Act (1948), and although his reign was of little direct consequence to *The Bell*, indirectly the day of his coronation mattered greatly to the form this magazine would take. Coronation day was chosen by Charles Madge and Humphrey Jennings to inaugurate their ground-breaking social research into the lives of ordinary people in England, research that provided the inspiration for many subsequent studies and laid the foundations of the Mass Observation movement. Their findings were published in *May the Twelfth Mass Observation Day-Surveys by over Two Hundred Observers* (1937).[2] The Mass Observation movement was a new form of collective research, and it promised to categorise the responses of ordinary people: in this instance to the coronation of King George VI. Its approach, which involved using untrained observers to record conversations in public houses and factories, was to prove instrumental to the development of sociology, and reinvigorated anthropology as a discipline. By 1943 it had been identified as an important movement and one in which human group behaviour could be fruitfully studied for analysis of deeper significance in societal structures.[3]

Although *The Bell* was ostensibly a literary journal, equal weight was given to articles of a socio-political bent, and many submissions crossed both fields. So far, criticism has tended to focus on *The Bell* as an organ of literary excellence, or reduced its sociological output to a series of isolated problems, as is the case with its protests against censorship.[4] Although it was not a sociology journal *The Bell* was deeply influenced by the Mass Observation movement, particularly as it tied in with O'Faoláin's theory of the novel. The idea that life as it is lived, and not in any abstraction, should be the arbiter of all our decisions, was an effective mantra for *The Bell*. O'Faoláin was clear on what he wanted for its content, and he insisted on an open and pragmatic approach to

his editorial policy. However, as early as the second issue he was appealing to
contributors to maintain an interest in ordinary life, and to write only of subjects which they knew: 'every contributor writes from actual experience ... do
not write on abstract subjects ... We are writing about our own people, our own
generation, our own institutions.'[5] Such a position makes his later hostility to
Patrick Kavanagh's poetry of 'ordinary plenty' all the more baffling, considering Kavanagh's commitment to writing of what he knew.

Mass Observation in its popularity as a sociological movement, and the way
in which it conflated with one of O'Faoláin's own theories on Irish society,
would ensure that it contributed in interesting ways to keep *The Bell*'s articles a popular mix of high art and factual analysis. The success of *The Bell*
and its endurance must, in some part, be down to the breadth of its interests.
What O'Faoláin understood to be the conditions for the production of literary
excellence would cause him to search for articles on other aspects of Irish life.
Consequently, the Mass Observation movement provided him with a ready-
made example to emulate in his attempt to build up Irish literary standards
and tastes, as embodied in *The Bell*. O'Faoláin already had the example of
Left Review (1934–38) and *Fact* (1937–39) as British journals with sociological
underpinnings, and these magazines offered him a template on which to base
The Bell. Their influence becomes apparent bearing in mind that magazines
such as *Fact* contained articles with titles such as 'Colliery Disaster: Evidence
of J.E. Samuel', a no-nonsense insight into the dangers faced by miners working in Britain.[6]

Such factual dramatisations would become commonplace in *The Bell* and
formed a staple of its output. Perhaps its most famous Mass Observation
inspired series of articles was 'I Did Penal Servitude' by D83222, which would
go on to inspire the book of the same title. D83222 was the journalist Walter
Mahon Smith, who had been sentenced to three years for embezzlement from
the bank in which he worked. His prison number, D83222, was O'Faoláin's
Dublin phone number and had been used to conceal his identity.[7] Mass
Observation left *The Bell* a rich depository for social historians, who could use
its hard-hitting factual analysis to articulate the social conditions of de Valera's
Ireland from a first-person perspective. However, *The Bell* was much more
than a simple journal of social observation, it aimed to develop and enhance the
society around it by building up standards and tastes from within. To this end
O'Faoláin was influenced by another social theory which finds its reification in
the magazine itself.

One issue that O'Faoláin saw as affecting Irish writing was the idea that the
country's society was thinly composed. That is to say that culture is developed layer upon layer, with each artistic movement or achievement adding
to the depth of that culture. In Ireland's case, as a new society, that depth of
culture was yet to develop. O'Faoláin was struck by this idea in his reading of

Henry James's 'Nathaniel Hawthorne',[8] a critical interpretation of one famous American author by another. James felt that Hawthorne's work was limited by the environment from which he was writing; the genius of Hawthorne was his ability to define and therefore to produce his own aesthetic atmosphere, one that was to nourish future artists. Hawthorne's *The Scarlet Letter* (1850) reflected the society from which it was produced, and in so doing, it captured some of what was essential to that society. Puritanism, hypocrisy and a frugality of living are all excellently rendered, along with the beauty and romanticism of New England life. For James, it had taken years of social interaction for a sufficiently established society to form, one that was capable of producing a work that would define that society, as well elucidating its limitations.

The Scarlet Letter was the work of genius that defined a generation and the culture from which it was born. According to James, Hawthorne was the author for whom 'the qualities of his ancestors *filtered* down through generations into his composition, *The Scarlet Letter* was, as it were, the vessel that gathered up the last of the precious drops'. For our purposes here, it is also of note that James understood Hawthorne's achievements as something of a model for the future. Hawthorne was provincial and idiosyncratic, his terms of reference were limited, and his horizons were restricted to the nuances of the society that he described. However, he also stood alongside the greatest of writers in the English language; he triumphed in his ability to make the particular universal, to offer hope and inspiration for other American writers. Hawthorne's was a local contribution of substantial merit to the field of literature: 'the idea of America having produced a novel that belonged to literature, and to the forefront of it. Something might at last be sent to Europe as exquisite in quality as anything that had been received, and the best of it was that the thing was absolutely American; it belonged to the soil, to the air; it came out of the very heart of New England.'[9] O'Faoláin identified the relevance of James's theory to the situation of the Irish writer, and it has been much repeated since he first promoted it.[10]

This theory runs that an author is nourished in his own work by the richness and depth of the outstanding work that has come before him.[11] In additions, the writer requires a rich and complex social environment in which to flourish, one that can produce the tensions and social mores required to give any work its depth. O'Faoláin looked at the fledgling Irish democracy and was unimpressed: 'We can see very clearly in Ireland to-day where the stratified, and fairly complex social life which a writer of 1915, say, could have known in Dublin has given way to a far more simple and uncomplex, a much "thinner" social life.'

As the Irish writer was now writing from the position of a man in a society that had formed itself anew from the ashes of separation with the United Kingdom, he must look to himself to source his material. The Irish writer was in a difficult place, having to choose his muse, and this burden imposed

limitations on his ability to produce works of outstanding merit without appeal
to the old tropes of nationalism and an idealised Gaelic past, as was the case
with the Irish literary revival. Prior to separation from the United Kingdom,
the Irish writer had the rich cultural heritage of a substantial body of English
work, and to the important writings of the Anglo-Irish, of which he could feel
a part, and from which he could draw inspiration. O'Faoláin used this theory
to explain why the short story was a better suited artistic mode than the novel
to apply to writing in Ireland. It did not require the complexity of society, or
the knowledge of tradition that he perceived as necessary in the construction
of the novel. However, this is not to say that O'Faoláin was unaware of some of
the difficulties with this theory, rather he was content to see it as another push
factor in the tradition of the Irish artist seeking sustenance in exile:

> Goldsmith, Wilde, Joyce, Shaw and Moore worked well in exile. Synge, Yeats
> and O'Casey worked best at home. One cannot draw the noose tight. All we must
> conclude is that there are circumstances in Irish life that perturb and that drive
> some to flight; just as they perturbed Hawthorne (he is not entirely silent about
> his discomforts) and drove James into exile.[12]

How much of all this is linked to a comprehensive theory of Irish writing, and
how much it is about what O'Faoláin perceived to be his own failure to produce
a novel of international significance is open to debate.

It is best to see these tensions as the source of his aesthetic output rather
than as their result. O'Faoláin himself oscillated between seeing this theory as
justification for his own shortcomings and from pride in the work that he produced. More often than not, and this is true of his fiction as well as his criticism,
he struggled with his demons and was left only with a profound questioning:
'Was Henry James right after all when he said that the flower of art blooms
only where the soil is deep? That "the coldness, the thinness, the blankness"
in life surrounding a writer can only evoke compassion for his lot? Was I mad
to propose to spend the rest of my life rooted in this sour and shallow soil?'
This theory of a thinly composed society is directly linked to O'Faoláin's concerns with the need to develop a sufficient aesthetic model for Irish writing.
O'Faoláin seemed personally unable to resolve this issue, and was either forced
into expressing contradictions, or into an evasive ploy of seeing success in failure, that is, of hoping that his failed attempts at artistic expression would fertil-
ise the imaginations of the artists to come. It is in this light that we should see
the artistic policy of *The Bell*. Consider this appeal, one that opposes his claims
that an Irish writer must only be concerned with facts, and express his artistic
subject with a cold objective eye:

> In Ireland the two dissolvents of this earthy material have always been hitherto,
> humour and poetry. The humour, thank heaven, is always welcome with us;
> sometimes low; sometimes not so low; always welcome. The poetry has ebbed;

poetry in the sense in which we warm, because of it ... lifts us out of the toils of naturalism; poetry which is partly wit, partly romanticism, partly fancy ... is an element which cannot be brought back into literature by an act of will. All we can do, in this period of pause, is to experiment with it, to be empirics, to incite writers coming after us, by our very failure, to see and to say how much better it could be done.[13]

All these contradictions and complexities serve to highlight the ambition with which O'Faoláin viewed his work, and the value to other aspiring Irish artists. The frustrations that he felt with the production of a distinctly Irish body of literature, and with the general paucity of activity among Irish writers goes some way towards explaining why he decided to attempt to publish *The Bell*. That he should go so far as to see the Mass Observation of Irish society as it was lived as necessary is a testament to what he perceived as the barrenness of Irish culture.

O'Faoláin was starting from first principles, asking: what is Irish culture, how do the Irish actually live? Without such information a comprehensive picture of Ireland would be obfuscated by abstractions and idealists. O'Faoláin's own writing should not be seen outside this context, although he might have been highly critical of it himself, he was an accomplished artist and set the bar for artistic merit high. It is easy to see O'Faoláin's criticisms of Irish aesthetic achievement as the bitter cries of a man who was perceptive enough to accurately survey the Irish literary landscape but too impotent to significantly alter it himself. This is perhaps a reductive reading and does not consider the complexities of O'Faoláin's character, nor take account of the myriad influences acting on it. Beneath his consistent attacks on the government, and his constant searching for external inspiration, lay a profound devotion to Ireland. Augustine Martin wrote that he was a writer who 'could never manage to conceal his deep love and concern for the country and its people, [and he] has written as devastatingly as any artist of his generation about the position of the artist here'.[14] O'Faoláin's concern for Irish artists is evidenced by the fact that he still considered himself 'as a Republican anxious for a united Ireland', and that this position was linked to his hope that a unified Ireland would produce a unified culture, one that was capable of emulating the artistic achievements of its esteemed past.[15] Such a hope is evident in *The Bell*'s special Ulster issues, which O'Faoláin saw as a project designed to assist in cultural unification.

O'Faoláin's concerns about the nature of Irish cultural heritage and the role of the artist in Irish society may have a different source from his own personal perception that the new Ireland was 'thinly composed'. During the years following the First World War and leading up to the Second World War the value of artistic endeavour was being questioned throughout the western world. Industrialisation had brought mass production and a commodification of the aesthetic; with that came a questioning of the proper place of art within a highly modernised society. This was a European literary landscape dominated

by the high modernist works of T.S. Eliot and Joyce, the concept of the frag-
mented self had already obtained literary orthodoxy. The tendency towards
self-questioning was exacerbated by the onset of war and Éire's subsequent
policy of neutrality. A sudden isolation from European artistic exchange left
some Irish artists, and O'Faoláin in particular, bemoaning the lack of cross-cul-
tural exchange. Seen in this light, his calls for aesthetic dialogue might be
perceived as a case of Nero fiddling while Rome burned. However, O'Faoláin
was not alone in seeing the war as a critical impediment to artistic expression;
Cyril Connolly at *Horizon* also felt the war was affecting writers' scope and his
magazine, like *The Bell*, was in part a rallying call on behalf of beleaguered artists.[16] Although O'Faoláin's demands for better support of the artist in society
are noble in themselves, it is unsurprising that they fell on deaf ears. As Clair
Wills points out:

> The idea that intelligence went along with being more 'Europeanly–minded', and
> had been devastated by the difficulty of getting across the Irish Sea, was scarcely
> guaranteed to please the more 'nationally – minded'. The would-be Europeans
> were suffering from a loss of dignity, and from their lack of confidence in Dublin
> as a cultural capital in its own right. The sense of being cut off from the European
> mainstream went to the heart of the cultural predicament of neutrality.[17]

That O'Faoláin should see this isolation as an aspect of Ireland's own failure
to produce an artistic environment that would sustain a new generation of
artists is not outside the realm of possibility, following as it did his post-independence disillusionment. However, it would be wrong to assume that he
was being disingenuous; rather his writing, both criticism and fiction, reflect
this underlying tension between international artistic isolation, and the inner
examination of Irish identity. It is within these three dominant strands – Mass
Observation, fears of a 'thinly composed' culture, and intellectual self-doubt
exacerbated by neutrality – that *The Bell* should be considered. These factors
dominate O'Faoláin's editorial vision for the magazine and, complimented by
O'Donnell's socialism, form the bulk of articles submitted for publication.

Early in his stay in England Seán O'Faoláin confessed to Edward Garnett
that he was 'thinking of doing a Ph.D. at London, working on Yeats' youth'.[18]
This idea never materialised although he maintained sufficient interest in Yeats
to contemplate writing a biography of him later, which too had to be abandoned:
'I gave it up when I gave up trying to be a scholar, and anyway found that W.B.
had, in his time, dived down so many caverns of knowledge and as quickly
returned, bringing many pearls with him, that if I were to write about him with
any authority of knowledge I should have to dive down the same caverns, stay
much too long, and bring back very little.'[19] O'Faoláin's insight into his own
limitations is revealing, in that he acknowledged his unwillingness to follow a
poet, albeit one of intimidating genius, into the deeper layers of his thought.

That O'Faoláin was aware of this limitation is evidenced by the succession of poetry editors at *The Bell*, whom he relied on to promote poetry of note and cover his own artistic blind spot. Fortunately, O'Faoláin's ability as an editor was excellent and he delegated these responsibilities to those capable, if different, deputies in Frank O'Connor, Geoffrey Taylor and Louis MacNeice.[20]

Taylor, in particular, was completely committed to poetry and remained an insightful critic of modern practitioners, while doing much work in the promotion of Irish poets long since fallen out of favour. Although his tastes were deeply wedded to tradition, he still found room in *The Bell* to promote the work of those deliberately experimenting with form and style.[21] He had moved from an iconoclastic youth where he haughtily claimed, 'I want to attack Yeats if only I can get some paper to print an article on him', to an established anthologist, working with John Betjeman by the launch of *The Bell* in 1940.[22] Taylor was instrumental in the promotion of a young English poet, Freda Laughton, in *The Bell*. Today, little is known about Laughton, and she is remembered − where she is recognised at all − as a war poet, published in a couple of war anthologies. The only biographical information about Laughton in these works is that she was born in Bristol in 1907 and studied art in London, before moving to Ireland in 1932. She was married twice, firstly to L.E.G. Laughton and then to John Midgley.[23] Laughton first appeared in *The Bell* in March 1944, where Taylor published three of her poems. Later in that year, she also published in the *Irish Times* and would go on to publish for that newspaper a further four times.

It was also in 1944 that Taylor published *Irish Poems of To-Day*, an anthology of the best poetry from the first seven volumes of *The Bell*, which included Laughton.[24] Her exposure in *The Bell* was short, occurring between March 1944 and July 1945, and she only published one poem there that would not appear in her first solo collection *A Transitory House* (1945).[25] Laughton's publication of *A Transitory House* at Jonathan Cape is likely to have been due to O'Faoláin and Taylor advocating on her behalf. On the dust jacket she is referred to, as 'a new writer from Ireland'. As we have seen, Taylor had connections to Jonathan Cape through David 'Bunny' Garnett who was also a reader for the company along with his father Edward. Despite their unusual history, Taylor had remained on speaking terms with Cape's reader. Whatever the source of the initial connection, Laughton's first and only collection was a work of some merit, and needs to be revisited in light of the support she received from *The Bell* and, more widely, within the canon of Irish literature. Laughton is now primarily remembered as a war poet, and some of her works are a testament to the sympathy she felt for those who were actively involved. Although her poetry demands that she be included in the wider debate on Irish literary modernisms as well, she is simply among the best poets working in an experimental mode in Ireland during the decade of the 1940s.

Her poem 'When from the Calyx-Canopy of Night', first published in *The*

Bell in 1944, portrays an assertive female sexuality, which although couched in the language of romantic fancy, nevertheless is remarkable for what would have been considered risqué depictions of the sexual act in Ireland during that time. Indeed, a substantial section of Laughton's collection is devoted to such thinly veiled accounts of sex. Poems such as 'To the Bride', advises a virginal young subject to 'Discard all timid blisses, kisses faint and shy. / ... Be proud reserve to shed / In a cloudy bed.'[26] Poetry of such emotional content was bound to draw attention and after winning *The Bell*'s poetry competition in 1944 she also drew vocal debate from among Ireland's critics. Austin Clarke again displayed his hostility to *The Bell* and its contributors in his review of *A Transitory House* for the *Irish Times*. Clarke claimed that although *The Bell*'s prose fiction was very specifically grounded in Ireland and in Irish experience, its poetry ran at a different tangent and was frequently more abstract and modernist: 'the short stories and prose sketches in it [*The Bell*] are so racy of the soil that they are at times embarrassing, but many of the poems might have been selected from *Horizon* or any other English modernist compilation'.

Although Clarke's identification of the more abstract preferences of Geoffrey Taylor as poetry editor have some credibility, his contention that *The Bell*'s prose was 'racy of the soil' is a bit more difficult to justify. If *The Bell*'s prose dealt with Ireland and the Irish then that was present at the conception of the magazine rather than as an accidental afterthought. Clarke's lazy reading of *The Bell*'s prose fiction is similar to Flann O'Brien's in that he chooses to focus on those descriptive of Irish life. This attack on *The Bell*'s fiction and on O'Faoláin's and O'Connor's own writing by other writers of their own generation in part explains why their writings fell from favour after their deaths, by setting the critical environment in which they were received. Clarke further expressed his dissatisfaction with Laughton's work by saying its place was outside of Irish letters entirely: 'there is nothing in this collection which has the slightest relation to this country'. Aside from questioning Laughton's right to be included among Irish letters, Clarke felt that her work was, at times, just plain bad: 'examples of the horrible ingenuities of the contemporary English poetic mind will be found in the book ... "bleating ocean," "indigestible furniture," "emasculated food," and all other prefabricated images'. Although Clarke conceded that the collection contained 'an occasional one which is both delicate and subtle' his overall opinion was entirely dismissive.[27] In these opinions he was supported by Frank Harvey in a letter to *The Bell*; writing in 'Public Opinion' Harvey claimed that Laughton was only 'an addition to English letters. She derives entirely from the modern school of young English poets ... To those working for a distinctive Anglo-Irish literature she can be no help. Her work is indistinguishable from the mass of contemporary English poetry by modernists.' Although Harvey was quick to attempt to dismiss any hint of prejudice by finishing his letter with: 'I by no means wish to detract from the value of Ms. Laughton's work. Undoubtedly she is a poet of fine promise', such naked anti-English prejudice surfaces occasionally in *The Bell*'s contributions, although it is more commonly remembered for its anti-Gaelic stance.[28]

Valentin Iremonger in the same issue was much kinder to Laughton in his article on the effects of war on Irish poetry. He dismissed both Clarke and Harvey as missing the point of Laughton's writing: 'Freda Laughton, in common with most of the other younger poets, draws her inspiration from the depths of her experience: that it happens to have taken place in Ireland is of no importance to what she has to say ... I should not like my poetry to be judged by its "Irishness".'[29] Iremonger had been so taken with Laughton's poetry that he had earlier written an appreciation of it for *The Bell*. He saw Laughton as 'one of the most important new Irish poets' whose work was of vital significance to Ireland at that time: 'in her realisation that the forces of the individual life engineer the instances of poetic experience and, consequently, of poetry, lies her validity just here and just now'. Iremonger was of the impression that Laughton's work had the potential to endure, her ability to intellectualise her subjects, and to offer a serious take on the ordinary boded well for her future: 'there is a great deal of intellection in her work – which is as it should be. Poetry is not a game ... in her recognition of it lies Freda Laughton's promise for the future.'[30] That Laughton's work has not endured in any meaningful way is an accident of history. Certainly her work compares favourably with other submissions to *The Bell*. Perhaps her portrayal as a distinctively 'English' writer as opposed to an 'Irish' one prevented her work finding a place within either tradition. Her overtly sexualised imagery certainly made many readers at that time uncomfortable – in a thinly veiled reference to this, one reader from Killybegs complained that her writing was 'sensuousness for the sake of sensuousness'.[31] In any case, her reputation as a native poet, deserving of a place apart from foreign modernism would not have been helped by her association with another controversial poet and artist in *The Bell*, Nick Nicholls.

On Wednesday 25 April 1945, Geoffrey Taylor chaired a poetry recital from the works of Freda Laughton and Nick Nicholls at the Contemporary Picture Galleries, at 113 Lower Baggot Street.[32] On display were some of Nicholls's most recent paintings, and the venue had a suitably avant-garde setting, being one of the most prominent art galleries that 'aimed to further the cause of Modernism by exhibiting more radical works than could be seen elsewhere'.[33] Nicholls was an English poet and painter who had moved to Ireland in 1939. There, he had gathered around Basil Rakoczi and Kenneth Hall who had formed the White Stag Group for the advancement of psychological analysis and art.[34] The group proved very influential in the history of Irish art; composed mainly of English expatriates it was free to explore art unconstrained by the historical legacy that weighed on Irish artists, and thus offered a much needed fresh perspective for Irish painting. The White Stag Group received

support from *The Bell* as a progressive and modern movement, particularly as it
offered an alternative to the Royal Hibernian Academy's yearly exhibits which
were much criticised as conservative and bland.[35] *The Bell* published articles on
the group's 'Exhibition of Living Art' and their 'White Stag' exhibition, and
followed their productions with enthusiasm, printing glossy examples from
their work.[36] That *The Bell* would promote their painting is perhaps unsurprising considering the group was associated with Mainie Jellett, Nano Reid
and Nigel Heseltine. Jellett was a close personal friend of Elizabeth Bowen, and
Bowen published a touching obituary of her in *The Bell* in December of 1944.
Nano Reid also featured frequently in *The Bell*, and O'Faoláin published an
article on her work to date in November of 1941.[37] Nigel Heseltine was the son
of the English composer Peter Warlock, he was in Ireland for the duration of
the Second World War as his father had been during the First World War, and
contributed articles to *The Bell* on contemporary Welsh writing.[38]

   O'Faoláin delegated responsibility for the coverage of painting to others,
with Anna Sheehy, Elizabeth Curran and Arthur Power submitting the bulk
of articles on Irish painting. Arthur Power was a Waterford-born painter, who
befriended James Joyce in Paris. He later published his memoirs of Joyce.[39]
O'Faoláin's own tastes were less inclined towards modernist or abstract painting, preferring the Italian masters and his close friend Paul Henry.[40] As we
have seen, Austin Clarke felt that *The Bell* travelled in two directions when one
looked at its poetry and its prose, between backward-looking short stories and
experimental modern English poetry. *The Bell*'s taste in the plastic arts were
also modern, promoting examples of new directions in town planning, architecture, painting, sculpture and even furniture making.[41] However, Clarke's
distinction is reductive and does not do justice to the breadth of writing that
appeared in what was, after all, primarily a literary journal. Today we are still
living with the critical legacy of Clarke's view of *The Bell* and its writers, which
positions them as outside movements within European literature as a whole
and only existing in a reactionary capacity to advances which had taken place
around them. As at least one critic has argued, writers of post-independence
Ireland were busy adjusting to the difficulties of the disappointment of their
new reality and this was 'shown in the commitment by many to what were
essentially mimetic modes of writing – the short stories of Seán O'Faolain and
Frank O'Connor and, in the war years, Patrick Kavanagh's *The Great Hunger*
(1942)'.[42] Yet such a view is problematic, in that it establishes a false distinction
between progressive experimental writing and an imitative 'mimetic' writing.

   Admittedly, O'Faoláin's writing was not deliberately hostile to the literary
conventions of their period. However, this is not to suggest that he was igno-
rant of them, or that he did not have his own reasons for choosing to work in
the manner in which he did, in sticking to a predominantly realist mode. This
depiction of O'Faoláin's writing as being outside the European tradition of

literature and directly oppositional to a monolithic high-modernist movement is problematic as O'Faoláin was alive to the possibilities that modernist experimentation afforded. He was deeply immersed in the traditions of European literature and his writing should be seen as operating within that tradition; his reasons for rejecting overtly experimental writing were clear. He chose to operate within the realist mode as he attempted to develop a specific challenge to that tradition, namely in the Catholic novel. To depict his writing as an inward-looking reaction to literary movements elsewhere would be to do a disservice to him and to the entire project of *The Bell*. Its contributors were, as often as not, offering challenging and subversive writing, and Clarke's accusations ring hollow when one considers O'Faoláin's own reasoned analysis of his position and the potential to view his short stories as existing within it. This position was explicitly outlined in the debate surrounding the publication of Nick Nicholls's 'The Bone and The Flower'.[43]

Its experimental format and obvious similarity to the avant-garde poetry of the modernist movement should alert us to the risky strategy which O'Faoláin was following in trying to promote writing that had the potential to alienate much of his readership through its opacity. O'Faoláin stated as much in his 'Sense and Nonsense in Poetry' debate with Geoffrey Taylor which he published alongside the poem: 'The present discussion centres around the old problem of "meaning" in poetry and it arose when the editor was presented with a very long, and interesting, series of verses which the Poetry Editor admires but of which the Editor confesses that he understands but little.' Taylor was a strong advocate for Nicholls's poem and argued that it operated on two levels, that of surface meaning conveyed through its language but also through association of those words which operate on an emotional level. For Taylor, the first level was the poem's 'sense', and the second emotional effect was a poem's 'nonsense'. O'Faoláin agreed with Taylor that poetry can often challenge the limits of our interpretation. However, he diverged with the poetry editor if only in degree rather than in fundamentals. For O'Faoláin, the distinction lay with 'a mind that concentrates on communication outward and of a mind content with communication inward'. In the case of the latter, he argued, their poetry became the 'poetry of frustration, and their meanings became highly equivocal and debateable. They had lost touch with universals.'[44] It is here that O'Faoláin's theory of the novel crosses his theory of poetry, in that although he allows for ineffable truths, he expects them to be the universals of human experience and not the workings of the creative mind reflecting itself.[45]

We can see his own attempt at a Catholic novel of universal truth in *Bird Alone* (1936), which failed to receive the critical understanding he had hoped for. In the end, O'Faoláin and Taylor came to a rough consensus on the issue, with O'Faoláin happy to concede to his poetry editor's authority, and in a final paragraph which is important in the way it delineates his attitude to modernism: 'I think the Poetry Editor has me here, because if he had, by some strange fortune, got hold of "The Wasteland" [*sic*] in manuscript, and brought it to me, I admit that I would have fought against that too. I also refuse to believe in Joyce's "Finnegans Wake".'[46] However, O'Faoláin's easy dismissal here of two of the supreme examples of literary modernism should not be taken as straightforwardly as it might first seem. Whatever O'Faoláin's stated public opinion, the fact remains that *The Bell* published a distinguished set of modern poets, all of whom had interesting and diverging relationships with the writings of the previous four decades. Alexandra Harris has demonstrated the way in which English artists had assimilated modernism and used its achievements and paradoxes in idiosyncratic ways to develop an English cultural flowering in the 1930s.[47] Similarly, *The Bell* should be considered as part of an Irish renaissance which interpreted modernism for the needs and hopes of Irish society. Ironically, despite O'Faoláin's consistent claims in his editorials about the paucity of Irish letters and Irish culture, *The Bell* itself stands as a direct challenge to the veracity of that sentiment. As the poet and diplomat Valentin Iremonger complained: 'I turn over the pages of *The Bell* since its inception and I list the following names: *W.R. Rodgers, John Hewitt, Maurice Craig, G.M. Brady, Margaret Corrigan, Maurice Farley, Robert Greacen, Sean Jennett, Patrick Kavanagh, Donagh McDonagh, John MacDonagh, Roy McFadden, Patrick Madden, Colin Middleton, Patrick Maybin, Bruce Williamson, Nick Nicholls, D.J. O'Sullivan, Brenda Chamberlain*, and others – ... all of them very good, some first rankers. This is some achievement for *three years*.'

Iremonger continued to deny O'Faoláin's assertions and, as his list attests, demonstrated the rude health of Irish letters in those years. He, for one, was upbeat and enthusiastic for the future, and criticised O'Faoláin's attempt to distinguish between older writers and those working today:

> You speak of 'revolutionary poets' being on 'one side of the Poetry Editor.' For my own part, being, and considering myself to be, a conservative poet working within the limitations of the English tradition, I disclaim the label; as I think all the poets you have published would. It was all very fine in the 'twenties and 'thirties to be revolutionary: there was a lot of debris to be cleared away and the vorticists, futurists, mechanists and other -sts and -aries were useful – but not to-day. To-day there is a war on.[48]

Add to Iremonger's list names such as Austin Clarke, Louis Aragon, Cecil Day Lewis, Freda Laughton and Louis MacNeice, who succeeded Taylor as poetry editor (March 1946–May 1947) in *The Bell*, and one begins to question O'Faoláin's motives in denying the strength of Irish letters.[49] Iremonger was able to demonstrate O'Faoláin's blind spot when it came to poetry, an arena in which he was least accomplished, but also to explode the division which

O'Faoláin chose to reinforce between early modernist writing and that being produced during the war. Weary of such dangers, Iremonger was determined to emulate O'Faoláin's wisdom in choosing a specialist editor for poetry when it came to his own involvement with the literary magazine *Envoy* (1949–51): 'I suggest that you should not function without a special Poetry Editor. *The Bell* found that they had to have such a being. It has the advantage that it gives the poetry section of the magazine some direction and objective and enables the magazine to lay down a line and to observe some standards.'[50] Although Iremonger was right to identify O'Faoláin's difficulties with regard to modernist poetry, O'Faoláin at least had the vision to allow its publication in *The Bell*. This was a significant legacy to leave Irish culture, and the magazine remains a high watermark of good writing during the war.

In 1948 O'Faoláin published *The Short Story* which had been previously serialised as 'The Craft of the Short Story' in *The Bell*.[51] This was a guide to the writing of short stories, and a theory as to their difference from the novel as a form; *The Short Story* reveals just how deeply immersed O'Faoláin was in the tradition of creative European literature. O'Faoláin selected several short story writers to illustrate his theories on the form; they include names as diverse and eclectic as Alphonse Daudet, Anton Chekhov, Guy de Maupassant, Robert Louis Stevenson, Frank O'Connor, Elizabeth Bowen, Ernest Hemingway and Henry James. O'Faoláin even went as far as adding his own improvements in square brackets to James's story 'The Real Thing' to demonstrate how it could have been better moved towards a conventional climax.[52]

In this book, two of O'Faoláin's recurring concerns – racial identity and a thinly composed society – conflate to give us a unified theory of the short story. For him, English society better lent itself to the format of the novel and was too conventional to produce great short story writers. Also, according to O'Faoláin, the English themselves did not value art, being more pragmatic and less exhibitionist than their Irish or continental neighbours: 'the fact is that the English do not admire the artistic temperament: they certainly do not demonstrate it'. Ironically, here O'Faoláin reproduced some of the worst excesses of Arnoldian Celticism, which he so despised in the work of Daniel Corkery by distinguishing between the two nations based on their aesthetic temperaments. O'Faoláin listed fourteen of the most interesting modern writers of short stories and found that only three were English. According to O'Faoláin, 'James Joyce, George Moore, Liam O'Flaherty, Elizabeth Bowen, Frank O'Connor, Lord Dunsany, H.E. Bates, A.E. Coppard, V.S. Pritchett, Ernest Hemingway, William Saroyan, Ring Lardner, John Steinbeck, Eudora Welty' were the most fascinating writers of short stories in the modern period.

This list, coupled with the list of authors whose stories he chose to illustrate his theory, points to a man who was deeply immersed in the literature of that period, and whose connection with an international literary tradition needs to be looked at more sympathetically.[53] Certainly, contemporaneous critics saw O'Faoláin's writing as at the forefront of the literary avant-garde; he was the first artist in the collection *New World Writing: Fifth Mentor Selection* (1954), an anthology that selected from the best of the ground-breaking American literary journal *New World Writing* and ran with the banner 'Avant Garde Means You!' The lesser lights in this book include Samuel Beckett, Dylan Thomas and Wallace Stevens, all now remembered as stars firmly within the literary firmament of modernism.[54] The American dramatist and Pulitzer prize-winning author William Saroyan felt confident in claiming: 'I believe O'Faoláin is one of the best writers of stories in the world.'[55]

As previously argued, not all of O'Faoláin's short stories should be considered as examples of a continuation in developments in European literature, some like 'Eden' were direct political metaphors. 'Childybawn' is the story of Benjy Spillane, the 50-year-old bachelor who only marries his long-suffering girlfriend after his mother dies, and is most likely an artistic response to the controversy surrounding his journalistic writings on falling Irish marriage rates, first published in Ireland as 'The Vanishing Irish' in the *Irish Times*.[56] 'The Silence of the Valley' was first published in *The Bell* in 1946, and is probably based on the death of Timothy Buckley who was best known as 'The Tailor', immortalised in Eric Cross's censored book *The Tailor and Ansty* (1942). Here, a motley crew of characters collect in the bar of a small hotel in some rural part of Ireland. They are present for the funeral of a local cobbler who lived in a small cottage with his sharp-tongued wife. Honor Tracy, who was an editorial assistant on *The Bell*, is the likely model for one of the characters, described as 'a sturdy, red mopped young woman in blue slacks now sitting on the counter drinking whiskey. She sometimes seemed not at all beautiful, and sometimes her heavy features seemed to have a strong beauty of their own.'[57] At the time of its writing O'Faoláin had begun an affair with Tracy, and the story was almost certainly based on his recollection of attending the Tailor's funeral with her.[58] Tracy is also almost certainly the model for the lover in one of O'Faoláin's most accomplished short stories 'Lovers of the Lake'. Frank O'Connor recalled the robust Tracy calling around to discuss her successful libel over her Irish sketchbook *Mind You, I've Said Nothing* (1953) and playfully discussing O'Faoláin's story:

> Honor Tracy has been discovered to be a near neighbour of ours and came to dinner the other night to say Sean has written a long story about Lough Derg in which two lovers discuss the fleash [*sic*] at interminable length – to Honor's mind, as she believes the Irish do far too much of that. She has finished a book on Ireland, the title of which is 'Mind, I Didn't Say Anything' the parish priest of Doneraile has added to his extensive premises and given up Mass or indeed emerging at all, while Honor is suing the Sunday Times for libel in settling her action out of court.[59]

Not all of O'Faoláin's short stories have such clear-cut autobiographical or political elements and some defy neat interpretation along such lines.[60] At this time the increasing pressure on O'Faoláin's private life led him to reconsider his position and the workload involved in editing a magazine, and he therefore decided to hand over editorial control to O'Donnell.

When Peadar O'Donnell inherited this position at *The Bell* in April 1946 the magazine had just passed its fifth year of production and gone through the Second World War. This should have been a time for consolidation and expansion. However, *The Bell* had never known financial stability, and it had always struggled to keep its circulation numbers up. Yet O'Faoláin's absence gave cause for optimism, and allowed for a radical restructure of *The Bell*'s editorial board and key players within it. O'Faoláin stepped back to accept the position of books editor, a role he had fulfilled at *Ireland To-Day* and which would not require the demands that a full-time editorial role entailed. However, this new position did not last long. He remained as books editor only for a year before handing over his responsibilities to Earnán [Ernie] O'Malley in April 1947. O'Malley's role in *The Bell* might explain Louis MacNeice's supposed role as poetry editor. The pair were close friends and it is conceivable that O'Malley asked MacNeice to lend his name to the journal in order to bring some critical credibility to the magazine; MacNeice's *The Poetry of W.B. Yeats* had been published in 1941 to widespread acclaim. But this restructuring offered opportunities for younger writers to assume a greater role. Honor Tracy became a direct assistant to O'Donnell and she stated that an entirely new format for *The Bell* was being envisaged under his editorial guidance. Writing to Sean O'Casey, Tracy informed him: 'Thank you so much for your subscription to the new *Bell*. The first number is November [1946] and I suppose you will start with that one ... we hope very much indeed that the new *Bell* will be the kind of magazine that you would feel inclined to write for. The Censorship will not worry us as far as the English edition is concerned.'[61] However, hopes for a successful reinvigoration under this new management were short-lived.

The Bell faced difficulties almost immediately, and no distinctive change in the format was noticeable. O'Donnell had always been the general manager of the magazine and he struggled to outgrow this role. His initial reaction to becoming editor was to turn to those figures he had known from his early career to ask for support. To this end he wrote to Liam O'Flaherty and Sean O'Casey asking for articles. Although O'Casey subscribed to *The Bell*, he never submitted an article under O'Donnell's time as editor. However, undeterred, O'Donnell asked him to review Lennox Robinson's edited collection, *Lady Gregory's Journals* (1946). O'Casey was reluctant, replying 'I'm not a reviewer', before noting that he was not very suited to the balanced criticism which reviewing required: 'it does not take kindly to me – in short, I'm not good at the job'. Despite his own misgivings O'Casey was willing to make an exception

in order to help O'Donnell out, but was worried that the magazine was struggling and its editor was personally keeping it afloat: 'By the way, where are you
boys getting the money for *The Bell*? I heard you were backing THIS, but that
the Gaels let you down. They would, as they let down O'Hickey, and set up
[Douglas] Hyde on Presidential Throne. I hear O'Flaherty has gone to Paris.
O'Faoláin's article on [Wolfe] Tone was a damn fine one.'[62]

It is enticing to imagine who O'Casey was referring to as the 'Gaels', but it is
most likely to be a reference to the Irish home market, which he perceived to be
dominated both intellectually and socially by conservative Catholic nationalists.
Whatever O'Casey was implying, he was right to be concerned; if O'Donnell
was personally making up the shortfall in *The Bell*, within a year he had decided
it was unsustainable. He again wrote to O'Casey and asked him for a contribution as the magazine was in imminent danger of closure:

> I am scrounging. I had decided on winding up *The Bell* but our friends in the
> States assure me that if I come out there I can probably rescue it and I am accord-
> ingly thumbing a lift across early in January. I am asking a group of writers to let
> me have breathing space by gifting me an article or short story out of which col-
> lection I could put together three issues and have a crack at finding the American
> outlet without which we must fail; we might with luck, even be able to afford
> an editor! If you have anything on hand that you could let me have in this way I
> should very much appreciate your sending it along.[63]

Such a begging letter is revealing as to the lowly financial condition in which
the magazine found itself and to the limited faith which it placed in its Irish
readership to provide sufficient support.

In the end, O'Donnell kept the magazine running for four more issues,
before closing it in May 1948 for a period of thirty months. O'Donnell never
managed to make the trip to the United States in order to find distributors
for the journal. The American consulate had received a copy of Professor
James Hogan's book, *Could Ireland Become Communist* (1935), which paints
O'Donnell as a seditious agitator, and his visa was refused because of this.
As O'Donnell explained with his typical laconic understatement, in an era of
fervent American McCarthyism: 'that book makes horrible reading to certain
strains of people'.[64]

O'Donnell should not have been surprised by his refusal on these grounds.
As early as 1932 he had taken the editor of *The Irish Rosary*, the Very Rev. H.V.
Casey, OP, to the high court for libel and damages for claiming he had been to
Russia to attend the Lenin College in Moscow to be instructed in revolution.
The defendant's solicitors argued that it was not a libel to 'say of a Catholic that
he is engaged in an anti-God campaign, that he went to Russia to study revolu-
tionary tactics with a view to setting up an anti-God communistic Government
in this country; they say it is not a libel to say of a man who has never been to

Russia that he went there in 1929'.[65] However, O'Donnell's resilience should not be underestimated, and such a setback was never going to keep a man as determined as him down for long. By October 1950, O'Donnell announced the triumphant return of *The Bell* to publication, and explained unequivocally that the reasons for its closure had not been financial, but due to its lack of a proper means of distribution in foreign markets: 'We closed in 1948, not from insolvency, but because of distribution difficulties in Britain and America.' This logistical problem had been overcome and the magazine could now grow in a more globalised marketplace, after O'Donnell had secured distribution agreements open to any Irish journal: 'No Irish magazine can live without external circulation, and in the new *Bell* we hope to solve this problem, not only for ourselves, but for all Irish periodicals going into the United States by organising a distribution service, open to all publishers.'. He also revealed that the prominence of Ulster Protestant voices was a deliberate editorial policy choice, and he hoped: 'to direct writers to deal with the more neglected aspects of Irish Life, and in this field, has asked partitionist Northern Protestants to write why they cannot reconcile their Protestantism to the idea of a united Ireland'.[66] Sean O'Casey, who had aided O'Donnell with his review before its closure, was happy to see the magazine back in publication: 'By implication of your tel. I assume that *The Bell* is to appear again, and to ring once more. I am very glad.'[67]

Faced with such obvious practical difficulties it is little wonder that O'Donnell's editorials suffered. His less than rigorous approach to his editorial duties, and his warm-hearted but disorganised personality, have been captured in Val Mulkerns's short account of that time.[68] Mulkerns began her writing career in *The Bell* and she belonged to a group of Dublin-based young writers, such as Anthony Cronin, who had felt that they were not being given sufficient exposure in the magazine. O'Donnell agreed to publish six of their short stories which, 'their committee judged to be the best they can offer', and began with Mulkerns's own submission, 'Girls'.[69] Mulkerns's story describes the tension of a house party where young women are competing for the attention of the boys present. The girls of the story are caught in a game of slur and counter slur, and the social tension is well rendered by Mulkerns. Certainly this story showed some of the promise which young Irish writers possessed, and Mulkerns's own career is testament to O'Donnell's decision to support her. David Marcus, another young writer who had founded the literary journal, *Irish Writing* (1946–54), submitted a short story called 'A Strange Woman'. This is a tale told through the perspective of a young boy, whose mother has died and whose father brings home another woman in her place.[70] Marcus recalled in his autobiography that when he first established *Irish Writing* he had contacted Seán O'Faoláin with a view to getting him to edit it. However, O'Faoláin declined having just retired from his editorial role in *The Bell*. He

also relates being contacted by O'Donnell who asked him to edit the literary
section of *The Bell*:

> Peadar eventually offered me what would be an extremely helpful monthly pay-
> ment, I was more than happy to agree. We shook hands on it, Peadar saying, 'I'll
> be in touch', and we parted. He wasn't in touch. That was the last I heard of the
> matter, the beginning and end of my reign as 'editor' of *The Bell*.[71]

Marcus's proven track record as an editor in *Irish Writing* obviously appealed
to O'Donnell who must have been searching for a new editor in the mould of
O'Faoláin, and it says something of the degree to which O'Donnell struggled
to reconcile the two roles of editor and general manager that he should be
searching so soon into the re-launch of *The Bell*. Presumably Marcus was not
contacted again because O'Donnell had found his own protégé in Anthony
Cronin. Tellingly, a month after Marcus's story first appeared, Cronin had
been installed as assistant editor. Cronin's first task was to issue a clarion call
for new Irish talent to come forward for publication. Cronin's article was perhaps a little too jaded and cynical for a man who was only 23 at the time of its
publication. Echoing the earlier editorials of O'Donnell and O'Faoláin, for him
the young Irish artist was trapped in a country doomed with a cultural inertia,
where the only escape was to take flight in emigration and exile: 'Exile might
be good for many young writers, I think, because Ireland at the moment is a
country where the general feeling is much more one of despair than of hope ...
the atmosphere is not favourable to life of any kind, and any method of escape
would surely be justified.'[72] Cronin's article is written with all the passion of
youth and with romanticism about exile that only one who had not experienced
emigration could cherish. He admitted as much when he later described his
first attempts at literary exile, writing a mock-heroic account of his time in Paris
with Brendan Behan in *Dead As Doornails* (1976).[73] Despite his later criticism
of his experience at *The Bell*, Cronin and the writers who appeared during his
time as assistant editor are worth considering.

To give some context to the standard of publication to which O'Donnell,
Cronin and *The Bell* aspired, it is necessary to look at the three international
numbers which were published under O'Faoláin and the quality of writers it
could attract. The first was initially conceived as an English number to corre-
spond to the Irish number of Cyril Connolly's *Horizon*. However, O'Faoláin
changed it to an international number when he was unable to secure a sufficient number of English contributors. Published in March 1943, the first
international number was hampered by the war from access to many writers
and artists. Nevertheless, it contained contributions from Sir Arnold Bax, the
composer and poet; a theatre review from the American theatre critic Richard
Watts; and a short story from the old Etonian, baronet and writer, Osbert
Sitwell. It also included a review of the works of Franz Werfel, whose *Song of*

Bernadette (1941) was a Catholic bestseller.[74] The second international number was also of surprising strength, containing a poem by the French socialist poet and resistance fighter Louis Aragon; a short story by the German writer Ernst Wiechert, who had been interned in Buchenwald by the Nazis for his dissident stance; and a review of the Catholic view of art by English writer and translator Edward Ingram Watkin.[75] The third international number contained John V. Kelleher's review of the Irish literary scene 'Irish Literature To-Day' which was critical of state censorship and had been informed by his friendship with O'Faoláin and Frank O'Connor.[76] This collection of diverse writers and public figures demonstrates the standard of submission which *The Bell* could draw from an international audience.

Alongside these international submissions was the work of Irish authors, several of whom appeared in the magazine's 'Work in Progress' series. The series began in December 1945 and finished with O'Faoláin's last edition as editor in April 1946. It opened with an extract called 'Doorstep to a Story' written by Peadar O'Donnell which marked the beginning of what would eventually become, ten years later, *The Big Windows* (1955).[77] It is an early version of *The Big Windows* bearing substantial differences from the published novel.[78] Also included in this series were works that would become Maura Laverty's *Lift Up Your Gates* (1946); Dr Robert Collis's account of struggling to find a home for dying Jewish children liberated from the Buchenwald, later published as *Straight On* (1947); an extract from Monk Gibbon's *Mount Ida* (1948); before finishing with a long section of Kate O'Brien's *That Lady* (1946). O'Brien's *That Lady* was a historical novel, similar to those popularised by Robert Graves's *I Claudius* (1934), set in sixteenth-century Spain under the reign of King Philip II. It was one of her more successful novels and was commissioned as a Hollywood film in 1955. O'Brien's *The Land of Spices* had already been banned by the censorship board, and her presence here was a deliberate act of support for the artist, whom O'Faoláin had considered a rival earlier in his publishing career.

Another writer who was supported by *The Bell* and whose work – like Maura Laverty's – made the transition to television, was James Plunkett. Plunkett can be considered among *The Bell*'s most enduring success stories. His work first came to national attention in *The Bell*, where he published twelve short stories and contributed throughout its entire lifespan. His writing is informed with a committed socialism and, encouraged by Peadar O'Donnell, he undertook a much criticised trip to the Soviet Union in 1955.[79] His novel *Strumpet City* (1969) was set in the build-up to the 1913 Dublin lockout, and is concerned with the effects of poverty on the inner-city poor, of which Plunkett himself was part; it was broadcast in 1980 by Raidió Teilifís Éireann as a television series to much critical acclaim. Plunkett bridges the transition between two Irelands, between rich and poor, and past and present. His work is layered with a strong social critique and with a wonderful skill in characterisation similar to Sean O'Casey in its execution. The third-last edition of *The Bell* is devoted entirely to him and consists of his five stories, 'The Eagles and the Trumpets', 'Weep for Our Pride', 'Mercy', 'The Dublin Fusilier' and 'The Half-Crown', which would all later appear in his short story collection, *The Trusting and the Maimed* (1955).[80] Though Plunkett's writing was often set in times past and looked backwards in its search for contemporary relevance, *The Bell* also published writing which was indicative of changes which were yet to be popularised in literature.

The June 1952 edition carried a strange story by John Hewitt called 'Mould'. It is unusual in its format and sits awkwardly with the other writings of the Northern Irish poet. Set in a remote suburb of Belfast this is the tale of Alexander Gaites, a recluse with a routine life and esoteric scholarly interests. Gaites's tale is written in his diary, which he completes at the end of every evening, much like his uncle John Curwood, whose voluminous memoirs the narrator still possesses. Curwood's diaries are written in a secret code or short-hand which makes Gaites suspicious of his uncle. He wonders if any person who 'makes such a record to have been superlatively secretive or to have been engaged in activity of thought too horrible to communicate at first hand'. The sinister mood of this story is reinforced when Gaites begins to notice strange goings on in his home and, in particular, a soft grey mould which begins to form on one of his books. Eventually, Gaites starts to see the mould everywhere and it slowly begins to occupy his home and belongings. Throughout, Gaites questions his own sanity and faithfully records his own responses to the terror which surrounds him. Finally, his radio dies, the electricity fails and he has only enough food left for one day. The entire street 'lay grey as under a thick grey frost of a gentle fall of snow'. The mould continues to cover the entire house and the whole city, and the short story ends with the author questioning his own testament: 'I do not know if what I have written makes sense …'[81]

This story is remarkable because it is at odds with the rest of Hewitt's work as the champion of poetic regionalism. However, it is more than just a work of whimsy on the author's part. Hewitt's consistent undermining of the epistemic authority of the text, which hints at unimaginable evils summoned through esoteric knowledge of forgotten books and suggestions of insanity, shares tropes with the work of the American horror writer H.P. Lovecraft. In particular, 'Mould' has striking similarities to 'The Colour Out of Space' (1927), which outlines an indescribable colour left after a meteorite has fallen to earth, which begins to cover and kill everything it touches, turning men insane before they are reduced to a grey dust. In addition to belonging to the tradition of the Irish Gothic, as embodied by Sheridan Le Fanu's 'Green Tea' (1872), Hewitt's story is an early example of a trend which saw a post-war upswing of interest in horror writing. This movement was given further impetus by the popular counterculture movement in American universities in the 1960s, where alternative realities or states of being were being explored and horror and science fiction increasingly gained credibility as topics for academic research. Although he was writing in the first half of the twentieth century, Lovecraft is only now beginning to be accepted as a serious author, with established names such as Michel Houellebecq writing critical interpretations of him.[82] 'Mould', then, is an early milestone on the road that would lead to an explosion of interest in horror writing a decade later and is distinctive, although not unique, as an example of prescient writing in *The Bell*.

Another story remarkable for its horrific tone and sinister implications is Flann O'Brien's last contribution to *The Bell*, published under his pseudonym Myles Na gCopaleen, 'Two in One'. O'Brien's story is the tale of a taxidermist's assistant who is trapped in a loathsome job under his spiteful and overbearing boss Kelly. This story employs the humour typical of O'Brien, which undercuts the horror of the narrator's actions. For example, he is piqued when Kelly keeps all the exotic animals to work with and only leaves the domestic pets to his assistant. Set in a small rural town in Ireland, the narrator, Murphy, expresses his disgust that: 'If a crocodile came in, or a Great Borneo spider, or (as once happened) a giraffe – Kelly kept them all for himself.' He can no longer stand the mistreatment and kills Kelly by beating him to death with a taxidermy tool. It is at this point that a twisted idea forms: '*I would don his skin and when the need arose, BECOME Kelly!*' After a few days of trying out Kelly's skin, Murphy decides to sleep in it, but it is here that he realises that in mixing the preparation chemical with the warmth of his own skin, Kelly's flesh sticks and reanimates itself; it thereby gets to 'live again, to breathe, to perspire'. Although initially shocked by this development, Murphy realises that he can now keep the taxidermy shop as his own and say his assistant has left. However, he is soon seen as the prime suspect in the disappearance of himself and is put on trial for murder. Rather than explain what has happened and face charges for the death of Kelly anyway, he decides to face his fate, and 'be cherished in the public mind as the victim of this murderous monster, Kelly. He *was* a murderer, anyway.'[83]

This story fits nicely with the rest of O'Brien's experiments in literature, reflecting his morbid interest in crime and murder. It also utilises meta-fictional plot devices, with one character literally within another. This effect is similar to *At Swim-Two-Birds* (1939) where fictional characters revolt against the oppressive domination of their author and thus become authors in themselves. This story is again an early example of a meta-fictional trend in literature which would follow later and predates the grotesque, yet humorous, postmodern short stories of a writer like Angela Carter in *The Bloody Chamber* (1979). Such stories give the lie to received notions of *The Bell* as a bastion of conservative realism.

It is no coincidence that both of these stories were written when Anthony Cronin was working as the assistant editor for *The Bell*. He first appeared on the title sheet listed as associate editor in May 1951 and continued in that capacity until the magazine's closure, although he was first published in February 1951. O'Donnell was still present as editor throughout these final years, but his interest visibly waned and Cronin began to take a more central role, writing the opening articles and submitting several pieces of criticism. By this late stage *The Bell* had already been closed for thirty months between April 1948 and November 1950 and missed another ten monthly issues between November 1950 and the final issue in December 1954. In total, out of the 168 months between January 1940 and December 1954, *The Bell* published 128 issues. Its troubled publication record led Cronin to try some experiments, such as a quarterly format, or an edition devoted entirely to one author in James Plunkett. Cronin's experience of working in *The Bell* is captured by his unflattering parody of Peadar O'Donnell as Prunshios McGonaghy, the editor of the fictional journal *The Trumpet*, in his novel *The Life of Riley* (1964). The novel captures something of the problems faced by the declining magazine, even if it is harsh in its comic evaluation of its achievements, with notable slights at O'Donnell, O'Faoláin, Kavanagh and even Nick Nicholl's 'The Bone and The Flower':

> *The Trumpet* had been a smart literary and sociological journal during the war, when it had been edited by a peasant historian rather more sophisticated than Prunshios, and when Ireland itself had been the home of flourishing artistic movements. It had carried a deal of documentary reportage and statistics about fishing, as well as poems like abattoirs, full of bones and sinews and thighs and hearts, and jerky short-stories about unevenly articulate peasants whose utterances varied from monosyllabic grunts to phrases like, 'when you shook out the bright scarf of your laughter'. It had not thrived under Prunshios. For one thing, with the end of the war the cattle-boats had been crammed with departing writers, standing knee-deep amid the puke and porter, quietly forgetting about O'Flaherty and O'Faolain and rehearsing their line on Connolly, Kierkegaard, Kafka and Scotty Wilson.[84]

Yet Cronin's influence is undeniable in the later editions. Outside the experiments with form and format, his time at *The Bell* is notable for the publication of interesting new criticism, such as a critical article called 'James Joyce's *Stephen Hero*', an early example of work on Joyce's unfinished novel.[85]

Although it is impossible to tell what Cronin was directly responsible for, young poets such as Thomas Kinsella first appear under his tenure. Under Cronin there is also a turn to more sexualised criticism and prose, perhaps befitting the changing social mores since *The Bell* began publication. He printed an article on the legendary sexual deviant, the Earl of Rochester, a Seamus De Faoite short story called 'The Mansion Purples' which describes the desire of an adolescent boy for the flower arranger in a local church, and an unusual short story called 'The Awakening' by Richard Austin. This is the tale of a detached, rationalist, young man who is devoid of human emotion and who attempts to seduce a young girl in London's Hyde Park. The protagonist owes something to Albert Camus's *The Stranger* (1942) in his ability to rationalise his own feelings amid a complete indifference to those in society.

Despite the quality of submission which appeared under Cronin, his own editorials merely aped those of O'Faoláin and O'Donnell before him, bemoaning the lack of any direction or drive in other young writers.[86] The new young editor's complaints did not go unnoticed, and grated with some of Dublin's literary set, who might reluctantly have been prepared to accept criticism from artists as established as O'Donnell and O'Faoláin, but not from one with Cronin's meagre attainments. As Frank MacManus remarked in a letter to Sean O'Casey:

> Another tidal wave of narking and complaining that I hear every bloody week from Irish writers. For Tony Cronin, Peadar O'Donnell's bright boy, nothing is right with Irish writers, the women and the weather. He had an editorial or an associate-editorial in *The Bell* lately that was the essence of complaining. And I don't know what he has written except a few colourless poems and an article or two. And speaking of articles he had one in another *Bell* about the Earl of Rochester. The Earl, said Cronin, speaking of his profligacy, did all the <u>usual</u> things. I like that word 'usual'. It puts the earl in his place as a sinner. Cronin could show him a thing or two it seems to say. He's only one of the narkers and I'll be another if I worry about them.[87]

Yet despite such backbiting Cronin must be given some credit. Under his guidance *The Bell* managed to maintain the quality of its submissions even as its circulation was rapidly dwindling. While he was there, James Plunkett became more prominent, Kate O'Brien published her short story 'A Fit of Laughing', Brian Friel submitted an early story 'The Child' and *The Bell* embraced modern literary criticism with further articles on Joyce and Beckett. Despite this seeming robust health, the magazine gave no indication that the final issue was to be the last. When looked at from this perspective, *The Bell* seems to have enjoyed a frenetic descent into publishing oblivion.

Notes

1 Francis McManus, 'Looking Back in Love and Anger', *Sunday Press* (23 May 1965).

2 Humphrey Jennings and Charles Madge (eds), *May the Twelfth Mass-Observation Day-Surveys by over Two Hundred Observers* (London: Faber & Faber, 1937).

3 See H.D. Willcock, 'Mass-Observation', *The American Journal of Sociology*, 48:4 (January 1943), pp. 445–456.

4 For an example, see Seán Dunne (ed.), *The Cork Review* (Cork: Triskel Arts Centre, 1991).
5 Séan O'Faoláin, 'For the Future', *The Bell*, 1:2 (November 1940), p. 5.
6 J.E. Samuel, 'Colliery Disaster: Evidence of J.E. Samuel', *Fact*, 4 (July 1937), pp. 45–50.
7 D83222, 'I Did Penal Servitude' *The Bell*, 9:1 (October 1944). See Robert Greacen, *The Sash My Father Wore: An Autobiography* (Edinburgh: Mainstream Publishing, 1997), p. 193. See Dáire Keogh, '"There's no Such Thing as a Bad Boy": Fr Flanagan's Visit to Ireland, 1946', *History Ireland* (Spring 2004), p. 31; D83222, *I Did Penal Servitude* (Dublin: Metropolitan Publishing, 1945).
8 Henry James, *Henry James: Literary Criticism, Essays on Literature, American Writers, English Writers* (New York: The Library of America, 1984).
9 James, *Henry James: Literary Criticism*, pp. 404, 403.
10 Artists and critics as notable as Kevin Barry, Declan Kiberd and John McGahern have repeated this position when discussing the short story. See Helen Davies, 'Raise Your Glasses', *The Sunday Times* (Culture; 1 April 2012), p. 23; Declan Kiberd, 'John McGahern's *Amongst Women*', in Maria Tymoczko and Colin Ireland (eds), *Language and Tradition in Ireland: Continuities and Displacements* (Amherst and Boston: University of Massachusetts Press, 2003), pp. 195–214; Pat Collins (dir.), *John McGahern: A Private World* [DVD: PAL]. Ireland, Hummingbird Productions, 2006.
11 Harold Bloom has developed a theory of poetry which has a similar grounding; see Harold Bloom, *The Anxiety of Influence: A Theory of Poetry* (Oxford: Oxford University Press, 1973).
12 Seán O'Faoláin, 'The Dilemma of Irish Letters', *The Month*, 2:4 (July–December 1949), pp. 373, 372.
13 Seán O'Faoláin, *Vive Moi! An Autobiography* (London: Sinclair-Stephenson, 1993), pp. 267, 377.
14 Augustine Martin, *Bearing Witness: Essays on Anglo-Irish Literature* (Dublin: University College Dublin Press, 1996), p. 92.
15 Seán O'Faoláin, *De Valera* (London: Penguin Books, 1939), p. 158.
16 See Cyril Connolly, 'Comment', *Horizon*, 1:1 (1940).
17 Clair Wills, *That Neutral Island* (London: Faber & Faber, 2007), p. 280.
18 Seán O'Faoláin to Edward Garnett (n.d.) Garnett, MS 1542.
19 Seán O'Faoláin to Gwyneth Foden (21 October n.d.); quoted in R.F. Foster, *W.B. Yeats: A Life II: The Arch-Poet 1915–1939* (Oxford: Oxford University Press, 2003), p. xxi.
20 MacNeice became poetry editor just before O'Faoláin retired as editor, although his presence remains something of a mystery in both *The Bell* and MacNeice scholarship. For more on this, see Kelly Matthews, *The Bell Magazine and the Representation of Irish Identity* (Dublin: Four Courts Press: 2012), pp. 94–95.
21 For example, see Geoffrey Taylor, 'William Allingham', *The Bell*, 4:2 (May 1942); or Geoffrey Taylor, 'The Best "Nation" Poet', *The Bell*, 6:3 (June 1943).
22 Geoffrey Taylor to Norah McGuinness (n.d.), MS 1033, the Norah McGuinness archive at the Dublin Writers Museum.

23 See Catherine W. Reilly, *English Poetry of the Second World War: a Biobibliography* (London: Masell, 1986), p. 196; Gerald Dawe (ed.), *Earth Voices Whispering An Anthology of Irish War Poetry 1914–1945* (Belfast: Blackstaff Press, 2008); Anne Powell (ed.), *Shadows of War: British Women's Poetry of the Second World War* (Stroud: Sutton Publishing, 1999). While there Laughton wrote 'Afternoon in a Garden at Vinecash', *A Transitory House* (London: Jonathan Cape, 1945).

24 Geoffrey Taylor (ed.), *Irish Poems of To-Day: Chosen from the First Seven Volumes of "The Bell"* (London: Secker & Warburg, 1944).

25 Laughton, *A Transitory House.*

26 Freda Laughton, 'To the Bride', *A Transitory House*, p. 49.

27 Austin Clarke, 'Recent Verse', *Irish Times* (19 January 1946), p. 4.

28 Frank Harvey, 'Public Opinion', *The Bell*, 12:3 (June 1946), p. 257.

29 Valentin Iremonger, 'Aspects of Poetry To-Day', *The Bell*, 12:3 (June 1946), p. 247.

30 Valentin Iremonger, 'The Poems of Freda Laughton', *The Bell*, 11:4 (January 1946), pp. 897–900.

31 Patricia K. Harrison, 'Public Opinion', *The Bell*, 10:5 (August 1945), p. 446.

32 'Poetry Recital', *Irish Times* (23 April 1945), p. 3.

33 S.B. Kennedy, *Irish Art and Modernism 1880–1950* (Belfast: The Institute of Irish Studies, The Queen's University of Belfast, 1991), p. 68.

34 Information on the White Stag Group and its associates is taken from S.B. Kennedy, *Irish Art and Modernism 1880–1950*, pp. 90–114; Clair Wills, *That Neutral Island* (London: Faber & Faber, 2007), pp. 283–284. Fionna Barber, *Art in Ireland since 1910* (London: Reaktion Books, 2013), pp. 99–106; Róisín Kennedy, 'Experimentalism or Mere Chaos? The White Stag Group and the Reception of Subjective Art in Ireland', in Edwina Keown and Carol Taaffe (eds), *Irish Modernism: Origins, Contexts, Publics (Reimagining Ireland)* (London: Peter Lang, 2009), pp. 179–194.

35 For an example of *The Bell's* sustained criticism of the R.H.A., see Arthur Power, 'The R.H.A.', *The Bell*, 6:3 (June 1943).

36 Arthur Power, 'Exhibition on Living Art', *The Bell*, 7:1 (October 1943); Herbert Read, 'On Subjective Art', *The Bell*, 7:5 (February 1944).

37 Elizabeth Bowen, 'Mainie Jellett', *The Bell*, 9:3 (December 1944); Elizabeth Curran, 'The Art of Nano Reid', *The Bell*, 3:2 (November 1941).

38 See the Oxford Dictionary of National Biography: www.oxforddnb.com.ezproxy. liv.ac.uk/view/article/33843 (accessed 12 November 2011); Nigel Heseltine, 'Welsh Writing Today', *The Bell*, 6:5 (August 1943).

39 Arthur Power, *Conversations with James Joyce* (London: Millington Ltd, 1974).

40 See Seán O'Faoláin, *A Summer in Italy* (London: Eyre & Spottiswoode, 1949); Seán O'Faoláin, *South to Sicily* (London: Collins, 1953). O'Faoláin also wrote a heartfelt introduction to Paul Henry's autobiography: Paul Henry, *An Irish Portrait: The Autobiography of Paul Henry R.H.A.* (London: B.T. Batsford, 1951); see also Seán O'Faoláin, *The Story of Ireland* (London: Collins, 1943).

41 For an article that explains the significance of material culture in *The Bell*, see Kelly Mathews, '"Something Solid to Put your Heels on": Representation and transformation in *The Bell*', *Éire-Ireland*, 46:1 & 2 (Spring/Summer 2011), pp. 106–127.

42 Alex Davis, 'The Irish Modernists', in Matthew Campbell (ed.), *The Cambridge*

Companion to Contemporary Irish Poetry (Cambridge: Cambridge University Press, 2003), p. 78.

43 Nick Nicholls, 'The Bone and Flower', *The Bell*, 7:2 (November 1943).

44 Seán O'Faoláin and Geoffrey Taylor, ' Sense and Nonsense in Poetry', *The Bell*, 7:2 (November 1943), pp. 156–159.

45 See Seán O'Faoláin, 'Plea for a New Type of Novel', *The Virginia Quarterly Review*, 10:2 (April 1934), pp. 189–199.

46 Seán O'Faoláin and Geoffrey Taylor, 'Sense and Nonsense in Poetry', *The Bell*, 7:2 (November 1943), pp. 156–169.

47 Alexandra Harris, *Romantic Moderns: English Writers, Artists and the Imagination from Virginia Woolf to John Piper* (London: Thames & Hudson, 2010).

48 Valentin Iremonger, 'Public Opinion', *The Bell*, 7:3 (December 1943), pp. 255–257.

49 MacNeice's role as poetry editor remains something of a mystery. Although his name appears in the magazine neither his autobiography nor his biography mention this. See Louis MacNeice, *The Strings are False: An Unfinished Autobiography*, int. E.R. Dodds (London and Boston: Faber & Faber, 1965); Jon Stallworthy, *Louis MacNeice* (London: Faber & Faber, 1995). Frank Shovlin in *The Irish Literary Periodical 1923–1958* (Oxford: Clarendon Press, 2003), p. 121 argues for Ernie O'Malley being responsible for MacNeice's connection with the journal. However, there could also have been a connection through the British Broadcasting Corporation (BBC), with MacNeice, Denis Johnston, W.R. Rodgers, Seán O'Faoláin, Frank O'Connor, Joseph Tomelty and many other contributors to *The Bell* working there.

50 Valentin Iremonger to John Ryan (17 September 1949), quoted in Shovlin, *The Irish Literary Periodical*, p. 137.

51 Seán O'Faoláin, *The Short Story* (London: Collins, 1948).

52 Henry James, 'The Real Thing', in O'Faoláin, *The Short Story*, pp. 262–288.

53 O'Faoláin, *The Short Story*, pp. 37, 36.

54 Arabel J. Porter (ed.), *New World Writing: Fifth Mentor Selection* (New York: The New American Library, 1954).

55 William Saroyan, 'The Unholy Word', *The Bell*, 15:1 (October 1947), p. 36.

56 Seán O'Faoláin, 'The Vanishing Irish', *Irish Times* (15 March 1954), p. 8; Seán O'Faoláin, 'Childybawn', *The Bell*, 19:10 (November 1954).

57 Seán O'Faoláin, 'The Silence of the Valley', *The Bell*, 12:6 (September 1946), p. 466.

58 For Tracy's recollections of the Ireland of that time, see Honor Tracy, *Mind You, I've Said Nothing* (London: Methuen, 1953).

59 Frank O'Connor to Helen [Kelleher]? (n.d. [1953]?), UCC, BL/L/JVK/192.

60 Julia O'Faoláin confirms this reading of the story by recalling a particularly embarrassing situation when Tracy showed up at their family holiday in Gougane Barra. See Julia O'Faoláin, *Trespassers: A Memoir* (London: Faber & Faber, 2013). p. 87.

61 Honor Tracy to Sean O'Casey (16 August 1946), O'Casey, MS 37, 998.

62 Sean O'Casey to Peadar O'Donnell (21 November 1946), O'Casey, MS 37, 998. O'Casey did publish his review, See Sean O'Casey, 'A Protestant Bridget', *The Bell*, 13:5 (February 1947), pp. 64–72.

63 Peadar O'Donnell to Sean O'Casey (18 December 1947), O'Casey, MS 37, 998.

64 Peadar O'Donnell, '*The Bell* Suspends Publication', *The Bell*, 16:1 (April 1948), pp. 1–4.
65 See 'Peadar O'Donnell's Libel Action', *Irish Times* (4 June 1932), p. 3.
66 Quidnunc, 'An Irishman's Diary', *Irish Times* (26 October 1950), p. 5.
67 Sean O'Casey to Peadar O'Donnell (6 November 1950), O'Casey, MS 37, 998.
68 Val Mulkerns, '"Did You Once See Shelley Plain?" Dublin, *The Bell*, the Fifties', *New Hibernia Review*, 10:3 (Autumn 2006).
69 Val Mulkerns, 'Girls', *The Bell*, 14:4 (July 1947).
70 David Marcus, 'The Strange Woman', *The Bell*, 17:6 (September 1951).
71 David Marcus, *Oughtobiography: Leaves from the Diary of a Hyphenated Jew* (Dublin: Gill & Macmillan, 2001), p. 104.
72 Anthony Cronin, 'The Young Writer', *The Bell*, 17:6 (September 1951), p. 12.
73 Anthony Cronin, *Dead As Doornails* (Dublin: Dolmen Press, 1976).
74 *The Bell*, 5:6 (March 1943).
75 *The Bell*, 6:5 (August 1943).
76 John V. Kelleher, 'Irish Literature To-Day', *The Bell*, 10:4 (July 1945).
77 Peadar O'Donnell, *The Big Windows* (London: Jonathan Cape, 1955).
78 Peadar O'Donnell, 'Doorstep to a Story', *The Bell*, 11:3 (December 1945), pp. 752–761.
79 W.J. McCormack, 'James Plunkett', *Independent* (30 May 2003).
80 *The Bell*, 19:9 (August 1954); James Plunkett, *The Trusting and the Maimed* (New York: Devin-Adair, 1955).
81 John Hewitt, 'Mould', *The Bell*, 18:3 (June 1952), pp. 163–169.
82 Michel Houellebecq, *H.P. Lovecraft: Against the World, Against Life*, trans. Dorna Khazeni (London: Weidenfeld & Nicolson, 2006).
83 Myles Na Copaleen, 'Two in One', *The Bell*, 19:8 (July 1954), pp. 31–34.
84 Anthony Cronin, *The Life of Riley* (London: Secker & Warburg, 1964), p. 113. Julia O'Faoláin is equally unflattering in her account of Cronin. She recalls one instance where the young poet pulled a chair from under her at a party given by Oonagh, Lady Oranmore and Browne. See Julia O'Faoláin, *Trespassers*. p. 148.
85 Joseph Prescott, 'James Joyce's *Stephen Hero*', *The Bell*, 19:10 (November 1954).
86 Anthony Cronin, 'A Province Once Again', *The Bell*, 19:7 (June 1954); Anthony Cronin, 'This Time, This Place', *The Bell*, 19:8 (July 1954).
87 Frank MacManus to Sean O'Casey (9 August 1954), O'Casey, MS 38, 126.

6

Conclusion: Signing off

On 10 March 1966 Frank O'Connor died from a heart attack in Dublin. He had been unwell since suffering a stroke while teaching at Stanford University. For O'Faoláin, the loss of his oldest friend was a hard blow. He wrote to John Kelleher to commiserate and to try to articulate something of the loss:

> Well, that is theoretically all over! A sudden death blesses those who receive it and blasts those who bury them. If you have been feeling the same sense of blackness, blankness and emptiness I have, I have just about enough feeling left in me to be sorry for you with the kind of miserable sorrow relatives of the dead dully feel for one another – no more! And I think you, like me, feel more – regrets, the 'too-late' guilt, remorse, and unappeasable anger with certain among the living, more among the dead, and last of all and most of all with Whoever made us and kills us.
>
> It is not his genius I miss, that is in his books. It is not even the man – we had both lost <u>him</u> before now. I hate the simple fact of his not being alive; not solely but mainly because while he lived he was so <u>abundantly</u> alive. When Yeats died he was not only older but less alive, and he was at no time so vitally, combustibly, explosively alive. This fellow was the incarnation of living men.
>
> His genius depended on it. It was a flame. No alloy. No coldness of the intelligence to make it blend with some other forum of apprehension. Pure undiluted intuition. A rare marvel. Of course, death always telescopes and simplifies a man. We think of him only as his essence. You and I know his many many hours and days of near-lunacy from depression, boredom, fury, frustration; as we know too how his essential sensitivity and reasonability would leak away into their opposites – even into cruelty and brutality and beyond insensitivity. It had to be that way. He just had to be what he was – a receptacle for every emotional strain, as for every least gentle and tender whisper of the softest wind of feeling, of the mystery and the poetry of life ... Such men make their death our death. They fill life with life and death. It is all about me these days – this sense of waste. Whence my obscene rage – so futile, so frustrating, so unwarming.
>
> It is rounded off. The turbulent life, the mellowing – that did <u>not</u> decline into apathy, capable of fine indignation to the last – the big public ... the return to Ireland, the happy years with Harriet, not declining into mere dull domestic habit, the grand old man admired still (and intensely) by the young, his gifts

intact (not as with Yeats fading out slowly, perceptibly) – and then, the hammer blow. Leaving us all to sorrow for the loss of a <u>completed</u> man. The tree was in full leaf when it crashed.

My deep sympathy with you, dear John, is this <u>total</u> loss.[1]

This letter is worth quoting at length for its touching sincerity, but also for what it says about the changes that O'Connor and O'Faoláin faced as the grand old men of Irish letters. The reference to W.B. Yeats is telling; O'Connor's death sounded the death knell of a generation, a generation that had drawn to O'Faoláin and *The Bell*. As the 1960s faded into the 1970s O'Faoláin and his peers were giving way to a new group of writers both at home and abroad. The short story as a medium had lost the popularity and prestige it had enjoyed a decade previously and emerging talents like that of John McGahern and Seamus Heaney were beginning to take centre stage. *The Bell* itself had ceased production in 1954, but in many ways it began its decline once O'Faoláin relinquished editorial control.

O'Faoláin had left the magazine in April 1946 and was still disillusioned with it a year later. He took a dim view of its achievements and its chances for survival:

> P O'D [Peadar O'Donnell] says he's flying to the U.S.A. in January: he will be looking for 1000 subscribers to *The Bell*, which is against the ropes just now. Kavanagh in the December issue was disgraceful. F O'C [Frank O'Connor] was deeply hurt. And no wonder! P O'D is not a good editor: he is a marvellous scrounger and his scrounging ways have kept the old mag going for 6 or 7 years … I wish I had £5000. I'd run that magazine as it should be done. Not too Irish. Just a world standard magazine produced in Dublin and, so, Irish; as the *Cornhill* is English, and the *A. Monthly* [Atlantic Monthly] is American and *Les Deux Mondes* [Revue des Deux Mondes (1829–)] is French. It could be done and pay its way.[2]

This letter captures the tension which drove *The Bell* in the O'Faoláin years, a tension that was all too common to Irish literature in general. O'Faoláin in his career as a writer was consistently struggling with overcoming literary provincialism and achieving the universality which he perceived was the birthright of his international peers. His platonic ideal of a magazine was one that was Irish, but unselfconsciously so, one that could stand its ground with the best writers globally, but rooted in the particular. In this, he felt *The Bell* had failed. However, O'Faoláin was too close to make an objective judgement; *The Bell* at its best was comparable with any other literary journal from London to New York, and the generation of writers and contributors as excellent as could be found elsewhere. That said, its eclectic tastes meant it often lacked the direction and focus of other journals, and this was especially true during O'Donnell's editorial tenure. O'Faoláin's criticism of O'Donnell's editorial style was insightful, the magazine worked best in those first six years when the pair worked together, and O'Donnell never had the interest to take it in an entirely new direction.

On mature reflection, O'Donnell also felt his time as editor of the magazine had been a failure. In that telling public exchange in 1970 between O'Faoláin and O'Donnell, where they both denied their integral role in *The Bell*, he reiterated his belief that it should have closed with O'Faoláin's departure: 'I think – I even thought at the time – that the *Bell* should have ceased publication when O'Faolain decided to end his editorship of it.'[3] Such apathy from the editors is surprising, especially considering a steady, if superficial, interest in *The Bell* by the Irish academic and cultural elite. Yet O'Faoláin was not only disappointed with the format and content of the magazine, he would later question its entire validity as a project. The very things that now define *The Bell* in popular memory had failed according to O'Faoláin. His constant criticisms of the government, his run-ins with the Irish Catholic Church and his struggle to nurture Irish literary talent were instead symptomatic of his own sense of failure, failure to become the writer he had hoped to be in his youth:

> To return to change and revolution, do you know I haven't written a letter to the papers for three years, for nearly eight I think if I discount one: (about nothing at all.) And for Phwy? For because (a.) I am fedup, and (b.) because I am fedup because I have a fear that I have no reason to be fedup: in other words, since I went to Italy first I began to see that maybe (barring religion) the bloody country (this one) isn't doing so bad at all, and that we were wrong (which is a smooth way of saying I was all wrong) in our attitude to it ... Ireland has become infinitely more tolerable since we got the Free State – physically; and indeed in some ways morally. And was it so intellectually freer? And was the Church any better then? So, when I saay [*sic*] we were wrong (I was wrong) I think we were (I was): we should have taken the side of the politicians, mixed with them, pushed them not abused them, which, for a person like me, means the impossible. I have no business meddling, a bloody brainless dreamy dotty of a writer ... so we (I) shouldn't have butted in at all. They will get on, millimetre by m. ... and if I live and am not blasted I just barely might write those few satirical-lyrical novels that are all I now want to do.[4]

To the generation that grew to maturity with *The Bell*, such an opinion would have been clearly wrong. For them, *The Bell* stood as a herald for the vanguard of cultural change and as a strong voice of liberal secularism against the perceived hegemony of the Church and state, although if its editors saw it as that is not so clear. However, Ireland had changed dramatically in the fourteen years since *The Bell* first opened its pages to 'Gentile or Jew, Protestant or Catholic, priest or layman' to evaluate the culture in which it was based and to take up the fight for the Irish arts.[5]

O'Faoláin had grown disillusioned with all the causes which he championed during his time with *The Bell*. Even state censorship, which was a recurring theme in *The Bell*, had lost its ability to rouse his ire: 'I found I was <u>dragged</u> into uttering a few words against [Jack] Piggot and the Censorship. In my heart I really do not care. I think I'll start rereading Turgenev to see how he did it.'[6] Ironically, the area where O'Faoláin felt most personally involved was the one in which he had grounds for complaint, his Catholicism. Although he remained nominally a Catholic throughout his life and consistently returned to it as a source in his writings, he was a victim of direct persecution on the part of the Catholic Church in Ireland. Archbishop John Charles McQuaid personally detested O'Faoláin and interfered directly, although unsuccessfully, in a bid to prevent his nomination as the director of the Arts Council. Archbishop McQuaid had dismissively, though perhaps insightfully, described O'Faoláin and the group of writers around *The Bell* as 'infected with the liberalism that considers it may give reign to "realistic expression", that is, to the unworthy aspects of life in books. They suffer much from the disregard of the Irish Catholic public.'[7] Despite these minor interferences from the Church and state, the truth of the matter was that *The Bell*, with a lifespan of fourteen years, was only a short period in the careers of writers as prolific as O'Donnell and O'Faoláin.

Arguably, O'Donnell's time as editor of *An Phoblacht* between 1926 and 1929 was more influential than editorship of *The Bell*. After all, it was in *An Phoblacht* where O'Donnell first popularised withholding land annuity payments, a policy which would later become a staple of the de Valera administration. After *The Bell* had closed, O'Donnell published *The Big Windows* (1955), *Proud Island* (1975) and his second volume of autobiography *There Will Be Another Day* (1963), and this was in addition to his duties as a committed political activist. Similarly, O'Faoláin also went on to publish widely long after his official association with *The Bell* had ended, although he would never be as central to the public consciousness as when he edited the magazine. He produced an experimental novel, *And Again?*, as late as 1979, and a three-volume set of *The Collected Stories of Sean O'Faolain* appeared in 1982. Throughout the 1970s and 1980s he wrote for magazines as diverse as *Playboy*, *The Atlantic Monthly* and *London Review of Books*.

In light of their sustained success as authors then, it is unsurprising that O'Donnell and O'Faoláin would not rate their time with *The Bell* as among their most important achievements. After all, these two men had fought through the civil war, and both had been on the run, fearing for their lives. Yet today, O'Faoláin is arguably best remembered for his editorials in the magazine, and O'Donnell, by contrast, for his role as a political agitator. Any analysis of *The Bell* and those who wrote for it must seek to reconcile these two extremes and find some common ground to contextualise the magazine and the role it played in their lives.

Despite the editors' open disavowal and lack of interest, *The Bell* can claim some concrete achievements, and its place in Irish cultural history is assured. Outside of the commonly recalled attacks on state censorship, jousts with the Catholic Church, and the promotion of a remarkable group of writers, *The Bell* also played its part in the development of a new Ireland. The cultural ideology of the young state was still being openly debated when *The Bell* was launched in 1940, and it sent a strong, if sometimes conflicted, message that other voices were competing for a role in this new society. That Ireland later chose to reject the type of society that *The Bell* had also resisted is a historical fact, yet identifying the contribution it made to this change is more elusive. Ultimately, *The Bell* was not overcome by the exhaustion of its writers and editors, fighting the good fight against the oppressive forces of Church and state, but by external events which were reforming all western societies.

Gay Byrne's *The Late Late Show* was first broadcast in 1962, taking up some of the debates *The Bell* had discussed a decade before, and the death of journal culture as a whole had as much to do with the rise of new media in radio and television as it did with its editors' failure to find content that was relevant to a modern Irish market. O'Faoláin may have been idealistic in trying to start from scratch and build the edifice of Irish culture anew, but *The Bell* and its writers left an important mark on the Irish cultural imagination.

Ireland's youth in the decade when *The Bell* stumbled towards its demise, were not interested enough in the magazine to ensure its survival; it had lost its ability to engage and was overtaken by other fora. Yet its legacy remains assured because it uniquely crystallised the faults of an establishment whose influence was still being felt and resisted by a younger generation. Appropriately for two disillusioned revolutionaries, history has a way of overtaking the best laid plans, and the new Ireland which O'Donnell and O'Faoláin attempted to usher in with *The Bell* simply did not appreciate their efforts. As John Montague has suggested, even the most expert of campanologists must eventually ask for whom the bell tolls, and the young Ireland which they helped to nurture took for granted the freedoms which *The Bell* had so valiantly championed:

> At the Fleadh Cheoil in Mullingar
> There were two sounds, the breaking
> Of glass, and the background pulse
> Of music. Young girls roamed
> The streets with eager faces,
> Pushing for men. Bottles in
> Hand, they rowed out for a song:
> *Puritan Ireland's dead and gone,*
> *A myth of O'Connor and O'Faoláin.*[8]

Notes

1 Seán O'Faoláin to John V. Kelleher (14 March 1966), UCC, BL/L/JVK/102.
2 O'Faoláin to John V. Kelleher (14 December 1947), UCC, BL/L/JVK/19; the article O'Faoláin is referring to is Patrick Kavanagh's 'Coloured Balloons' discussed in Chapter 1.
3 Peadar O'Donnell, 'The Little Magazine', *Irish Times* (4 March 1970), p. 11.
4 O'Faoláin to John V. Kelleher (n.d. [1959]?), UCC, BL/L/JVK/93.
5 Seán O'Faoláin, 'This is Your Magazine', *The Bell*, 1:1 (October 1940), p. 9.
6 O'Faoláin to John V. Kelleher (15 January 1959), UCC, BL/L/JVK/83.
7 See John Cooney, *John Charles McQuaid: Ruler of Catholic Ireland* (Dublin: The O'Brien Press, 1999), pp. 159, 319.
8 John Montague, 'The Siege of Mullingar', *The Cork Review* (Cork: Triskel Arts Centre, 1991), p. 52.

Works cited

Contributors to journals often wrote under a pen name to maintain anonymity. In such cases the name is followed by *see* and their proper name appears elsewhere in the works cited list.

Electronic sources

Abbey Theatre Archive: www.abbeytheatre.ie/archives/.
The Blanket: A Journal of Protest and Dissent: http://indiamond6.ulib.iupui.edu:81/.
Dictionary of Irish Biography: http://dib.cambridge.org/.
Oxford Dictionary of National Biography: www.oxforddnb.com/.
The Franciscan Archive: www.franciscan-archive.org/.
The Guardian and Observer Digital Archive: www.theguardian.com/info/2012/jul/25/digital-archive-notice.
The Houses of the Oireachtas: www.oireachtas.ie/parliament/.
The Irish Newspapers Archive: www.irishnewsarchive.com/.
The Irish Times Newspaper Archive: www.irishtimes.com/archive.
Landed Estates Database: www.landedestates.ie/.
The National Archives of Great Britain: www.nationalarchives.gov.uk/.
The National Archives of Ireland: www.nationalarchives.ie/.
The Stormont Papers: http://stormontpapers.ahds.ac.uk/stormontpapers/index.html.
The Times Digital Archive: http://gale.cengage.co.uk/times.aspx/.
Bureau of Military History: www.bureauofmilitaryhistory.ie/.

Manuscript collections

Austin Clarke Papers, 1913–1974, National Library of Ireland.
Edward Garnett Collection, Harry Ransom Center, the University of Texas at Austin.
Elizabeth Bowen Collection, Harry Ransom Center, the University of Texas at Austin.
Frank O'Connor Collection, British Broadcasting Corporation Written Archive Centre, Reading.
Frank O'Connor Collection, Howard Gotlieb Archival Research Center, Boston University.
Frank O'Connor Collection, John J. Burns Library, Boston College.

George Weller/Seán O'Faoláin Letters, Boole Library, University College Cork.
John V. Kelleher Correspondence, Boole Library, University College Cork.
Piaras Béaslaí Papers, 1895–1965, National Library of Ireland.
Sean O'Casey Papers, 1917–1993, National Library of Ireland.
Seán O'Faoláin Collection, Archive of British Publishing and Printing, University of Reading.
Seán O'Faoláin Collection, British Broadcasting Corporation Written Archive Centre, Reading.
Seán O'Faoláin Correspondence 1926–1969, John J. Burns Library, Boston College.
The Norah McGuinness and Geoffrey Phibbs Collection, Dublin Writers Museum.

Periodicals

The Bell (October 1940–April 1948 [monthly] and November 1950–December 1954 [sporadically]).
Commonweal: A Weekly Review of Literature, the Arts, and Public Affairs (November 1924–September 2013 [biweekly]).
Fact (April 1937–June 1939 [monthly]).
Horizon: A Review of Literature and Art (January 1940–January 1950 [monthly]).
Ireland To-Day (June 1936–March 1938 [monthly]).

Printed primary sources

Anonymous, 'Announcements', *The Bell*, 5:5 (February 1943).
_____, 'Arranmore Disaster', *Irish Times* (28 November 1935).
_____, 'The Bothy Fire Victims', *Irish Times* (12 November 1937).
_____, 'Cruiskeen Lawn', *Irish Times* (4 October 1940).
_____, *The Dublin Magazine: A Quarterly Review of Literature, Science and Art*, 15:1 (January–March, 1940).
_____, 'Ireland's Crash: After the Race', *The Economist* (17 February 2011).
_____, 'Legal Notice', *The Bell*, 3:6 (March 1942).
_____, 'Lively Scenes at Lecture', *Irish Times* (4 March 1935).
_____, 'Modern Novels Criticised', *Irish Times* (5 November 1938).
_____, 'New Play at the Abbey: "The Money Doesn't Matter"', *Irish Times* (11 March 1941).
_____, 'Peadar O'Donnell's Libel Action', *Irish Times* (4 June 1932).
_____, 'Poetry Recital', *Irish Times* (23 April 1945).
_____, *Irish Times* (30 January 1922).
_____, *Irish Times* (14 November 1935).
_____, *Irish Times* (20 June 1942).
An Ulster Protestant: *see* Rodgers, W.R.
Auchmuty, James J., 'The Scottish Strain', *The Bell*, 3:1 (October 1941).
Behan, Brendan, 'I Become a Borstal Boy', *The Bell*, 4:3 (June 1942).
Bellman, The: *see* Morrow, H.L. (Larry)
Boston, Richard, 'Obituary: Anne Scott James', *Guardian* (15 May 2009).

Bowen, Elizabeth, 'The Big House', *The Bell*, 1:1 (October 1940).

___, 'James Joyce', *The Bell*, 1:6 (March 1941).

___, 'Mainie Jellett', *The Bell*, 9:3 (December 1944).

Clarke, Austin, 'The Green Helicon', *Irish Times* (24 February 1951).

___, 'Letters to the Editor', *Irish Times* (21 November 1951).

___, 'Recent Verse', *Irish Times* (19 January 1946).

Connolly, Cyril, 'Comment', *Horizon: A Review of Literature and Art*, 5:25 (January 1942).

___, Comment', *Horizon: A Review of Literature and Art*, 1:1 (January 1940)

___, *Enemies of Promise* (London: Routledge & Kegan Paul, 1938).

Cronin, Anthony, *Dead As Doornails* (Dublin: Dolmen Press, 1976).

___, *The Life of Riley* (London: Secker & Warburg, 1964).

___, *No Laughing Matter: The Life and Times of Flann O'Brien* (London: Paladin, 1990).

___, 'A Province Once Again', *The Bell*, 19:7 (June 1954).

___, 'This Time, This Place', *The Bell*, 19:8 (July 1954).

___, 'The Young Writer', *The Bell*, 17:6 (September 1951).

D83222: *see* Smith, Walter Mahon.

D'Alton, Louis Lynch, 'Public Opinion', *The Bell*, 2:4 (July 1941).

Daiken, Leslie (ed.), *They Go, The Irish: A Miscellany of War Time Writing* (London: Nicholson & Watson, 1944).

Davies, Helen, 'Raise Your Glasses', *Culture, The Sunday Times* (1 April 2012).

Farrell, Michael, *Thy Tears Might Cease*, int. Monk Gibbon (London: Arena Books, 1984).

Ferriter, Diarmaid, 'The Not So Swinging Sixties', *Irish Times* (15 September 2009).

Fitzurse, R.: *see* Taylor, Geoffrey.

Furze, Richard A. Jr, *A Desirable Vision of Life: A Study of The Bell, 1940–1954*, unpublished PhD thesis, National University of Ireland, University College Dublin, 1974.

Garnett, Edward, 'Foreword', in Seán O'Faoláin, *Midsummer Night Madness and Other Stories* (London: Jonathan Cape, 1932).

Gibbon, Monk, 'In Defence of Censorship', *The Bell*, 9:4 (January 1945).

___, 'Introduction', in Michael Farrell, *Thy Tears Might Cease*.

___, 'Public Opinion', *The Bell*, 9:6 (March 1945).

Hackett, Francis, *I Chose Denmark* (New York: Doubleday, Doran & Co., 1940).

___, 'A Muzzle Made in Ireland', *Dublin Magazine* (October–December 1936).

Harrison, Patrick K., 'Public Opinion', *The Bell*, 10:5 (August 1945).

Harvey, Frank, 'Public Opinion', *The Bell*, 12:3 (June 1946).

Hayes, Stephen, 'My Strange Story', *The Bell*, 17:4 (July 1951).

Heseltine, Nigel, 'Welsh Writing Today', *The Bell*, 6:5 (August 1943).

Hewitt, John, 'Mould', *The Bell*, 18:3 (June 1952).

Hogan, James, *Could Ireland Become Communist? The Facts of The Case* (Dublin: Cahill and Co., 1935).

Ireland, Denis, 'The Abbey Theatre', *The Bell*, 2:3 (June 1941).

Iremonger, Valentin, 'Aspects of Poetry To-Day', *The Bell*, 12:3 (June 1946).

___, 'The Poems of Freda Laughton', *The Bell*, 11:4 (January 1946).

_____, 'Public Opinion', *The Bell*, 7:3 (December 1943).

Johnston, Dennis, 'Plays of the Quarter', *The Bell*, 2:1 (April 1941),

_____, 'The Theatre', *The Bell*, 2:4 (July 1941).

Kavanagh, Patrick, 'Advent', in Antoinette Quinn, *Patrick Kavanagh: Collected Poems*.

_____, 'Coloured Balloons: A Study of Frank O'Connor', *The Bell*, 15:3 (December 1947).

_____, 'O Stony Grey Soil', *The Bell*, 1:1 (October 1940).

_____, 'The Wake of Books: A Mummery', *The Bell*, 15:2 (November 1947).

Kelleher, John V., 'Irish Literature To-Day', *The Bell*, 10:4 (July 1945).

Laughton, Freda, 'To the Bride', *A Transitory House* (London: Jonathan Cape, 1945).

_____, *A Transitory House* (London: Jonathan Cape, 1945).

MacManus, Francis, 'Looking Back in Love and Anger', *Sunday Press* (23 May 1965).

MacManus, M.J., *Eamon De Valera: A Biography* (Dublin: The Talbot Press, 1944).

MacNeice, Louis, *The Strings are False: An Unfinished Autobiography*, int. E.R. Dodds (London and Boston: Faber & Faber, 1965).

Marcus, David, 'The Strange Woman', *The Bell*, 17:6 (September 1951).

McCormack, W.J., 'James Plunkett', *Independent* (30 May 2003).

Mercier, Vivian, 'The Fourth Estate – Verdict on The Bell', *The Bell*, 10:2 (May 1945).

Montague, John, 'A Literary Gentleman', *The Cork Review* (Cork: Triskel Arts Centre, 1991).

_____, 'The Siege of Mullingar', *The Cork Review* (Cork: Triskel Arts Centre, 1991).

Morrow, H.L., 'Meet Elizabeth Bowen', *The Bell*, 4:6 (September 1952).

_____, 'Meet Maurice Walsh', *The Bell*, 4:2 (May 1942).

Mulkerns, Val, 'Girls', *The Bell*, 14:4 (July 1947).

Mulkerns, Val, le Brocquy, Louis and Roth, Andreas, 'Francis Stuart and Aosdána', *Irish Times* (1 December 1997).

Murphy, C.B., 'Sex, Censorship and The Church', *The Bell*, 2:6 (September 1941).

Murphy, Shea, 'The Saddest Sight', *The Bell*, 13:6 (March 1947).

Na gCopaleen, Myles: *see* O'Brien, Flann.

Nicholls, Nick, 'The Bone and Flower', *The Bell*, 7:2 (November 1943).

O'Brien, Flann, 'Cruiskeen Lawn', *Irish Times* (4 October 1954).

_____, 'Going to the Dogs', *The Bell*, 1:1 (October 1940).

_____, 'Letters to the Editor', *Irish Times* (8 November 1938).

_____, 'Two in One', *The Bell*, 19:8 (July 1954).

O'Casey, Sean, 'Censorship', *The Bell*, 9:5 (February 1945).

_____, 'A Protestant Bridget', *The Bell*, 13:5 (February 1947).

O'Connor, Frank, 'The Gaelic Tradition in Literature', *Ireland To-Day*, 1:1 (June 1936).

_____, *Leinster, Munster, and Connaught* (London: Robert Hale, 1950).

_____, *My Father's Son* (Belfast: The Blackstaff Press, 1994).

_____, 'The Stone Dolls', *The Bell*, 2:3 (June 1941).

O'Donnell, Peadar, 'Achill, Arranmore and Kirkintilloch', *Ireland To-Day*, 2:10 (October 1937).

_____, 'At the Sign of the Donkey Cart', *The Bell*, 12:2 (May 1946).

_____, '*The Bell* Suspends Publication', *The Bell*, 16:1 (April 1948).

_____, *The Big Windows* (London: Jonathan Cape, 1955).

_____, *The Bothy Fire and All That* (Dublin: Irish People Publications, 1937).

_____, 'Call the Exiles Home', *The Bell*, 9:5 (February 1945).

_____, 'Commentary: Tarry Flynn', *The Bell*, 14:2 (May 1947).

_____, 'Doorstep to a Story', *The Bell*, 11:3 (December 1945).

_____, 'German Spies in Ireland', *Irish Times* (14 June 1958).

_____, 'The Irish in Britain', *The Bell*, 6:5 (August 1943).

_____, 'The Little Magazine', *Irish Times* (4 March 1970).

_____, 'Migration is a Way of Keeping a Grip', *The Bell*, 3:2 (November 1941).

_____, *Monkeys in the Superstructure: Reminiscences of Peadar O'Donell*, int. Michael D. Higgins (Galway: Salmon Publishing, 1986).

_____, *The Role of the Industrial Workers in the Problems of the West* (Dublin: Dochas Co-Operative Society, 1965).

_____, *Salud! An Irishman in Spain* (London: Methuen, 1937).

_____, 'Under the Writer's Torch', *The Bell*, 12:6 (September 1946).

_____, 'What I Saw in Spain', *Ireland To-Day*, 1:4 (September 1936).

_____, 'Young Irish Writers', *Commonweal* (26 April 1933).

O'Faoláin, Seán, '1916–1941: Tradition and Creation', *The Bell*, 2:1 (April 1941).

_____, 'Beginnings and Blind Alleys', *The Bell*, 3:1 (October 1941).

_____, *Bird Alone* (London: Jonathan Cape, 1936).

_____, 'Book Reviews', *Ireland To-Day*, 1:1 (June 1936).

_____, 'Book Reviews', *Ireland To-Day*, 1:2 (July 1936).

_____, 'Childybawn', *The Bell*, 19:10 (November 1954).

_____, *Come Back to Erin* (New York: Viking Press, 1940).

_____, *Constance Markievicz* (London: Jonathan Cape, 1934).

_____, 'The Countess Markievicz', *Sunday Chronicle* (27 November 1932).

_____, 'The Dail and the Bishops', *The Bell*, 17:3 (June 1951).

_____, 'The Dangers of Censorship', *Ireland To-Day*, 1:6 (November 1936).

_____, *De Valera* (London: Penguin Books, 1939).

_____, 'De Valera's Life Story', *Sunday Chronicle* (13 March 1932).

_____, 'The Dilemma of Irish Letters', *Month*, 2:4 (July–December 1949).

_____, 'Don Quixote O'Flaherty', *London Mercury*, 37:218 (December 1937).

_____, 'Eamon De Valera', *The Bell*, 10:1 (April 1945).

_____, 'Eden', *The Bell*, 17:9 (December 1951).

_____, 'F.R. Higgins', *The Bell*, 1:5 (February 1941).

_____, 'For the Future', *The Bell*, 1:2 (November 1940).

_____, 'Imaginary Conversation', *The Bell*, 18:5 (October 1952).

_____, 'The Liberal Ethic', *The Bell*, 16:5 (February 1951).

_____, *The Life Story of Eamon de Valera* (Dublin: Talbot Press, 1933).

_____, 'Literary Provincialism', *Commonweal* (21 December 1932).

_____, 'The Little Magazine', *Irish Times* (25 February 1970).

_____, *Midsummer Night Madness and Other Stories*, foreword Edward Garnett (London: Jonathan Cape, 1932).

_____, 'Midsummer Night Madness', *The Collected Stories of Sean O'Faolain Volume 1* (London: Constable, 1980).

____, 'The Modern Novel: A Catholic Point of View', *Virginia Quarterly Review*, 11:3 (July 1935).

____, 'A Neglected Autobiography', *Irish Times* (3 April 1943).

____, 'Neutral?', *Authors Take Sides on the Spanish War* (London: Left Review, 1936).

____, *Newman's Way* (London: Longmans, 1952).

____, 'One World', *The Bell*, 7:4 (January 1944).

____, 'One World', *The Bell*, 7:5 (February 1944).

____, 'One World', *The Bell*, 7:6 (March 1944).

____, 'One World', *The Bell*, 8:2 (May 1944).

____, 'One World', *The Bell*, 9:4 (January 1945).

____, 'One World: The Next Geneva?', *The Bell*, 10:2 (May 1945).

____, 'Pigeon-Holing the Modern Novel', *London Mercury*, 33:194 (December 1935).

____, 'Plea for a New Type of Novel', *Virginia Quarterly Review*, 10:2 (April 1934).

____, 'The Priests and the People', *Ireland To-Day*, 2:7 (July 1937).

____, 'Provincialism', *The Bell*, 2:2 (May 1941).

____, 'Public Opinion: Coloured Balloons', *The Bell*, 15:4 (January 1948).

____, 'Roxana', *Irish Times* (23 December 1957).

____, *The Short Story* (London: Collins, 1948).

____, 'Signing Off', *The Bell*, 12:1 (April 1946).

____, 'The Silence of the Valley', *The Bell* 12:6 (September 1946).

____, *South to Sicily* (London: Collins, 1953).

____, *The Story of Ireland* (London: Collins, 1943).

____, *A Summer in Italy* (London: Eyre & Spottiswoode, 1949).

____, 'The Talking Trees', *Playboy* (January 1969).

____, *The Talking Trees* (London: Jonathan Cape, 1971).

____, 'This is your Magazine', *The Bell*, 1:1 (October 1940).

____, 'The True Story of Michael Collins', *Sunday Chronicle* (15 May 1932).

____, 'The Vanishing Irish', *Irish Times* (15 March 1954).

____, *Vive Moi! An Autobiography* (London: Rupert Hart-Davis, 1965).

____, *Vive Moi! An Autobiography*, ed. Julia O'Faoláin (London: Sinclair-Stevenson, 1993).

O'Faoláin, Seán, and Taylor, Geoffrey, 'Sense and Nonsense in Poetry', *The Bell*, 7:2 (November 1943).

O'Neill, Henry, 'Another "Life-Story" of Eamon de Valera', *Irish Press* (27 March 1933).

Phibbs, Geoffrey: *see* Taylor, Geoffrey.

Plunkett, James, *The Trusting and the Maimed* (New York: Devin-Adair, 1955).

Porter, Arabel J. (ed.), *New World Writing: Fifth Mentor Selection* (New York: The New American Library, 1954).

Power, Arthur, 'Exhibition on Living Art', *The Bell*, 7:1 (October 1943).

____, 'The R.H.A.', *The Bell*, 6:3 (June 1943).

Prescott, Joseph, 'James Joyce's *Stephen Hero*', *The Bell*, 19:10 (November 1954).

Quidnunc, 'An Irishman's Diary', *Irish Times* (26 October 1950).

Read, Herbert, 'On Subjective Art', *The Bell*, 7:5 (February 1944).

Reddin, Kenneth, 'Roisin Walsh', *Irish Times* (12 July 1949).

Robinson, Lennox, 'How the County Libraries Began', *The Bell*, 1:1 (October 1940).
Rodgers, W.R., 'Conversation Piece', *The Bell*, 4:5 (August 1942).
_____, 'Ireland', *The Bell*, 2:4 (July 1941).
Samuel, J.E., 'Colliery Disaster: Evidence of J.E. Samuel', *Fact*, 4 (July 1937).
Saroyan, William, 'The Unholy Word', *The Bell*, 15:1 (October 1947).
Shaw, George Bernard, 'Censorship', *The Bell*, 9:5 (February 1945).
Smith, Walter Mahon, 'I Did Penal Servitude' *The Bell*, 9:1 (October 1944).
_____, *I Did Penal Servitude*, preface Seán O'Faoláin (Dublin: Metropolitan Publishing, 1945).
Stuart, Francis, 'Frank Ryan in Germany', *The Bell*, 16:2 (November 1950).
Taylor, Geoffrey, 'The Best "Nation" Poet', *The Bell*, 6:3 (June 1943).
_____, 'The Quality', *Irish Times* (12 January 1952).
_____,'William Allingham', *The Bell*, 4:2 (May 1942).
_____ (ed.), *Irish Poems of To-Day: Chosen from the First Seven Volumes of "The Bell"* (London: Secker & Warburg, 1944).
Tracy, Honor, *Mind You, I've Said Nothing* (London: Methuen, 1953).
Wood Richardson, Caleb, *That is Only War: Irish Writers and The Emergency*, unpublished PhD thesis, Stanford University, May 2006.

Printed secondary sources

Adams, Michael, *Censorship: The Irish Experience* (Tuscaloosa: University of Alabama Press, 1968).
Arrington, Lauren, *W.B. Yeats, the Abbey Theatre, Censorship, and the Irish State: Adding the Half-Pence to the Pence* (Oxford: Oxford University Press, 2010).
Auden, W.H. and Isherwood, Christopher, 'Young British Writers – On the Way Up', in Edward Mendelson (ed.), *The Complete Works of W.H. Auden Prose: Volume II 1939–1948* (Princeton: Princeton University Press, 2002).
Baden, Donatella Abbate (ed.), *Seán O'Faoláin: A Centenary Celebration: Proceedings of the Turin Conference, Università di Torino, 7–9 aprile 2000* (Torino: Centro studi celtici, Dipartamento di scienze del linguaggio, 2001).
Baker, Deborah, *In Extremis: The Life of Laura Riding* (London: Hamish Hamilton, 1993).
Ballin, Malcolm, *Irish Periodical Culture 1937–1972: Genre in Ireland, Wales, and Scotland* (New York: Palgrave Macmillan, 2008).
Barber, Fionna, *Art in Ireland since 1910* (London: Reaktion, 2013).
Bell, Bowyer J., *The Secret Army: The IRA* (Piscataway, NJ: Transaction Publishers, 1997).
Bloom, Harold, *The Anxiety of Influence: A Theory of Poetry* (Oxford: Oxford University Press, 1973).
Bowman, John, *De Valera and the Ulster Question 1917–1973* (Oxford: Oxford University Press, 1989).
Brooker, Peter and Thacker, Andrew (eds), *The Oxford Critical and Cultural History of Modernist Magazines: Volume 1, Britain and Ireland 1880–1955* (Oxford: Oxford University Press, 2009).

Brown, Terence, 'Geoffrey Taylor: A Portrait', *Ireland's Literature: Selected Essays* (Mullingar: The Lilliput Press, 1988).

____, *Ireland: A Social and Cultural History 1922–2002* (London: Harper Perennial, 2004).

Campbell, Matthew (ed.), *The Cambridge Companion to Contemporary Irish Poetry* (Cambridge: Cambridge University Press, 2003).

Carlson, Julia (ed.), *Banned in Ireland: Censorship and the Irish Writer* (Athens: University of Georgia Press, 1990).

Carson, Niall, 'The Barbaric Note: Seán O'Faoláin's Early Years at the BBC', *Irish University Review*, 43:2 (Autumn/Winter 2013).

Cleary, Joe, *Outrageous Fortune: Capital and Culture in Modern Ireland* (Dublin: Field Day Publications, 2007).

____ (ed.), *The Cambridge Companion to Irish Modernism* (Cambridge: Cambridge University Press, 2014).

Clissmann, Anne, *Flann O'Brien: A Critical Introduction to his Writings* (Dublin: Gill & Macmillan, 1975).

Coleman, Marie, *The Irish Sweep: A History of the Irish Hospitals Sweepstake 1930–87* (Dublin: University College Dublin Press, 2009).

Collins, Pat (dir.), *John McGahern: A Private World* [DVD: PAL]. Ireland, Hummingbird Productions, 2006.

Cooney, John, *John Charles McQuaid: Ruler of Catholic Ireland* (Dublin: The O'Brien Press, 1999).

Cronin, Seán, *Frank Ryan: The Search for the Republic* (Dublin: Repsol Press, 1980).

Cunningham, Valentine, *British Writers of the Thirties* (Oxford: Oxford University Press, 1988).

Davis, Alex, 'The Irish Modernists', in Matthew Campbell, *The Cambridge Companion to Contemporary Irish Poetry* (Cambridge: Cambridge University Press, 2003).

Dawe, Gerald (ed.), *Earth Voices Whispering An Anthology of Irish War Poetry 1914–1945* (Belfast: Blackstaff Press, 2008).

Deane, Seamus, 'Boredom and the Apocalypse: A National Paradigm', *Strange Country: Modernity and Nationhood in Irish Writing since 1790* (Oxford: Clarendon Press, 1997).

____, *Strange Country: Modernity and Nationhood in Irish Writing Since 1790* (Oxford: Clarendon Press, 1997).

Delaney, Paul, *Seán O'Faoláin: Literature, Inheritance and the 1930s* (Dublin: Irish Academic Press, 2014).

Denson, Alan (ed.), *Letters from AE* (London: Abelard-Schuman, 1961).

Dow Fehsenfeld, Martha and More Overbeck, Lois (eds), *The Letters of Samuel Beckett: Volume 1: 1929–1940* (Cambridge: Cambridge University Press, 2009).

Dunne, Seán (ed.), *The Cork Review* (Cork: Triskel Arts Centre, 1991).

Elborn, Geoffrey, *Francis Stuart: a Life* (Dublin: Raven Arts Press, 1990).

Ellmann, Richard, *James Joyce* (London: Contemporary Fiction; Oxford University Press, 1961).

Evans, Bryce, *Ireland During the Second World War: Farewell to Plato's Cave* (Manchester: Manchester University Press, 2014).

Fanning, Brian, *The Quest for Modern Ireland: The Battle for Ideas, 1912–1986* (Dublin: Irish Academic Press, 2008).

Ferriter, Diarmaid, *Judging Dev: A Reassessment of the Life and Legacy of Eamon de Valera* (Dublin: Royal Irish Academy, 2007).

Foster, R.F., *Modern Ireland 1600–1972* (London: Penguin, 1988).

____, *Vivid Faces: The Revolutionary Generation in Ireland 1890–1923* (London: Allen Lane, 2014).

____, *W.B. Yeats: A Life I: The Apprentice Mage 1865–1914* (Oxford: Oxford University Press, 1998).

____, *W.B. Yeats: A Life II. The Arch-Poet* (Oxford: Oxford University Press, 2003).

Gibbons, Luke, *The Quiet Man* (Cork: Cork University Press, 2002).

Girvin, Brian, *The Emergency, Neutral Ireland 1939–45* (London: Macmillan, 2006).

Glendinning, Victoria, *Elizabeth Bowen: Portrait of a Writer* (London: Weidenfeld & Nicolson, 1977).

Graves, Richard Perceval, *Robert Graves: The Years With Laura Riding 1926–1940* (London: Weidenfeld & Nicolson, 1990).

Greacen, Robert, *The Sash My Father Wore* (Edinburgh: Mainstream Publishing, 1997).

Hamovitch, Mitzi Berger (ed.), *The Hound & Horn Letters* (Athens: University of Georgia Press, 1982).

Hanley, Brian, *The IRA, 1926–1936* (Dublin: Four Courts Press, 2002).

Harmon, Maurice, *Seán O'Faoláin: A Critical Introduction* (Dublin: Wolfhound Press, 1984).

____, *Seán O'Faoláin: A Life* (London: Constable, 1994).

Harris, Alexandra, *Romantic Moderns: English Writers, Artists and the Imagination from Virginia Woolf to John Piper* (London: Thames & Hudson, 2010).

Hartigan, Marianne, 'The Commercial Design Career of Norah McGuinness', *Irish Arts Review*, 3:3 (Autumn 1986).

Heaney, Seamus, *Finders Keepers: Selected Prose 1971–2001* (London: Faber & Faber, 2002).

Hegarty, Peter, *Peadar O'Donnell* (Cork: Mercier Press, 1999).

Henry, Paul, *An Irish Portrait: The Autobiography of Paul Henry R.H.A.*, int. Seán O'Faoláin (London: B.T. Batsford, 1951).

Houellebecq, Michel, *H.P. Lovecraft: Against the World, Against Life*, trans. Dorna Khazeni, intro. Stephen King (London: Weidenfeld & Nicolson, 2006).

Hutton, Clare and Walsh, Patrick (eds), *The Oxford History of the Irish Book Volume V: The Irish Book in English 1891–2000* (Oxford: Oxford University Press, 2011).

Hynes, Samuel, *The Auden Generation: Literature and Politics in England in the 1930s* (London: Viking Press, 1977).

James, Henry, *Henry James: Literary Criticism, Essays on Literature, American Writers, English Writers* (New York: The Library of America, 1984).

Jenkins, Hilary, 'Newman's Way and O'Faoláin's Way', *The Irish University Review*, 6:1 (Spring 1976).

Jennings, Humphrey and Madge, Charles (eds), *May the Twelfth Mass-Observation Day-Surveys by over Two Hundred Observers* (London: Faber & Faber, 1937).

Kelly, A.A. (ed.), *The Letters of Liam O'Flaherty* (Dublin: The Wolfhound Press, 1996).

Kennedy, Róisín, 'Experimentalism or Mere Chaos? The White Stag Group and the Reception of Subjective Art in Ireland', in Edwina Keown and Carole Taaffe, *Irish Modernism: Origins, Contexts, Publics (Reimagining Ireland)* (London: Peter Lang, 2009).

Kennedy, S.B., *Irish Art and Modernism 1880–1950* (Belfast: The Institute of Irish Studies, The Queen's University of Belfast, 1991).

Keogh, Dáire, '"There's No Such Thing as a Bad Boy": Fr Flanagan's Visit to Ireland, 1946', *History Ireland* (Spring 2004).

Keogh, Dermot, *The Vatican, the Irish Bishops and Irish Politics* (Cambridge: Cambridge University Press, 1986).

Keown, Edwina and Taaffe, Carole (eds), *Irish Modernism: Origins, Contexts, Publics (Reimagining Ireland)* (London: Peter Lang, 2009).

Kiberd, Declan, *The Irish Writer and the World* (Cambridge: Cambridge University Press, 2005).

Lane, Jack and Clifford, Brendan (eds), *Elizabeth Bowen: 'Notes on Eire' Espionage Reports to Winston Churchill, 1940–42, with a review of Irish neutrality during World War 2* (Aubane: Aubane Historical Society, 2008),

Lewis, Jeremy, *Cyril Connolly: A Life* (London: Jonathan Cape, 1997).

Longley, Edna, *Yeats and Modern Poetry* (Cambridge: Cambridge University Press, 2013).

Lycett Green, Candida (ed.), *John Betjeman, Letters: Volume One: 1926–1951* (London: Methuen, 1994).

_____, *John Betjeman: Letters Volume Two: 1951–1984* (London: Methuen, 1995).

Marcus, David, *Oughtobiography: Leaves from the Diary of a Hyphenated Jew* (Dublin: Gill & Macmillan, 2001).

Martin, Augustine, *Bearing Witness: Essays on Anglo-Irish Literature* (Dublin: University College Dublin Press, 1996).

Martin, Peter, *Censorship in the Two Irelands 1922–1939* (Dublin: Irish Academic Press, 2006).

Matthews, James, *Voices: A Life of Frank O'Connor* (New York: Atheneum, 1983).

Matthews, Kelly, *The Bell Magazine and the Representation of Irish Identity* (Dublin: Four Courts Press, 2012).

_____, '"Something Solid to Put your Heels on": Representation and Transformation in *The Bell*', *Éire-Ireland*, 46:1 and 2 (Spring/Summer 2011).

McCann, Sean, *The Story of the Abbey Theatre* (London: Four Square Books, 1967).

McGuire, James and Quinn, James (eds), *The Dictionary of Irish Biography from the Earliest Times to the Year 2002*, vols 1–8 (Cambridge: Cambridge University Press, 2009).

McKeon, Jim, *Frank O'Connor: A Life* (Edinburgh: Mainstream Publishing, 1998).

McIntosh, Gillian, *The Force of Culture: Unionist Identities in Twentieth-Century Ireland* (Cork: Cork University Press 1999),

Mendelson, Edward (ed.), *The Complete Works of W.H. Auden Prose: Volume II 1939–1948* (Princeton: Princeton University Press, 2002).

Mulkerns, Val, '"Did You Once See Shelley Plain?" Dublin, *The Bell*, the Fifties', *New Hibernia Review*, 10:3 (Autumn 2006).

Murphy, Daniel, 'Religion and Realism in Seán O'Faolain's Prose', *Imagination & Religion in Anglo-Irish Literature 1930–1980* (Dublin: Irish Academic Press, 1987).

Murphy, Richard, *The Kick: A Life Among Writers* (London: Granta Books, 2002).

Mutran, Munira H. (ed.), *Sean O'Faoláin's Letters to Brazil* (São Paulo: Associacão Editorial, 2005).

O'Brien, Mark and Larkin, Felix M. (eds), *Periodicals and Journalism in Twentieth-Century Ireland: Writing Against the Grain* (Dublin: Four Courts Press, 2014).

Ó'Drisceoil, Donal, 'Appendix A: Irish Books Banned under the Censorship of Publications Acts 1929–67', in Clare Hutton and Patrick Walsh (eds), *The Oxford History of the Irish Book Volume V: The Irish Book in English 1891–2000* (Oxford: Oxford University Press, 2011).

——, *Censorship in Ireland 1939–1945: Neutrality, Politics and Society* (Cork: Cork University Press, 1996).

——, *Peadar O'Donnell* (Cork: Cork University Press, 2001).

O'Faoláin, Julia, 'O'Faoláin at Eighty and Post Mortem', *Cork Review* (Cork: Triskel Arts Centre, 1991).

——, *Trespassers: A Memoir* (London: Faber & Faber, 2013).

O'Ferrall, Fergus, 'Christian Sensibility and Intelligence: the Witness of Seán O'Faoláin', *The Cork Review* (Cork: Triskel Arts Centre, 1991).

O'Halpin, Eunan, *Spying on Ireland: British Intelligence and Irish Neutrality During the Second World War* (Oxford: Oxford University Press, 2008).

O'Malley, K.H. and Dolan, Anne (eds), *'No Surrender Here!': The Civil War Papers of Ernie O'Malley 1922–1924* (Dublin: The Lilliput Press, 2007).

O'Malley, K.H. and Allen, Nicholas (eds), *Broken Landscapes: The Civil War Papers of Ernie O'Malley 1924–1957* (Dublin: The Lilliput Press, 2011).

O'Sullivan, Michael, *Brendan Behan: A Life* (Colorado: Roberts Rinehart Publishers, 1999).

O'Toole, Fintan, 'A Portrait of Peadar O'Donnell As an Old Soldier', *Magill*, 6:5 (February 1983), p. 28.

Pihl, Lis, '"A Muzzle Made in Ireland": Irish Censorship and Signe Toksvig', *Studies: An Irish Quarterly Review*, 88:352 (Winter 1999).

Powell, Anne (ed.), *Shadows of War: British Women's Poetry of the Second World War* (Stroud: Sutton Publishing, 1999).

Power, Arthur, *Conversations with James Joyce* (London: Millington, 1974).

Powers, Katherine A. (ed.), *Suitable Accommodations: An Autobiographical Story of Family Life: the Letters of J.F. Powers, 1942–1963* (New York: Farrar, Straus and Giroux, 2013).

Quigley, Mark, *Empire's Wake: Postcolonial Irish Writing and the Politics of Modern Literary Form* (New York: Fordham University Press, 2013).

Quinn, Antoinette, *Patrick Kavanagh: A Biography* (Dublin: Gill & Macmillan, 2001).

——, *Patrick Kavanagh: Collected Poems* (London: Penguin Books, 2005).

——, (ed.), *A Poet's Country: Selected Prose* (Dublin: Lilliput Press, 2003),

Reilly, Catherine, *English Poetry of the Second World War: a Biobibliography* (London: Masell, 1986).

Riordan, Susannah, 'The Unpopular Front: Catholic Revival and Irish Cultural Identity, 1932–48', in Mike Cronin and John M. Regan (eds), *Ireland: the Politics of Independence, 1922–49* (Basingstoke: Palgrave Macmillan, 2000).

Shelden, Michael, *Friends of Promise: Cyril Connolly and the World of Horizon* (London: Minerva, 1990).

Shovlin, Frank, 'From Revolution to Republic: Magazines, Modernism, and Modernity in Ireland', in Andrew Thacker and Peter Brooker (eds), *The Oxford Critical and Cultural History of Modernist Magazines: Volume 1, Britain and Ireland 1880–1955* (Oxford: Oxford University Press, 2009).

____, *The Irish Literary Periodical 1923–1958* (Oxford: Clarendon Press, 2003).

____, 'The Struggle for Form: Seán O'Faoláin's Autobiographies', *The Yearbook of English Studies*, 35 (2005).

Skeffington, Andrée Sheehy, *Skeff: The Life of Owen Sheehy Skeffington 1909–1970* (Dublin: Lilliput Press, 1991).

Snoddy, Theo, *Dictionary of Irish Artists: 20th Century* (Dublin: Wolfhound Press, 1996).

Stallworthy, Jon, *Louis MacNeice* (London: Faber & Faber, 1995).

Stewart, Bruce, 'On the Necessity of De-Hydifying Irish Cultural Criticism', *New Hibernia Review/Iris Éireannach Nua*, 4:1 (Spring, 2000).

Thacker, Andrew and Brooker, Peter (eds), *The Oxford Critical and Cultural History of Modernist Magazines: Volume 1, Britain and Ireland 1880–1955* (Oxford: Oxford University Press, 2009).

Travis, Alan, 'Postcard Wars', *Index on Censorship*, 29:6 (November–December 2000).

Tymoczko, Maria and Ireland, Colin (eds), *Language and Tradition in Ireland: Continuities and Displacements* (Amherst and Boston: University of Massachusetts Press, 2003).

Ward, Margaret, *Hanna Sheehy Skeffington: A Life* (Cork: Cork University Press, 1997),

Willcock, H.D., 'Mass-Observation', *The American Journal of Sociology*, 48:4 (January 1943).

Wills, Clair, *That Neutral Island* (London: Faber & Faber, 2007).

Woolmer, Howard J., *A Checklist of THE HOGARTH PRESS 1917–1946* (Pennsylvania: Woolmer/Brotherson, 1986).

Index

Abbey Theatre 2, 16, 17, 25, 97, 103, 104
  dispute with *The Bell* 30–40
AE (George Russell) 7, 18, 28, 36, 39, 68,
  98, 103, 104
Aiken, Frank 73
Allingham, William 108
Aragon, Louis 20, 140, 147
Arnold, Matthew 141
Auden, Wystan Hugh 4, 8, 44, 120
Austin, Richard 151

Balzac, Honoré 69, 119
Barrington, Margaret 123
Bates, H.E. 141
Bax, Arnold 146
Beckett, Samuel 2, 5, 142, 151
Behan, Brendan 7, 54, 146
Berlin, Isaiah 41
Betjeman, John 28–30, 107, 135
Blackmur, Richard Palmer 4, 28
Blythe, Ernest 25, 34, 35
Bowen, Elizabeth 6, 13, 29, 40–45, 96, 100,
  138, 141
Bowen, Evelyn 100
Brady, G.M. 140
Brennan, Robert 51
Browne, Noel 82, 83
Butler, Hubert 84, 113, 123
Byrne, Gay 160

Campbell, Joseph 109
Camus, Albert 151
Carter, Angela 149
Casey, H.V. 144
censorship 1, 5, 8, 13, 14, 19, 21, 25, 28, 32,
  33, 66, 68, 70, 72, 97, 102, 112, 113,
  129, 143, 147, 159, 160
  O'Faoláin's attitude towards 114–124

Chamberlain, Brenda 140
Chekhov, Anton 42, 141
Churchill, Winston 114
Clarke, Austin 102, 103
  dispute with O'Faoláin 108–113
  criticism of poetry in *The Bell* 136–140
Collins, Michael 25, 61, 62
Collis, Robert 147
Commonweal 12, 21–23, 102
communism 21, 22, 52, 53, 56, 115, 120,
  122, 144
Connolly, Cyril 3, 8, 24, 29, 39, 40, 41, 44,
  134, 146, 150
Coppard, A.E. 39, 141
Corkery, Daniel 3, 13, 19, 141
  radicalisation of O'Faoláin 51–52
Corrigan, Margaret 140
Cosgrave, William T. 25
Craig, Maurice 140
Craigavon, James 64
Cromwell, Oliver 88
Cronin, Anthony 97, 100, 101
  editorship of *The Bell* 145–146 , 150–151
Cross, Eric 142
Curran, Elizabeth 138

D'Alton, Louis Lynch 30–39
Daiken, Leslie 43
Dalton, Charles 25
Daudet, Alphonse 141
Defoe, Daniel 116
Derrig, Thomas 73
de Brún, Pádraig 89
de Faoite, Seamus 150
de Maupassant, Guy 141
de Valera, Eamon 69, 70, 71, 75, 130, 159
  O'Faoláin's attitude towards 61–66
Dillwyn, Mary 107

Dostoyevsky, Fyodor 82
Dryden, John 69

Eliot, T.S. 5, 6, 20, 78, 134
Envoy 101, 141
European literature 5, 6, 44, 52, 58, 89, 116, 118, 119, 123, 133, 134, 138, 139, 141

Farley, Maurice 140
Farrell, Michael (Gulliver) 2, 16, 30, 55
Farren, Robert (Roibéard Ó Farachain) 35, 102
Flaubert, Gustave 69, 119
Fleming, P.J. 25
Ford, John 50
Friel, Brian 151

Garnett, Constance 2, 15
Garnett, David 105, 107, 135
Garnett, Edward 23, 28, 63, 76, 78, 80, 105, 117, 134, 135
  readership at Jonathan Cape 11–15
  support of O'Flaherty 56, 57
Gibbon, Monk 26, 109, 147
  role in censorship debate 119–124
Gilmore, George 52–54, 56
Gogarty, Oliver St John 109
Gogol, Nikolai 42
Goldsmith, Oliver 132
Gollancz, Victor 56
Gonne, Iseult 54
Grant, Duncan 105
Graves, Robert 112, 147
  ménage and scandal 105–107
Graves, Sally 41
Greacen, Robert 140

Hackett, Francis 68
Hampshire, Stuart 41
Harvey, Frank 136, 137
Hawthorne, Nathaniel 131, 132
Hayes, Richard Francis 25
Hayes, Stephen 57
Heaney, Seamus 7, 157
Hemingway, Ernest 141
Henry, Paul 138
Heseltine, Nigel 138
Hewitt, John 60, 140, 148
Higgins, F.R. 16, 36, 109
Hogan, James 122, 123, 144
  Could Ireland Become Communist? 52, 53, 115

Hogan, Mick 53
Hogarth Press 104
Houellebecq, Michel 149
Howard, George Wren 12
Hull, Cordell 69
Hyde, Douglas 144

IRA (Irish Republican Army) 23, 25, 29, 63, 117
  The Bell's republican background 50–58
Ireland, Denis 31, 33, 36
Ireland To-Day 12, 24, 28, 33, 63, 73, 80, 84, 116, 143
  O'Faoláin's and O'Donnell's role in 18–20
Iremonger, Valentin 35, 112, 137, 140
Irish Academy of Letters 16
Irish neutrality 29, 41, 43, 54, 66, 70, 134
Irish Writing 145, 146

James, Anne Scott 41
James, Henry 141
  theory of literature 131, 132
Jellett, Mainie 138
Jennett, Sean 140
Jennings, Humphrey 129
Johnston, Denis 30, 32, 34, 35, 37, 39
Joyce, James 11, 13, 78, 86, 98, 109, 115, 132, 134, 138, 140, 141, 150, 151
  influence on younger generation 1–6

Kafka, Franz 150
Kavanagh, Patrick 3, 6, 7, 29, 109, 111, 112, 130, 138, 140, 150, 157
  relationship with *The Bell* 98–103
Kelleher, John V. 6, 19, 39, 58, 61, 112, 147, 156
Kettle, Mary 50
Kierkegaard, Soren 150
Kingsmill Moore, T.C. 122
Kinsella, Thomas 150

Lardner, Ring 141
Larkin, Jim Jnr 123
Laughton, Freda 6, 135–37, 140
Laughton, L.E.G. 135
Laverty, Maura 147
le Fanu, Sheridan 148
Lewis, Cecil Day 44, 140
Lewis, C.S. 44
Lovecraft, H.P. 148, 149
Lover, Samuel 6

Madden, Patrick 140
Madge, Charles 129
Marcus, David 145, 146
Markievicz, Constance 62
Markievicz, Maeve 62
Markievicz, Stanislaus 62
Martin, Augustine 133
Martin, Eamon 25–27, 50, 54
Mass Observation 8, 33, 66, 114, 129, 130,
    133, 134
Maybin, Patrick 140
McBride, Maud Gonne 50
MacDonagh, John 140
McFadden, Roy 140
McGahern, John 157
McGill, Donald 114
McGrath, Joe 25–27, 53
McGreevy, Thomas 2, 109
McGuinness, Norah 104
MacHugh, Roger 35
MacManus, Frank 112, 151
MacManus, M.J. 65
MacNamara, Brinsley 16, 17, 111, 112
MacNeice, Louis 44, 59, 109, 135, 140
    role as poetry editor of *The Bell* 143
MacNeil, Eoin 25
McQuaid, John Charles 159
MacRory, Joseph 72
Mercier, Vivian 11, 108
Middleton, Colin 140
Midgley, John 135
Miller, Henry 6, 118
modernism 2–7, 90
    modernist poetry in *The Bell* 135–142
Montague, John 100, 160
Moore, George 132, 141
Morrow, H.L. (The Bellman) 33, 44
Mulkearns, Val 145
Murphy, C.B. 118, 119
Murphy, Shea 56
Murray, Sean 53, 56

naturalism 4, 5
Newman, John Henry 81, 82, 85, 87
Nicholls, Nick 6, 107, 137–139, 140,
    150
Nicholson, Nancy 105, 106, 107

O'Brien, Flann (Brian O'Nolan) 2, 17, 100,
    136, 149
    dispute with *The Bell* 96–98
O'Brien, Kate 15, 117–119, 147, 151

O'Casey, Sean 36, 37, 51, 56, 62, 101, 112,
    122,123, 132, 143, 144, 145, 148, 151
O'Connell, Daniel 85
O'Connor, Frank (Michael O'Donovan)
    1–4, 7, 16–19, 25, 28, 29, 40, 58, 59,
    61, 96–103, 106, 108, 109, 111, 112,
    116, 119, 135, 136, 138, 141, 142, 147,
    156, 157
    The Big Fellow 62
    dispute with the Abbey Theatre, *see*
        Abbey Theatre
    dispute with Patrick Kavanagh, *see*
        Kavanagh
    Guests of the Nation 104
    The Invincibles 37
    republican background, *see* IRA
O'Dea, Denis 30–38
O'Donnell, Peadar 1, 8, 11, 12, 14, 16–18,
    20–23, 25–27, 28, 64, 70, 98, 99, 102,
    103, 113–115, 121, 123, 134, 143–145,
    146, 150, 151, 157, 158
    The Big Windows 147, 159
    The Bothy Fire and All That 71
    criticism of the state 71–77
    The Gates Flew Open 23
    Proud Island 159
    republican background, *see* IRA
    Salud! An Irishman in Spain 20
    There Will Be Another Day 159
O'Donovan, James L. 18, 63
O'Faoláin, Seán (John Whelan) 1–4, 8, 9,
    11, 16–19, 25–27, 32–39, 58, 59, 72,
    76, 96–104, 129, 135, 136, 138–147,
    150, 151, 156–158
    affair with Elizabeth Bowen, *see* Bowen
    affair with Honor Tracy, *see* Tracy
    And Again? 159
    Bird Alone 6, 21, 28, 80, 116, 139
    Catholicism 5, 21, 77–90
    censorship, *see* censorship
    The Collected Stories of Sean O'Faolain
        159
    Come Back to Erin 23
    Constance Markievicz 61
    De Valera 63
    and Eamon de Valera, *see* de Valera
    dispute with Austin Clarke, *see* Clarke
    The Great O'Neill 58
    The Irish 58
    An Irish Journey 27
    Jonathan Cape 12–16
    The Life Story of Eamon de Valera 61

Midsummer Night Madness 12, 14, 28, 41, 42, 117, 118
A Nest of Simple Folk 13, 14
Newman's Way 87
One World editorials 66–71
republican background, *see* IRA
She Had to Do Something 17
A Summer in Italy 78, 89
Talking Trees and Other Stories
thinly composed society 130–134
O'Faoláin, Julia 77
O'Flaherty, Liam 2, 56, 141, 143, 144, 150
O'Hegarty, P.S. 35
O'Higgins, Kevin 25
O'Leary, J.J. 24, 37, 53, 110
O'Malley, Ernie 24, 27, 52, 143
O'Rahilly, Alfred 25
O'Sheehan, Jack 25
O'Sullivan, D.J. 140
O'Sullivan, Seumas 109

Pearse, Patrick 52, 53
Peters, Augustus Dudley 16
Plomer, William 41
Plunkett, Edward (Lord Dunsany) 18, 141
Plunkett, James 147, 148, 150, 151
Pound, Ezra 5, 20
Power, Arthur 138
Powers, J.F. 39
Pritchett, V.S. 141

Reid, Nano 138
republicanism 50, 52, 65, 66, 68, 90
Rich, Harriet 156
Riding, Laura 105, 106, 107
Robinson, Lennox 24, 50, 103, 143
scandal in *The Bell, see* Abbey
Rodgers, W.R. 140
relationship with O'Faoláin and
O'Connor 59–61
Russell, Seán 54, 57
Ruttledge, P.J. 73
Ryan, Desmond 53
Ryan, Frank 52, 54, 55, 73
Ryan, John 101

Saroyan, William 20, 39, 141, 142
Sartre, Jean-Paul 20
Savonarola, Girolamo 87, 88
Schroedinger, Ernst 20
Second World War 3, 4, 12, 28, 61, 75, 84, 114, 133, 138, 143

sexuality 4, 106, 117, 118, 119, 124, 136, 137, 150
Shaw, George Bernard 20, 29, 59, 119, 121, 122, 132
Sheng-Tao, Yeh 20
Sheehy, Anna 138
Shiels, George 31
Sitwell, Osbert 20, 78, 146
Skeffington, Hannah Sheehy 50, 62
Skeffington, Owen Sheehy 20, 84
Smith, Walter Mahon (D83222) 130
Smyllie, R.M. 33
Spanish Civil War 29, 54, 55, 85
O'Faoláin's and O'Donnell's attitude towards 20, 21
Stalin, Joseph 122
Steinbeck, John 141
Stephens, Wallace 142
Stephenson, Robert Louis 141
Strindberg, August 122
Strong, L.A.G. 109
Stuart, Francis 54, 55
Synge, J.M. 132

Taylor, Geoffrey (Geoffrey Phibbs) 29, 38, 51, 112, 113
ménage and scandal 103–108
modernist poetry, *see* modernism
Thomas, Dylan 142
Tierney, Michael 25
Toksvig, Signe 68
Tone, Wolfe 144
Tracy, Honor 142, 143
Turgenev, Ivan 2, 6, 14, 15, 40, 159
Tyrrell, George 81, 82

unionism 133, 145
Ulster edition of *The Bell* 59, 60

Verschoyle, Derek 41, 62

Walsh, Maurice 26, 50, 53
Walsh, Róisín 8, 26, 50, 51, 54, 98
Warlock, Peter 138
Watkin, Edward Ingram 147
Watts, Richard 146
Weller, George 59
Welty, Eudora 141
Werfel, Franz 147
White, J.R. 62
White Stag Group 137–138
Wiechert, Ernst 20, 147

Wilde, Oscar 132
Williamson, Bruce 140
Wilmot, John (Earl of Rochester) 150
Wilson, Scotty 150
Woolf, Leonard 104
Woolf, Virginia 5

Yeats, Jack B. 24
Yeats, W.B. 1–7, 8, 11, 15, 18, 28, 31–36,
    59, 103, 104, 109, 111, 132, 134, 135,
    143, 156, 157

Zola, Émile 4